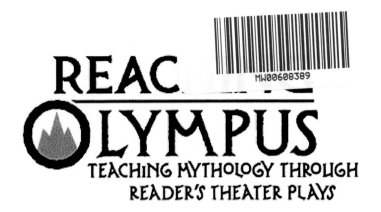

# REACHING OLYMPUS

## TEACHING MYTHOLOGY THROUGH READER'S THEATER PLAYS

THE *REACHING OLYMPUS* SERIES PRESENTS

# REACHING VALHALLA

## TALES AND SAGAS FROM NORSE MYTHOLOGY

WRITTEN AND ILLUSTRATED BY ZACHARY HAMBY

# DEDICATION

*For Oscar (God-Spear) and Otto (the Rich)*

"Cattle die. Kinsmen die. I myself shall die, but there is one thing I know never dies—the reputation we leave behind at our deaths."

*-Havamal*, Old Norse poem-

ISBN-10:  0-9827049-2-5
ISBN-13:  978-0-9827049-2-9
LCCN:  2013903371

The *Reaching Olympus* Series Presents, *Reaching Valhalla:* Tales and Sagas from Norse Mythology

Written and Illustrated by Zachary Hamby

Edited by Rachel Hamby

Published by Hamby Publishing in the United States of America

# TABLE OF CONTENTS

## INTRODUCTORY MATERIALS

## SCRIPT·STORIES: TALES FROM NORSE MYTHOLOGY

## GAMES, PUZZLES, AND EXTRA STORIES

## APPENDICES

# REACHING OLYMPUS:
## AN INTRODUCTION TO THE SERIES

The faces of the souls of the Underworld could not have been more death-like. It was several years ago, but I remember it well. In a matter of weeks, I had gone from inexperienced student to full-time teacher. Smack dab in the midst of my student teaching experience, my cooperating teacher gave me some startling news. Because of a worsening medical condition, she would be leaving soon—then it would be all me. Even more startling: four long years of college had not prepared me for the subject matter I would be required to teach—a class called World Short Stories and (gulp) Mythology. I remembered a few short stories from my survey literature courses, but with mythology, I was drawing a blank. In my cobwebbed memory there stood a woman with snake-hair and a psychedelic image of a wingéd horse—but that was it. Not to worry though. I had two whole weeks to prepare. After that I needed to fill a whole semester with mythological learning.

As any competent educator would, I turned to my textbook for aid. At first things looked promising. The book had a classy cover—black with the afore-mentioned wingéd horse on it. Bold gold letters tastefully titled it Mythology. Edith Hamilton—in the same lettering—was apparently the author. Yes, my judgment of the cover was encouraging, but what I found inside was anything but.

When I opened the text to read, I quickly realized I was doomed. Edith Hamilton had written her book in code. It was the same indecipherable language used by those who write literary criticism or owner manuals for electronic devices. Every sentence was a labyrinth, curving back in on itself, confusing the reader with many a subordinate clause and cutting him off completely from context with an outdated aphorism. If she wasn't randomly quoting Milton or Shakespeare, she was spending a paragraph differentiating between the poetic styles of Pindar and Ovid. It was as if Edith Hamilton was annoyed at having been born in the twentieth century and was using her writing style as some kind of literary time travel. Originally published in 1942, Mythology reflects the writing style of the day—a style that has grown increasingly more difficult for modern readers to comprehend. I knew if I could barely understand Hamilton's language, my students were going to be even more lost than I was.

Designed for average learners, Mythology was a junior-senior elective—the kind of class that was supposed to be entertaining and somewhat interesting. With Edith Hamilton tied around my neck, I was going down—and going down fast. It was at this point that the stupidly optimistic part of my brain cut in. "Maybe it won't be so bad," it said. "Don't underestimate your students." My ambitions renewed thanks to this still, small voice, and I laid Edith to the side, somehow sure that everything would turn out all right in the end. This was still more proof that I knew nothing about mythology.

Before I continue to tell how my tragic flaw of youthful optimism led to my ultimate downfall, I should take a minute to say a kind word about Edith Hamilton. In a time when interest in the classical writings of Greece and Rome was waning, Edith Hamilton revitalized this interest by writing several works that attempted to capture the creativity and majesty of Greco-Roman civilization. Hamilton's Mythology was one of the first books to take a comprehensive look at the Greco-Roman myths. The popularity of mythology today owes a great deal of debt to this book and its author. Fifty years after its publication, it is still the most commonly used mythology textbook in high school classrooms. Ironically, Mythology is no longer on an average high-schooler's reading level. As I mentioned earlier, Hamilton's writing style, with its ponderous vocabulary and sphinx-worthy inscrutability, further alienates any but the most intrepid of readers.

My first semester of teaching Mythology was a disaster. If I hadn't been so idealistic and gung-ho, I probably would have given up. Instead the new teacher within me stood up and said, "No! I'm going to do this, and we're going to make it fun! After all, Mythology is filled with all kinds of teenage interests: family murder, bestiality, incest, etc. It'll be just like watching MTV for them."

Utilizing every creative project idea under the sun, I threw myself into making the class work. We drew pictures, we read aloud, we watched related videos, wrote alternate endings to the stories—yet every time I kept coming up against the same brick wall: the text. It did not matter how enjoyable the activities were. Whenever we turned to the actual stories and cracked open that dreaded book, the life was sucked out of my students, and I was staring at their Underworld faces once again.

My last resort was boiling the stories down to outlines and writing these out on the whiteboard. Even that was better than actually reading them. At least the students would get the basic facts of the story. One student, possibly sensing I was seconds away from the breaking point, made the comment, "I didn't know this class would be a bunch of notes. I thought it would be fun."

Then I gave up.

When I look back on that semester, I realize that I failed a whole batch of students. They came and went thinking that studying mythology was a brainless exercise in rote memorization. Perhaps the failure of that first experience would not have been so stark if a success hadn't come along the next year.

The second time through the class, I was determined not to repeat the mistakes of the past. There must be some way of avoiding the text—somehow relating the stories without actually reading them. But then I thought, "Isn't this supposed to be an English class? If we don't actually read, can it be called English? What has this outdated text driven me to?"

When I looked into the stories, I could see excellent tales trapped behind stuffy prose. How could I get the students to see what I saw? How could I set those good stories free?

On a whim I decided to try my hand at rewriting one of the myths. I had dabbled in creative writing in college, so surely I could spin one of these tales better than Edith Hamilton had. The idea of dividing the story into parts struck me as a good one. Maybe that would foster more student involvement. A few hours later, I had created my first Reader's Theater script. (At the time I had no idea that there was an actual term for this type of thing or that there was sound educational research behind reading aloud.) Part of me was excited. The other part was skeptical. "These kids are high-schoolers," I said to myself. "They'll never go for this." I looked at some of the elements I had included in my script: overly-dramatic dialogue, sound effects, cheesy jokes. What was I thinking? Since I had already spent the time and energy, I decided to give it a shot.

There are those grand moments in education when something clicks, and those moments are the reason that teachers teach. My script clicked. It clicked quite well, in fact. The students loved reading aloud. They were thrilled beyond belief to not be reading silently or taking notes or even watching a video. They performed better than I ever dreamed possible. They did funny voices. They laughed at the cheesy jokes. They inhabited the characters. They even did the sound effects.

As I looked around the room, I noticed something that was a rarity: My students were having fun. Not only that, but they were getting all the information that Edith Hamilton could have offered them. When the script was done, I encountered a barrage of questions: "Why did Zeus act like that to Hera? What is an heir? Why did Aphrodite choose to marry Hephaestus? Did the Greeks have any respect for marriage?" Did my ears deceive me? Intelligent questions—questions about character motivation, vocabulary, and even historical context? I couldn't believe it.

I was also struck by another startling fact: The students were asking about these characters as if they were real people. They were able to treat the characters as real people because real people had inhabited their roles. Zeus was not some dusty god from 3,000 years ago. He was Joe in the second row doing a funny voice. Something had come from the abstract world of mythology and become real. And as for the quiz scores, my students might not remember the difference between Perseus and Theseus, but they definitely remembered the difference between Josh and Eric, the two students who played those roles. On top of all this, the class had changed from a group of isolated learners to a team that experiences, laughs, and learns together.

After the success of that first script, I realized I had created some kind of teaching drug. It was an incredible teaching experience, one that I wanted to recreate over and over again. I wouldn't and couldn't go back to the old world of bland reading. So I didn't.

The great moments of Greek mythology flew from my keyboard, and I created play after play. Despite my overweening enthusiasm, I knew that too much of a good thing could definitely be bad, so I chose stories that would spread out the read-aloud experience. We would still use Edith Hamilton in moderation. After all, a few vegetables make you enjoy the sweet stuff all the more.

Over the course of that semester, I discovered a new enthusiasm in the students and myself. They enjoyed learning, and I enjoyed teaching. I had students arguing over who would read which parts—an unbelievable sight for juniors and seniors. Laughter was a constant in the classroom. As the Greeks would say, it was a golden age of learning.

Now I have the chance to share this technique with other teachers. With these plays, I hope my experiences will be recreated in other classrooms. Mythology should not be an old dead thing of the past, but a living, breathing, exciting experience.

# USING THIS BOOK IN THE CLASSROOM

Script-stories (also known as Reader's Theater) are a highly motivational learning strategy that blends oral reading, literature, and drama. Unlike traditional theater, script-stories do not require costumes, make-up, props, stage sets, or memorization. Only the script and a healthy imagination are needed. As students read the script aloud, they interpret the emotions, beliefs, attitudes, and motives of the characters. A narrator conveys the story's setting and action and provides the commentary necessary for the transitions between scenes.

While Reader's Theater has been enormously successful with lower grade-levels, it is also a great fit for older learners as well. Students of any age enjoy and appreciate the chance to *experience* a story rather than having it read to them. For years now script-stories have been the tool that I use to teach mythology to high-schoolers. I wouldn't have it any other way. Below are the answers to some of the most frequently asked questions concerning the use of script-stories in the classroom.

**How do you stage these stories in the classroom?** Hand out photocopies of the particular script for that day. (Note: It is perfectly legal for you to photocopy pages from this book. That is what it was designed for!) Certain copies of the plays should be highlighted for particular characters, so that whichever students you pick to read parts will have their lines readily available. (This is not necessary, but it does make things run more smoothly.) Some teachers who use script-stories require their students to stand when reading their lines or even incorporate physical acting. As for the sound effects in the plays *(fanfare)*, noisemakers can be distributed to the students and used when prompted. Otherwise, students can make the noises with their own voices.

**How do you structure a class around script-stories? How often do you use them?** Too much of a good thing can be bad. In my own classroom I do employ the script-stories frequently—in some units we read a story every day of the week—but I do supplement with other notes, texts, activities, and self-created worksheets. Some of these activities are included in the back of the book. For other examples of these activities, check out my website *www.mythologyteacher.com*.

**How do you assess script-stories?** A quick reading quiz after the completion of a script is an easy way to assess comprehension. In my own classroom I ask five questions that hit the high-points of the story. I never make the questions overly specific (for example, asking a student to remember a character's name like Agamemnon or Polydectes). Each play in this book comes with five recall questions for this purpose.

Another form of assessment is by trying to foster as much discussion as possible. How well students discuss will tell you how well they have comprehended the story. The discussion questions included in this book have seen success in my own classroom.

I hope you find this book to be a great resource. It was designed with the intent of helping a much wider audience experience the timeless tales of world mythology in a new manner. Below I have listed some further notes concerning the script-stories. Thanks for purchasing this book. Please feel free to contact me if you have any questions.

Sincerely,

Zachary Hamby
mr.mythology@gmail.com
www.mythologyteacher.com

## FURTHER NOTES FOR TEACHERS

**UNIT PLAN** The script-stories in this book are organized in the order in which they should be read. Teaching one a day and including some of the suggested activities (see individual teacher pages) should yield at least a 13-day unit. Supplemental activities from the back can be inserted as well.

**INTENDED AUDIENCE:** 6th-12th grade

**LENGTH:** Script-stories range between 25-45 minutes in length

## SCRIPT-STORY PROCESS

- Every student will need a copy of the script-story.
- Reading parts may be highlighted for greater reading ease.

- As the teacher, you are the casting director. Assign the parts as you deem best.
- Give your largest parts to your strongest readers but still try to draw out the reluctant participant.
- As the teacher, you should take the part of the narrator. Actively participating only makes it more fun for you and the students.
- Cut loose and have fun. Script-stories allow students to see their teacher in a whole new light.

## POSSIBLE MODIFICATIONS

- Costumes, props, and even sets can be added to any script-story to make it more engaging.
- Requiring the students to stand while reading their parts creates a stronger dynamic between speaking roles.
- Encouraging students to write their own script-stories gets them thinking about the elements of storytelling and the use of dialogue.
- Assigning one student to be responsible for all the sound effects in a play can involve someone who is not a strong reader in the performance. Including certain tools that actually make the indicated sound effects (noise-makers, coconuts, etc.) is another excellent way to add interest.

# REACHING VALHALLA

"No one may escape dying, and it is my counsel that we not flee, but for our part act the bravest."

**~Saga of the Volsungs~**

A burly, bearded man tops the hill. He's wearing the hide of a bear. On his head is a fearsome helmet, and in his hand he carries an enormous broad-axe. When he sees you (his enemy), his eyes light up with an insane light, and he rushes forward. So much for your life!

This is the most common perception of the Norse people—violent barbarians. To an extent this perception is accurate. The Vikings, the most notorious members of the Norse people, were sailor-warriors, who raided the coasts of Europe mercilessly for nearly 300 years. But at home in Scandinavia—which includes modern day Denmark, Norway, and Sweden—life was simpler and more peaceful.

The term *Norse* means "Northern" as the Norse inhabited the northern lands of Europe and struggled to survive in the frigid, inhospitable climate. This lifestyle produced a hearty people—a people who valued ingenuity, bravery, and perseverance. The Norse were fantastic craftsmen. Elaborate pieces of jewelry, ornate weapons, and finely-crafted ships have all been unearthed from their burial mounds. They were master ship-builders, and this, coupled with their undaunted courage, led to their Viking exploits.

*Viking* means "bay-warrior"—making it the equivalent of our word for pirate, one who raids from the water. Vikings were young men from Scandinavia, who had no hope of gaining their fortune at home. Scandinavia had become over-populated, and a system of land passing from father to oldest son left younger sons out in the cold—sometimes quite literally. There was little for these disenfranchised men to do but take to the sea and search for wealth elsewhere. Unfortunately, the lands to which they traveled were already inhabited—by Christianized Europeans.

When the monks of Lindisfarne, an island off the coast of Britain referred to as "The Holy Island," saw boatloads of Viking warriors storm up their beaches, there can be no telling what went through their minds. Who would attack a holy site? Everyone knew what a supreme sin it would be to loot a church or even worse murder a monk. But the Norse warriors did not know the rules of Christianity. They worshipped Odin and Thor, who had taught them that the strong take the spoils. It was 793 A.D., and the Viking age had officially begun.

Vikings raided the coastlines of Europe for the next 300 years—ignoring any religious significance to holy sites. They saw the wealth of the church, gold that could be melted down into other objects, and took it as their own. Inevitably, the Vikings did more than simply raid. Some conquered and stayed—intermarrying with the Europeans—and bringing Norse culture into the European mainland.  The Norse had fair skin and blond to reddish hair.

The same adventuring spirit of the Norse led them further westward to Iceland and then to Greenland and beyond. Based on more recent discoveries, Norse settlements existed on the coasts of North America around 1,000 A.D., making them the first Europeans to reach the New World. And they did it all in a 70-foot-long ship handcrafted from wood.

The spirit of the Norse is still alive today—a tough grit that demands that we stand firm in the face of adversary. The myths of the Norse reflect this grim determination. If you can imagine a complete contrast to the frivolous Greek and Roman gods, it would be the Norse gods. They do not spend their days lightheartedly sipping nectar and eating ambrosia, starting petty quarrels between them for their own amusement. They feast in the halls of Asgard, but only because they know one day soon the time for feasting will be over. The day of Ragnarok will come, the gods will die, and the world will end.  And although they know it is a battle they cannot avoid or even win, they daily endeavor to delay its coming.

The script-stories contained in this book are retellings of the Norse myths. I have tried to make them a bit more lighthearted than the originals. Although the Norse enjoyed slapstick just as much as anyone else (for example, the gods dress Thor up as a bride for a giant!), on the whole the tone of their myths is somber. As with the other books in this series, I have sometimes condensed multiple characters into one,

rearranged events for continuity, and added some storytelling flourishes. That being said, the material is true to the spirit of the source, and all major plot points are in place. In other words, you could still pass a test on Norse mythology by reading these plays! If you want the full flavor of the original, you should seek out the Prose Edda of Snorri Sturluson (see recommended reading). I also highly recommend *Norse Myths* by Kevin Crossley-Holland as his retellings are faithful and informative, yet still entertaining.

The script-stories included here appear in chronological order. If you are reading them all, this is the order in which they should be read, yet almost any of them can be read as a stand-alone story. The exceptions are the final four script-stories, "Otter's Ransom," "The Sword of the Volsungs," "Sigurd the Dragonslayer," and "The Fallen Valkyrie," which comprise a story cycle of their own.

I hope you find this textbook useful and enjoyable.

## RECOMMENDED READING

- Clements, Jonathan. *A Brief History of the Vikings: The Last Pagans or the First Modern Europeans?* London: Robinson, 2005. Print.
- Crossley-Holland, Kevin. *The Norse Myths.* New York: Pantheon Books, 1980. Print.
- *The Saga of the Volsungs.* (Trans. Jesse Byock.) London: Penguin Books, 1990. Print.
- Sturluson, Snorri. *The Prose Edda.* (Trans. Jesse L. Byock.) London: Penguin Books, 2005. Print.

# GALLERY OF THE GODS

## ODIN, GOD OF THE SKY AND THE BRINGER OF RAIN

Odin is known as the "All-Father" or leader of the Æsir gods. He is also a battle-god as he determines the outcomes of earthly battles through the help of the valkyries, his immortal shield-maidens. From his high throne he can see down into all of the Nine Worlds. Two ravens, Hugin and Munin, bring him news from these worlds. He rides an eight-legged steed named Sleipnir. He is the husband of Frigga and the father of many of the gods. Odin learned the secret of runes (mystical symbols) by spending three days hanging from a tree with a spear in his side. Then he passed this knowledge onto men. Wednesday (Odin or Woden's day) is named for him.

## FRIGGA, GODDESS OF MARRIAGE

Frigga is the stately wife of Odin and the queen of the Æsir. She spends her day sitting at her magical spinning wheel, spinning out the clouds of the sky. She is also the mother of Balder, who is also her favorite son. Friday (Frigga day) is possibly named after her or the goddess Freya.

## BALDER, THE MOST BELOVED OF THE GODS

Balder (also called "the Shining One") is the favorite son of both Odin and Frigga. He is the kindest, most gracious, most handsome of the gods and has no enemies among them. He is literally the "golden child" of Asgard. Balder has a twin brother named Hodur, who was born blind. Apart from Odin, Balder is the wisest of the gods.

## THOR, GOD OF THUNDER

Thor is brave, strong, and true, but not necessarily the smartest of the gods. His sworn enemies are the giants. Thor wears a magical girdle that doubles his strength and wields a dwarf-crafted hammer called Mjolnir that returns each time he throws it (a symbolic reference to the thunderbolt). Thor is married to Sif, a household goddess with golden hair. Thursday (Thor's day) is named for him.

## FREYA, GODDESS OF BEAUTY AND FERTILITY

A goddess from the tribe of the Vanir (another race of immortals), Freya comes to live in Asgard with the Æsir after a deadly war between their peoples. She is described as being so beautiful that only Odin could stand to look directly at her. She is often the object of attraction for many gods, giants, and other creatures. She wears a dwarf-crafted necklace called Brisingamen. Her brother is Frey, a valiant swordsman, also from the Vanir tribe. Friday (Freya's day) is possibly named for her.

## TYR, GOD OF BATTLE

A valiant swordsman and a brave warrior, Tyr shares the title of God of Battle with Odin. Along with many other of the gods, he is the son of Odin. Tuesday (Tyr's day) is named for him.

## HEIMDALL, WATCHMAN OF THE GODS

Sporting a pair of solid-gold teeth, Heimdall is a god with super-senses. He can hear grass growing and spot things from miles away. These talents made him the perfect choice to guard Bifrost, the Rainbow Bridge that connects Asgard to Midgard (the human world). Heimdall carries a horn that can be heard through all Nine Worlds.

## LOKI THE TRICKSTER

A half-giant, half-god outcast, Loki possesses shape-changing abilities. He was adopted into the Æsir tribe of immortals, although not all the gods agree with this decision. He becomes the favorite companion to Odin and Thor when they go adventuring in Midgard or Jotunheim, the land of the giants, because of his cunning abilities. He is referred to as "The Doer of Good, and the Doer of Evil."

## GIANTS, DWARVES, ELVES, AND VALKYRIES

The **frost giants** or "jotuns" are the arch-enemies of the gods and are constantly plotting to overthrow them. Some are extremely large, violent, and grotesque, while others appear human-sized, wise, and fair. In some stories, gods and giants even intermarry. The **dwarves** are a race of underground blacksmiths who can create amazing treasures. The **elves** are a mysterious race of wise beings, who rarely leave their world of Alfheim. The **valkyries** are Odin's supernatural shield-maidens, who carry warriors who die valiantly in battle to Valhalla, his mighty mead-hall in Asgard.

# YGGDRASIL, THE WORLD TREE

# THE BUILDING OF THE WALL
## TEACHER GUIDE

## BACKGROUND

Yggdrasil is the name of the mighty ash tree whose branches support the Nine Worlds of the Norse universe. Prominent among these worlds are Asgard (the home of the gods), Midgard (literally "middle-earth," the human world), Jotunheim (the land of the giants), Svartalfheim (the land of the dwarves), and Niflheim (the realm of the dead). Bifrost the Rainbow Bridge connects Asgard to Midgard.

The World Tree is also host to a number of supernatural animals. Perched in the highest branches is an eagle (actually a wind giant in disguise) whose flapping wings cause the winds of the world. Beneath the ground a serpent named Nidhogg gnaws at the tree's roots. Daily skittering up and down the trunk is a squirrel named Ratatoskr. Various deer and goats chew at the tree's leaves. These animals cause harm to the World Tree. Like any tree, Yggdrasil is alive and must be tended properly. Three wise beings known as the Norns (the Norse Fates) water the tree and keep it healthy. But as everything else in the Norse cosmology, the World Tree is not eternal and will eventually burn in the fires of Ragnarok, the Day of Doom.

## SUMMARY

Odin and the other Norse gods (called the Æsir) have just finished a violent war with another tribe of gods called the Vanir. The war has completely destroyed their home, Asgard. They begin to rebuild their home, and as they do, Odin tells them about the creation of the world. He goes into great detail about how the first gods formed the world from the dead body of Ymir the frost giant. He also tells of the origin of the various races that exist in the Nine Worlds.

After Odin finishes telling his story of creation, the gods complete the construction of Asgard. They are proud of their new home, but they have no wall to protect it. The gods discuss how to build a wall that can protect it. The god, Heimdall, is sent to the Rainbow Bridge to watch for a creature who could build a wall for them. Heimdall brings a Vanir god and goddess to Odin. They ask to come live with the Æsir as a show of peace between the tribes. The gods accept these as their own. Soon after, Heimdall apprehends a creature named Loki, a giant half-breed, who also asks to come live among the gods. He shows them that he can change his shape and vows to help them in any way he can. The gods are distrustful of him, but Odin allows him to stay. Finally, Heimdall brings a strange stonemason before the gods, who says he can build an impenetrable wall around Asgard. The gods fear that the mason is actually a giant in disguise, but they recognize that he is the only creature capable of such a task. The giant asks for the sun and the moon, along with goddess, Freya, if he completes the wall by the first day of summer. All of the gods are dubious of the deal except for Loki, who says that there is no way the builder—giant or not—can complete the wall in the time he says he can. Loki stakes his reputation on it. The gods take the giant's deal.

Soon it becomes apparent that the giant will complete his work because he has an enormous horse that does as much work as he does. The gods angrily confront Loki, telling him to find a solution to the problem. Loki realizes that the giant cannot complete the wall without his horse-helper. Loki transforms into a mare in order to lure the giant's steed away. Without his helper the giant is not able to complete the wall. Now the gods have their new wall but do not have to pay their enemy his outlandish price. The giant's true identity is revealed, and Thor, the God of Thunder, ends his life. The gods hail Loki as the newest member of their group.

## ESSENTIAL QUESTIONS

- What does *home* mean?
- How much risk is *too much* risk?
- Is it fair to win through a trick (even when it's for a good cause)?

## ANTICIPATORY QUESTIONS

- Who were the Vikings?
- What are some of the various stories about how the world began?
- In the past why was it important to have walls around a city? Why do cities *not* have walls today?

## CONNECT

**Mythological Archetypes** Archetypes are specific character-types found in stories from cultures all across the world.  For example, the heroic warrior is a common archetype. Loki is an example of another common archetype, the trickster, one who overcomes obstacles through tricks and deceit—usually to the misfortune of others. What other types of tricksters can you think of from other myths or stories? (Hermes and Odysseus from Greek mythology and Coyote from Native American mythology are good examples to consider.)

## TEACHABLE TERMS

- **Imagery** On pg. 21 the line "The once-powerful wall had been beaten down to a line of jagged nubs, and the surrounding meadow was charred from battle." uses imagery to appeal to the reader's sense of sight.
- **Backstory** On pg. 23 Odin beings to tell about the creation of the world as he remembers it happening. This is an example of establishing important details through backstory.
- **Culture** What does the Norse creation story that begins on pg. 23 have to say about Norse culture? What did the Norse people value? What did they see as important or powerful in the world?
- **Personification** Svadilfare the Horse, who first appears on pg. 30, is an example of personification. He is an animal with human characteristics such as speech.
- **Pun** When the god Tyr tells the giant that he is a "little horse" on pg. 34, he is making a pun (wordplay on similar-sounding words) using *hoarse* and *horse*.
- **Dialect** On pg. 34 Loki uses dialect when he says, "There ain't nothing like…"

## RECALL QUESTIONS

1. What type of bridge connects the various worlds of the World Tree?
2. What becomes the official duty of the god Heimdall?
3. What does the mysterious builder want in return for building a wall?
4. What disguise does Loki use to distract the builder's helper?
5. What happens to the giant builder?

# THE BUILDING OF THE WALL

## CAST

| | |
|---|---|
| **ODIN** | *All-Father of the Gods* |
| **LOKI** | *Half-god, Half-giant* |
| **FREY** | *God of the Vanir Tribe* |
| **FREYA** | *Goddess of Love and Beauty* |
| **HEIMDALL** | *Watchman of the Gods* |
| **TYR** | *God of Single Combat* |
| **THOR** | *God of Thunder* |
| **BALDER** | *Most Beloved of the Gods* |
| **FRIGGA** | *Wife of Odin* |
| **GIANT** | *Mysterious Builder* |
| **SVADILFARE** | *Gigantic Horse* |

**NARRATOR:** Odin, the All-Father of the Æsir, stared silently at the smoking ruins that had once been Asgard, the home of the gods. High-roofed halls now lay in blackened heaps. The once-powerful wall had been beaten down to a line of jagged nubs, and the surrounding meadow was charred from battle.

A great crowd of gods stood around Odin—looking to him for guidance.

**ODIN:** *(grimly)* So passes our home. All we worked for these many years—gone.

**NARRATOR:** The Æsir had been caught up in a violent war against another powerful tribe of gods, the Vanir. Lightning bolts had been hurled, mountains broken down, the very roots of the World Tree had been shaken, but at last, the conflict had ended, and the two tribes had made an uneasy peace—but not before Asgard had been completely destroyed.

Balder, the most beloved of the gods, stepped forward and smiled hopefully as he addressed his aged father.

**BALDER:** Iduna says that her magical apple orchard has not been harmed by the fires.

**NARRATOR:** The apples that the goddess Iduna grew in her orchard were what kept the gods from aging.

**BALDER:** All hope is not lost. We can rebuild Asgard.

**ODIN:** Rebuild? What's the use? Why rebuild when it will only be destroyed again?

**NARRATOR:** Another of Odin's sons, Tyr, a dark-haired warrior-god, pointed his sword toward the broken wall.

**TYR:** We must have better defenses. In our next home, Father, the walls must be solid. A fortress with weak walls is no fortress at all.

**ODIN:** But our beautiful halls are nothing but ash.

NARRATOR:  Thor, the God of Thunder, raised his fist into the air.

THOR:    Father, just as we crushed the Vanir, we will rebuild these halls! And we will build you a golden hall that will have no rival!

*(shouts of agreement from the gods)*

NARRATOR:  Heimdall, a burly, bearded god, held his growling stomach.

HEIMDALL:  But please, Father, not before we have had some dinner!

TYR:  Heimdall! You are always thinking with your stomach! Don't you care that we're now homeless?

HEIMDALL:   Homeless or not—I'm still hungry!

NARRATOR:  Odin began to smile but thought better of it.

ODIN:  Very well. We will rebuild. But for Heimdall's sake, we will feast first.

NARRATOR:  Heimdall grinned ear-to-ear—revealing his dazzling rows of golden teeth. Frigga, Odin's stately wife, led the other gods in a search for food among the ruins.

FRIGGA:  The livestock must have fled in the battle.

NARRATOR:  Thor raised a triumphant cry.

THOR:  Ha! Here is an unlucky goat who met his end! Thor likes a good goat leg! Start a fire.

HEIMDALL:  Now all we need is—

NARRATOR:    Tyr raised a blackened barrel from a pile of debris.

TYR:  *(triumphantly)* A barrel of mead!

THOR:  Ha-ha! Let the feast begin!

NARRATOR:  In the circle of debris that had once been the hall of the gods, the Æsir feasted. As Thor munched on a roasted goat-leg, he paused thoughtfully.

THOR:    *(mouthful)* Father, there are so many different creatures that live in the Nine Worlds—Æsir gods, Vanir gods, frost giants, wind giants, elves, men, and dwarves. Where did we all come from? And the Nine Worlds themselves?  What made them?

TYR: *(sarcastically)* There is a topic for some light dinner conversation—what is the meaning of life?

NARRATOR:  Thor ignored his brother's remark.

THOR:  I only ask, Father, because you're the oldest among us. If you're not old enough to remember how it all started, who is?

ODIN: *(annoyed)* Luckily, I have kept my memory in my old age! Yes, I was there at the beginning, and I saw all these things come to pass. But if I told you how it all happened, you wouldn't believe me.

THOR:  Try us. It cannot be as strange as all that.

ODIN:  Very well. *(pause)* As you know, the Nine Worlds are supported by the branches of the World Tree. But the World Tree did not always exist. Like any other tree, it had to grow. There was a time when all of this was—different.

**TYR:** I smell a long story coming on.

**ODIN:** In the beginning, there were only two things: fire and ice, floating in the midst of the wide gap of nothingness. And when these two things came together, they made—

**HEIMDALL:** Steam!

**NARRATOR:** Odin furrowed his bushy eyebrows.

**ODIN:** *(grumbling)* You are correct, Heimdall, but don't interrupt me again. From this mist came the first two creatures—Ymir the first frost giant and the Great Cow.

**THOR:** *(confused)* Great Cow?

**TYR:** Perhaps you should go more slowly, Father. Thor is having trouble keeping up.

**THOR:** *(defensively)* I am not! Continue with the story!

**ODIN:** As I was saying, Ymir the giant lived from the milk of the Great Cow. Losing her precious fluid, the Great Cow became thirsty, so she began to lick the ice to quench her thirst.

**NARRATOR:** The younger gods looked to one another in confusion.

**ODIN:** As the Great Cow licked the ice, a figure emerged. Slowly, lick by lick—appearing a bit at a time—came my father, and he was the first of the gods.

**BALDER:** *(thoughtfully)* Hmmm. Licked into existence by a cow. How interesting.

**NARRATOR:** Frigga smiled at her young son reassuringly and patted his head.

**FRIGGA:** It is true. Now, sweetheart, chew your meat more carefully. Small bites.

**THOR:** If there was only one male god and one male giant, where did more gods and giants come from?

**ODIN:** It was a magical time—one your generation can barely understand. But to answer your question, Ymir's children, the other frost giants, were born from his armpit.

**NARRATOR:** Heimdall nearly spewed his mead.

**HEIMDALL:** *(snickering)* Born from his armpit! I bet they were stinky children! Hee hee!

**TYR:** Heimdall, I'm surprised you weren't born from an armpit.

**HEIMDALL:** *(laughing)* Ha! Yeah! *(pause)* Hey! Wait a minute…

**ODIN:** Continuing…then my father mated with a she-giant. From this union came my brothers and I.

**THOR:** *(angrily)* Grrrr. I hate giants!

**BALDER:** Yes, Thor, but you weren't listening. All gods are part-giant.

**THOR:** Not me! I'm *all* god!

**TYR:** *(sigh)* Just continue with the story.

**ODIN:** As you know the giants have always been our mortal foes, and the conflict between our people and theirs started way back then. Jealousy fueled it, and we gods warred against Ymir and his children. It was a mighty fight. In the end, the giants fled, and Ymir lay dead.

**TYR:** Ah-ha! The gods won! As they always do!

**ODIN:** Yes, we had won, but there was still no world in which creatures of good could live. So from Ymir's body, we formed one. Working together, we took the giant's flesh and ground it into dirt. His blood flowed out and made the oceans, rivers, and lakes. His bones became stone, and we fluffed his brains until they lifted from the earth and became the clouds. The high dome of his skull formed the sky.

**NARRATOR:** The gods had stopped their meal. They were all staring at one another with disgusted looks.

**THOR:** You mean, we live in the corpse of a filthy, stinking giant?

**HEIMDALL:** I think I've lost my appetite.

**ODIN:** Oh, you young ones understand nothing! It was a beautiful thing! Anyway, Yggdrasil—the World Tree—grew from his body along with the new worlds. One was made for dwarves, one was made for men...

**THOR:** Where did *those* creatures come from?

**ODIN:** Well, the dwarves came from the maggots that had infested the body of the frost giant.

**TYR:** That's fitting. Dwarves are almost as disgusting as giants!

**ODIN:** And the first man and woman, Ask and Embla, were formed from two trees.

**FRIGGA:** Which explains man's hard-headedness!

**ODIN:** Anyway, the last addition—the crown of it all—was Bifrost, the Rainbow Bridge, connecting our world to the world of men.

**HEIMDALL:** (*excitedly*) Ah! The Rainbow Bridge! A lovely spot! I go there every night, you know.

**ODIN:** Really? Why is that?

**HEIMDALL:** I cannot sleep at night. I have excellent ears, you know. The sound of the grass growing keeps me awake. So I go there and use my far-sight to look down into the other worlds of the Great Tree. It helps me collect my thoughts. It's quite—*transcendent.*

**NARRATOR:** The gods stared at Heimdall. These were strange words to come from the oafish god.

**HEIMDALL:** What? I like it there!

**ODIN:** Since you spend so much time there, we should have you guard it. While we build, you will be our watchman. It will do little good for us to rebuild Asgard if it's destroyed again by our enemies.

**HEIMDALL:** Gladly!

**ODIN:** My story is complete. Perhaps now you see why we must always keep an eye on Jotunheim, the land of the frost giants.

They have never forgotten that we killed their ancestor, and they are ever seeking revenge for that deed. *(pause)* Now, let us build.

**NARRATOR:** And build they did. Odin controlled the clouds giving a respite from the wind and rain. As his father had suggested, Heimdall journeyed to Bifrost and kept watch for enemies. Tyr and Thor led the other gods in fashioning a great hall for each god and goddess. The greatest and most magnificent hall was reserved for Odin himself. It was called Valhalla, and it towered over the others—its shining roof thatched with golden shields. Frigga organized the goddesses, who spent their time spinning tapestries to hang in the halls. Balder, with the help of Iduna, planted trees and gardens to beautify the surroundings. Odin watched all of this progress with his wise eyes. At last, the new home of the gods was completed.

**ODIN:** Asgard is remade!

**BALDER:** It's perfect.

**TYR:** Ahem. Not quite *perfect* yet.

**ODIN:** What do you mean?

**TYR:** We have no wall.

**ODIN:** You are right. We need a wall—a taller and thicker wall—one that will hold firm. There has to be some skill in it. I won't see Asgard destroyed again! Send for Heimdall!

**NARRATOR:** Heimdall was sent for and soon arrived, grinning goldenly.

**ODIN:** Heimdall, we need a wall—a strong wall—one built with magic and cunning. As the watchman you look down into the other worlds. Have you seen any creature capable of building us such a wall?

**HEIMDALL:** The dwarves? I have seen that they are excellent craftsmen!

**ODIN:** No, no. They think only of jewels and gold. We need stone.

**HEIMDALL:** Hmmm. I will go to the Rainbow Bridge and watch.

**ODIN:** Then go! And report back when you find us our builder.

**NARRATOR:** Not many days afterward, the Æsir were feasting in Valhalla when Heimdall interrupted them. He was escorting a handsome youth and a shining maiden.

**HEIMDALL:** Father! I found these two trying to cross the Rainbow Bridge! They're Vanir gods!

**FRIGGA:** What beautiful children!

**TYR:** Enemies!

**BALDER:** Let them speak for themselves. Maybe they are friends!

**FREY:** I am Frey, and this is my sister Freya. It's true. We are from the tribe of the Vanir, but we come in peace. We heard that you rebuilt your halls here, and we are sent with a message from all our kin. They regret our former conflict, and never again will the Vanir war against you.

**ODIN:** This is good news—if it is true.

**NARRATOR:** Freya, the Vanir maiden, removed her muddied traveling cloak. Her beauty was so great that it stung the god's eyes. Only Odin could bear to look at her full glory.

**FREYA:** *(humbly)* As a sign of peace, we wish to reside here with you—with the Æsir—forever.

**TYR:** Convenient! Some of the Vanir—our enemies—want to live among us! Why? So you can spy on us?

**FREY:** The Vanir tribe lost as much as you in our conflict. We are ready for peace. If you do not believe me, here!

**NARRATOR:** He pulled his shining sword from his belt. The Æsir all moved for their weapons. *(murmuring from the gods)* But Frey turned the sword's handle toward Odin and offered it up to him.

**FREY:** Here is my sword—if you wish it.

**ODIN:** A noble gesture! But that won't be necessary. Keep your mighty blade. You two are most welcome! Join our ranks!

**NARRATOR:** The two Vanir smiled, and the Æsir let up a cheer. *(cheering from the gods)* Only Heimdall grimaced—somewhat miffed he had not caught two Vanir spies. Then suddenly his ears began to twitch.

**HEIMDALL:** Wait! What's that? I hear someone or *something* sneaking up the Rainbow Bridge! I knew I shouldn't have left my post!

**TYR:** *(sarcastically)* Are you sure it's not the sound of the grass growing?

**HEIMDALL:** Argh! I'll be back! And I'll bring the trespasser with me!

**NARRATOR:** The gods began their feasting anew—finding a place among the festivities for Frey and Freya. *(crashing sounds)* Soon the hall doors burst open, and Heimdall appeared again, struggling to keep a grip on the captive he carried in his burly arms.

**HEIMDALL:** *(to Loki)* Stop struggling! *(yelling)* Here is the trespasser! Now this one has to be a spy!

**LOKI:** *(yelling)* Let me go! Let me go!

**NARRATOR:** Heimdall dragged his skinny prisoner the length of Valhalla and threw him down at Odin's feet.

**HEIMDALL:** I don't know what this creature is. He looks like some sort of god, but he smells like a giant!

**LOKI:** *(moaning)* Mercy, mighty gods! Mercy! What have I done to deserve this kind of treatment?

**ODIN:** We'll ask the questions! Who are you, strange creature?

**LOKI:** *(moaning)* I am doomed! I expected to find hospitality here in Asgard! I hoped to find some shelter here—from the cruelty of the Nine Worlds!

**ODIN:** Answer my question, creature! Who or what are you?

**LOKI:** Oh, great Odin, I am Loki. My mother was one of your kind, and my father was a wind giant.

**TYR:** A half-breed giant!

**THOR:** What? A giant! You are lucky this is a place of peace, or I'd crack your head open! Giants are not welcome here! Jotunheim is their home!

**LOKI:** Why do you think I came here? The giants won't accept me either! I'm an outcast!

**ODIN:** Asgard is a place of safety for *friends*. But we are very careful here to accept friends—especially those who are giant-born.

**LOKI:** Friend! Yes, I am a friend!

**ODIN:** Everyone who resides here at Asgard has a use and a purpose. What can you do for us?

**LOKI:** (*helpfully*) I'm full of tricks, your majesty! Not evil tricks, but good ones! Let me show you!

**NARRATOR:** There was a flash of light in the hall, and where Loki had once stood there was nothing.

**HEIMDALL:** (*enraged*) Argh! I knew it! He has vanished! He must have transformed a hundred times on me when I dragged him here—but I held on!

**LOKI:** Buzzzzzzz. I'm *here*, you meathead!

**NARRATOR:** Heimdall looked down upon his shoulder, to where a horsefly perched. Its face looked very much like Loki's.

**LOKI:** (*small voice*) See? I'm very handy— good at spying, too!

**HEIMDALL:** He confesses it! He is a spy!

**NARRATOR:** The buzzing of Loki grew so loud that it reverberated from every wall.

There was a flash, and Loki stood in his original form before the throne.

**LOKI:** Oh, please, Odin! Please!

**ODIN:** Hmmm. Very well. You may stay in Asgard. We may find a use for you yet. You must always struggle to overcome that giant blood of yours. Your father was of the enemy, and part of him is left in you.

**NARRATOR:** Thor eyed Loki coldly.

**THOR:** I'll be watching you, giant-scum. Slip up and your head will be mine.

**NARRATOR:** Loki was allowed to remain among the gods, but they treated him with suspicion. It was not a week later when Heimdall escorted yet another stranger into Asgard.

**HEIMDALL:** Make way! This time I have done it! I have found a builder—a builder for our wall!

**NARRATOR:** The stranger was quite a sight. He was as tall as tree, yet spindly like a reed. His body was swathed in a concealing cloak, and a large hat covered his face. Heimdall led him before the throne of Odin.

**ODIN:** Heimdall, who is this?

**HEIMDALL:** A builder! Just look at him!

**GIANT:** Lord of the Æsir, I have heard from your watchman here that you are in need of a stonemason. I am the one you seek.

**NARRATOR:** Odin eyed the stranger suspiciously.

**ODIN:** Asgard needs a wall around it—a wall strong enough to withstand the giants of Jotunheim. Why are you suited for such a job?

**GIANT:** I swear by all my ancestors that I can build a wall tall enough and strong enough to withstand even the mightiest of gods and giants. I know secret spells— spells of binding—that could make it impenetrable.

**ODIN:** I see. But tell me, what is your price for such a project?

**GIANT:** You will give me six months. If I cannot complete the wall by summer, you will owe me nothing.

**ODIN:** But if you do…

**GIANT:** But if I do…you must give me Sol and Mani—the sun and the moon.

*(murmuring among the gods)*

**ODIN:** *(coolly)* The sun and the moon, huh? Is that all? *(laugh)* Your terms are ridiculous.

**GIANT:** *And* I want this female as my bride.

**NARRATOR:** The stranger pointed a knobby finger toward Freya, the Vanir maiden.

*(murmuring among the gods)*

**FREYA:** Me?

**FREY:** Never! You'll never get my sister!

**NARRATOR:** Frey rose and drew his sword.

**GIANT:** Fine. But know this—there is no one else among all the creatures of the Nine Worlds who could build a wall like I can.

**ODIN:** Leave us, stranger! We must discuss your offer.

**NARRATOR:** The stranger turned and left the hearing hall.

**TYR:** Father, this is not a good idea! That stranger is obviously a giant in disguise!

**ODIN:** Of course! Anyone but a complete idiot would know he was a giant!

**THOR:** *(in shock)* What? He was a giant? Here in Asgard?

**ODIN:** *(sarcastically)* I rest my case. Who else but a giant would ask for such an insane price for his work?

**BALDER:** What a horrible request! We'd have our wall, but without the sun and moon the world would be in darkness forever!

**LOKI:** Not necessarily.

**NARRATOR:** The creature Loki was lurking in the shadows of the hall. All the gods turned toward him.

**ODIN:** What do you mean?

**LOKI:** Not even a giant can build a massive wall in a year!

**ODIN:** How can you be so sure?

**LOKI:** It's impossible. He'll try and fail— and then you will have your wall. And who better to build a wall to keep giants out than a giant himself? Giants are the masters of many spells. If you enter this agreement, he is bound to keep his part of the oath just as you are.

**TYR:** *(snidely)* Great advice from the son of a giant! It's a trick. They're in cahoots!

**LOKI:** *(angrily)* I've seen my share of giants. They treated me like a slave! I barely escaped Jotunheim with my life! What do I owe them?

**TYR:** Hmph. A likely story.

**LOKI:** Does anybody else have a better idea?

**NARRATOR:** Thor scrunched up his face in thought.

**THOR:** The weird, little weasel-creature makes a good point.

**LOKI:** Um. Thank you…I guess. The giant will fail. I'd stake my reputation on it.

**TYR:** Your reputation? A *small* wager if I've ever seen one. You're almost as much a stranger as this giant-mason is!

**NARRATOR:** Loki addressed Odin directly.

**LOKI:** The fact remains, Odin, you need a wall—or this Asgard will fall just as quickly as the last one did.

**NARRATOR:** Odin sat thoughtfully.

**ODIN:** Very well.

**FREY:** Wait! Odin, you can't just marry my sister off to some giant!

**ODIN:** Loki is right. The giant will not be able to finish the job by summer.

**FREY:** But what if he does? Is this how the Vanir are treated by your people?

**ODIN:** I'm sorry, my boy, but you *did* put yourself under my command.

**NARRATOR:** Freya began to weep.

**FREYA:** I'll be the bride of a giant! Thank the Norns my father is dead, or he would die of shame!

**ODIN:** There is nothing to worry out.

**FREY:** Not for you anyway. It's easy to gamble with the fates of others.

**NARRATOR:** The giant stonemason was sent for, and when Odin declared that the gods would take his deal, he began to rub his massive hands together greedily.

**ODIN:** But you are required to complete the job alone! No one may help you!

**GIANT:** Fair enough. But surely you will allow me the use of my horse and cart.

**NARRATOR:** Odin shot Loki a questioning glance.

**LOKI:** What good is a horse?

**ODIN:** Fine. Use your horse and cart. It will not matter.

**GIANT:** As you say! The deal is struck. Farewell, fools! *(diabolical laugh)*

**NARRATOR:** The stranger turned and swept from the room. His evil laughter echoed down the hallway.

**BALDER:** *(happily)* That went well, don't you think?

**NARRATOR:** The Æsir followed the giant stonemason to see him begin his work. But instead of delving directly into his labor, the giant raised his long hands and cupped them around his mouth.

**GIANT:** *(horse whinny)* Neigh! Neigh!

**SVADILFARE:** *(horse whinny)* Neigh! Neigh! *(hoofbeats)*

**NARRATOR:** Down from the mountains thundered an enormous horse. Tufts of hair nearly covered its hooves, and its neck was as thick as an oak. Behind it rattled a wagon heaped with stone.

**HEIMDALL:** That's the biggest horse I've ever seen!

**GIANT:** Yes, stupid, puny god. He is my steed, Svadilfare.

**NARRATOR:** The horse and cart came to a stop before the gods. The beast gave them a wise glance, and much to their surprise unhooked itself from the wagon and stood upon its hind legs. It was now as tall as its giant master.

**HEIMDALL:** *(shocked)* By the Norns! It's a monster!

**SVADILFARE:** *(booming)* I am no monster, foolish gods! I am a lord among horses, and I have come to see that this wall is completed by the beginning of summer. You silly gods have played right into our trap! *(horse laugh)* Ha!

**THOR:** *(yelling)* Laugh it up, Horse-breath! It'll be hard to build a wall after Thor has ripped your hooves off! *(battlecry)* Argh!

**ODIN:** Thor! No! We have made our bargain. We have no choice but to leave them to their work and hope that they are not successful.

**NARRATOR:** Thor raised a menacing finger toward the giant-in-disguise.

**THOR:** Listen to me, giant! After this is over, you and I shall meet in battle, and only one of us will walk away with a head.

**GIANT:** *(laughs)* When this is over, puny one, you will live in a world of darkness, and the giants will overcome you at last! *(laughter)*

**NARRATOR:** The two giant beings fell into work. Stone upon stone was laid by the mason, who stayed true to his word and placed each one with precision and cunning. His craft was so great that when he would be finally finished, the wall would be as a cliff of solid stone around the halls of Asgard.

The giant's steed worked day and night—never sleeping—dragging loads of rock from the broken remains of a nearby mountain. He was worth even more work than his master. Using rope and pulley, he hoisted the heaviest stones into place, and the mason uttered strange spells over them—spells of binding. And so the gods began to despair.

**BALDER:** Perhaps life without the sun and moon will not be as bad as we think.

**ODIN:** We'll be living in total darkness!

**BALDER:**   *(confidently)* Well, even in darkness there is always hope.

**ODIN:**   Don't be ridiculous! There never has been hope, and there never will be.

**FREYA:**   I'll be thankful for the darkness, since it will spare me the sight of my monster husband!

**ODIN:**   *(angrily)* Enough! Where is that Loki creature? Bring him to me at once!

**NARRATOR:**   The Æsir combed the halls of Asgard, but no one could find Loki.

**TYR:**   I knew it! He's abandoned us! *(pause)* Wait!

**NARRATOR:**   Tyr cocked his head to listen.

**LOKI:**   Bzzzzzzzzzzzzz.

**NARRATOR:**   Tyr's hand shot out, snatching a fly from the air.

**TYR:**   There you are, you traitor!

**LOKI:**   *(tiny voice)* Zzzzz. Let go! Let go!

**TYR:**   Reveal yourself, or I'll squash you like—well, a bug!

**NARRATOR:**   The full-sized Loki appeared—folding his wings and legs back up into his body.

**TYR:**   Here's the traitor! I say we kill him for trying to desert us!

**ODIN:**   *(angrily)* Loki! Were you trying to escape?

**LOKI:**   Oh no! Not escape! I was just innocently eavesdropping. Just being a fly on the wall. *(forced laugh)* Heh heh. Get it?

**ODIN:**   *(booming)* This is no joke!

**NARRATOR:**   Odin rose from his throne in anger, and the atmosphere around him began to crackle with power.

**LOKI:**   *(cry of fright)* Please! Spare me!

**ODIN:**   I have declared that no god blood will ever be spilt in this holy hall, and I will not break my word!

**TYR:**   You could always take him outside…

**ODIN:**   But how dare you try to abandon us after we gave you friendship here in Asgard!

**NARRATOR:**   Odin raised his hand, and an invisible wind lifted Loki into the air. The helpless creature began to spin—caught in a whirlwind. *(whooshing of a whirlwind)*

**LOKI:**   Ah! Stop! Please!

**TYR:**   Hmmm. I was hoping he would smite him, but this is good, too.

**ODIN:**   Loki, you have gotten us into this mess, and you will get us out of it!

**LOKI:**   Please! Please! Stop!

**NARRATOR:**   Odin lowered his hand, and Loki fell in a heap upon the floor.

**LOKI:**   It's hopeless. What can I do?

**ODIN:**   *You* figure it out.

**NARRATOR:**   Loki rose—trembling.

**LOKI:** I will stop this giant—but I have my terms.

**TYR:** How dare you ask anything of us! Turn him over to me, Father! I'll drag him out of Asgard and then end his life!

**ODIN:** What do you ask—other than keeping your life?

**LOKI:** Make me one of you. No more of this half-breed business. I want to be a blood-brother of the gods. And give me one of the goddesses as my wife.

**NARRATOR:** Loki's beady eyes rested on Freya. Frey stepped angrily in front of his sister.

**TYR:** You'll never be one of us! Will he, Father?

**NARRATOR:** All the gods stared at Odin expectantly. As much as they loathed Loki, they knew he was their only hope.

**ODIN:** Very well, Loki. We will honor your terms.

**NARRATOR:** Loki smoothed down his mussed hair and cracked his bony knuckles.

**LOKI:** That's more like it. Hmmm. Now, tell me more about his horse. Is it a steed or a mare?

**ODIN:** (*angrily*) I haven't checked lately.

**TYR:** (*growling*) It is a steed.

**LOKI:** Perfect! I can solve your problem. You will have your wall—and light to shine upon it!

**NARRATOR:** Loki slunk out from the presence of the Æsir and into the courtyard of Asgard. The giant's wall had been built all the way around the halls of the gods. The only portion missing was the grand archway that was to hang above the gates. The two giant builders stood nearby humming to themselves as they prepared to put the final nail in the Æsir's coffin. The giant stonemason paused in his work, stretched, and yawned.

**GIANT:** (*yawn*) Svadilfare, all that is left is the archway, and we have a whole day left before summer is here. The sun is getting hot. I think I'll take a nap. Go ahead and drag the arch-piece over here while I'm napping. When I wake, we'll hoist it into place.

**SVADILFARE:** (*sarcastically*) Of course. Why would *I* need a break?

**GIANT:** (*angrily*) Silence, dumb beast! Do it immediately—or I'll turn you into glue for the bricks!

**NARRATOR:** The builder stretched and padded over to the shady side of the wall.

**SVADILFARE:** (*grumbling*) Where would he be without me to do his dirty work?

**LOKI:** My plan will work perfectly.

**NARRATOR:** Loki covered his mouth to stifle a giggle, and with a wiggle of his ears, he turned himself into the loveliest pink mare creation had ever seen. He made sure to make his coat extra shiny and his rump especially plump. With a feminine whinny he trotted out of hiding. (*hoofbeats*)

**LOKI:** (*feminine voice*) Oh, Svadilfare! Yoo-hoo! Svadilfare!

NARRATOR:  Svadilfare the steed looked up and neighed in shock.

SVADILFARE:  *(neigh of surprise)* By my hooves! A mare!

NARRATOR:  He ran to the side of the transformed Loki.

SVADILFARE:  Hey, there! I haven't seen you around here before. New in town?

LOKI:  I heard there was a stud farm in these parts, but I had no idea how true it would be. Tee hee.

SVADILFARE:  If I said you had a nice muzzle, would you hold it against me?

NARRATOR:  The pink mare put on a sudden pout.

LOKI:  *(suddenly hard-to-get)* No, thank you, slave.

NARRATOR:  Svadilfare looked at the mare with a puzzled look.

SVADILFARE:  *(confused)* Why did you call me a slave?

LOKI:  *(innocently)* Well, that's what you are, isn't it? I mean, you spend all day working and you never get paid for it. Isn't that a slave?

SVADILFARE: No—I—Uh...

LOKI:  Why don't you come away with me? We can frolic in the fields and feast on the grass and be free! Just the two of us. Tee hee.

SVADILFARE:  All right!

NARRATOR:  Svadilfare puckered his horse-lips up for a kiss.

LOKI:  *(under his breath)* Yuck. I've got to get out of here—and quick.

NARRATOR:  Loki the beautiful mare took off toward the mountains. *(hoofbeats)*

LOKI:  *(lovey-dovey)* Catch me if you can, big boy!

SVADILFARE:  I love it when they play hard-to-get!

NARRATOR:  The stallion charged off, hot on Loki's heels. *(hoofbeats)*

LOKI:  *(under his breath)* Those gods owe me big time for this.

NARRATOR:  And so the two horses disappeared from Asgard. Loki led Svadilfare for miles and miles, down the Rainbow Bridge—through world after world.

When the giant stonemason awoke from his nap and found his horse had vanished, his roars filled the entire valley.

GIANT:  *(roar)* Svadilfare! Svadilfare! Where are you? If I ever find you, you can kiss your flea-bitten hide goodbye!

ODIN:  *(coyly)* Ahem. Is there a problem?

NARRATOR:  Odin All-Father and the other Æsir strolled up nonchalantly.

GIANT:  *(ferociously)* Don't think that you have won! All I have left is this arch piece. I can finish this wall just as easily by myself!

**ODIN:** Can you? My, my. You know, that piece looks rather large. Make sure you lift with your legs. *(chuckle)*

**NARRATOR:** Try as he might, the giant could not lift the arch piece high enough to fit into place.

**GIANT:** *(grunting)* Curse that horse! Curse you gods! Curse the sun and the moon!

**NARRATOR:** All the night, he toiled—pushing it this way and that way—cursing every being under the sun. But he could not fit the piece into place.

   The first day of summer dawned. The Æsir were waiting by the wall to greet it. The giant was in a heap upon the ground, where he had fallen during the night—completely exhausted. His magic was fading, and his disguise had melted away. His true appearance surfaced—that of a being with grotesque features covered in boils and gangly limbs matted with foul hair.

**ODIN:** Thank you for the wall, giant. It will keep *your kind* safely out of our home forever.

**GIANT:** *(hoarsely)* You cheats may have won this time, but we will find another way to destroy you! I swear it!

**TYR:** *(playfully)* What's that? I can't hear you. You're a little *horse*.

*(laughter from all the gods)*

**ODIN:** Now, Thor—if you don't mind escorting our guest out of Asgard.

**THOR:** With pleasure!

**NARRATOR:** Thor ran forward and lifted the giant by his gangly limbs. He spun the giant around and around, and with a whoosh—released him—sending him flying up, up, up, over the mountains. *(whistling sound)* There was a slight cracking sound as he touched down far away.

*(polite clapping from the gods)*

**TYR:** Nice distance.

**THOR:** *(booming)* One giant down! Many more to go!

**ODIN:** Yes, we have averted certain disaster—for now. But the giant was right: They will come at us with other tricks, other deceptions. We must be on our guard.

**NARRATOR:** The attention of the gods was drawn to a bend in the path, where Loki, back in his normal form, staggered into view. All kinds of leaves and twigs were stuck to his body, and he looked three steps from dead.

**LOKI:** *(breathlessly)* I—I—I finally ditched him. There ain't nothing like outrunning an amorous horse.

**THOR:** I say, three cheers for Loki! His trick has saved the day!

**ALL:** Huzzah! Huzzah! Huzzah!

**NARRATOR:** Only Tyr refused to cheer.

**ODIN:** Loki, trickster, you have saved Asgard! We have a brand new wall, which will make us safe for generations to come—all thanks to you. We welcome you as one of our own!

**NARRATOR:** Through his panting breaths, the trickster gave a sly smile.

**LOKI:** It's about time!

**FREYA:** Thank you for saving me from such a monstrous husband!

**NARRATOR:** Freya ran forward to kiss Loki upon the cheek. Balder and Thor lifted the skinny trickster up on their shoulders and carried him between the mighty pillars of the newly-built wall. That day Loki was the toast of Asgard, and all was cheerful there for a time.

## DISCUSSION QUESTIONS

- What do you find interesting about the Norse creation story? Explain.
- Do the gods treat Loki fairly? Explain.
- What makes Loki a good ally for the Æsir?
- Were the Æsir wise for taking the giant's deal? Explain.
- Was it fair for the gods to win the way they did? Explain.
- What are the different personalities of the gods?
- Should the gods trust Loki? Explain.

# THE APPLES OF IDUNA
## TEACHER GUIDE

## BACKGROUND

Fountains and elixirs of youth are a type of magical element that shows up in many folktales and legends from a variety of lands. An item that gives the ability to stay eternally young and cheat death is a fascinating idea, and the Norse had their own youth-prolonging objects—the golden apples from the magical orchard of the goddess Iduna. If the gods eat of these apples, they will remain young and vital. If they don't, they will grow old as mortals do and eventually die.

Even though the Norse prized youth, they also valued wisdom and those who had lived long enough to attain it. But in a strange twist, it was considered almost a failure for a man to reach old age. Why? Early death was not a disappointment if it was done right. The battle-oriented world of the Norse people demanded that men die a valiant death (preferably in battle). Those who did were carried in the beautiful arms of the valkyries, Odin's handmaidens, to Valhalla "the hall of the Slain" in Asgard. There they would feast until the battle of Ragnarok at the end of time. This was the closest the Norse ever got to a heaven.

If a man were cowardly or otherwise unimpressive in his death, he would have to spend his afterlife in Niflheim, the frozen world of the dead. This realm is ruled by a hag named Hela, incidentally where the modern term *hell* originated. Nothing was more dishonorable to a Norse warrior than a "straw-death" or a death at home in bed from sickness or old age.

## SUMMARY

Iduna's magical apples give eternal youth to the Æsir as long as they are eaten every day. Although it is vital that Iduna stay in her orchard to keep it healthy, she often wonders what it would be like to get out and see the world.

Odin is bored with the happenings in Asgard, and Loki suggests they disguise themselves and go adventuring in Midgard, the human world. As they travel, they stop to cook their dinner over a campfire. Loki tries to cook the meat, but something prevents it from cooking. A giant eagle perched in the tree above their cook-fire declares that he is stealing the fire's heat through magic. He agrees to allow the meat to cook if Loki will give him a share. Loki agrees, and the eagle swoops down and begins to eat all the meat. In anger Loki attacks the eagle with a stick but finds himself magically bonded to the stick, which is in turn magically bonded to the eagle. The bird takes flight with Loki in tow.

Dragging Loki through forests and over rugged mountain peaks, the eagle demands that Loki aid him or die. Loki agrees. The eagle is really Thiazi the giant and needs Loki's assistance in stealing Iduna and her magic apples from Asgard. Loki returns to Asgard and lures Iduna down into Midgard, where she is abducted by the giant-eagle.

Weeks pass, and no one knows what has become of Iduna. The apples of youth begin to wither on the branch, and the gods grow old. Finally, they realize Loki is behind Iduna's disappearance and send him to fetch her. Loki takes Frigga's falcon-skin cloak and flies to the giant's mountain hideout. Iduna is there, and Loki transforms her into a nut to carry her back to Asgard in his claws. But the giant-eagle sees his escape and gives pursuit. As Loki is nearing

Asgard, the gods see his approach and build a fire on the walls. Loki swoops down through the fire, and as the giant-eagle follows behind, the gods cause the fire to blaze—setting their enemy on fire and killing him. Once restored to her true self, Iduna feeds the gods the apples she had stored in her basket, and they are restored to youthful vitality.

## ESSENTIAL QUESTIONS

- What is better—youth or old age?
- What are the benefits and drawbacks of both youth and old age?
- If you start a problem, should *you* have to solve it?

## ANTICIPATORY QUESTIONS

- What are some stories you have heard about the Fountain of Youth or other items that prevent aging?
- What usually happens in these types of stories?
- Is there a reason the gods live forever?
- What would happen if the gods aged?
- What types of problems would this cause?

## CONNECT

**Biblical Allusions** By the time the Norse myths were recorded, their chroniclers were men who had been converted to Christianity. Many parallels can be seen between some of the Norse stories and elements of the Bible. For example, Iduna's orchard of apples has similarities to the Garden of Eden. Also, Loki (not just in this story but in others) has many similarities to the Devil—a sly, shape-changing trickster. The question is debated among scholars: Were these Biblical elements originally in the myths? Or did the Christian men who first recorded the Norse myths add them in?

## TEACHABLE TERMS

- **Hyperbole** Bragi's ponderous poetry on pg. 39 is an example of hyperbole, something overdone for effect. In this case it's intended for humorous effect.
- **Stereotype** A common, but limiting, conception of a group of people is a stereotype. This play uses stereotypes about the elderly to generate humor in the story. Discuss how stereotypes work and why they often aren't accurate.
- **Colloquialism** When Odin says, "I can't hear it thunder," on pg. 52, this is a colloquialism (or regional saying) to indicate he is hard of hearing.
- **Cause and Effect** How do Loki's actions cause trouble for the gods? Does any good come from Loki's actions? Why is Loki called both "The Doer of Good and the Doer of Evil"? Discuss.
- **Complex Character** Loki is an excellent example of a complex character. As the stories progress, Loki will only become more complex. At times he is an ally, and at others, an enemy. Is Loki trying to do good but can't escape his evil nature? Or is he secretly evil and pretending to be good? What are his motivations? Discuss.

## RECALL QUESTIONS

1. How do the gods stay eternally young?
2. What keeps Loki's meat from cooking?
3. Why does Loki agree to help a giant?
4. Into what does Loki transform Iduna for their return voyage?
5. How do the gods defeat Thiazi?

# THE APPLES OF IDUNA

## CAST

| | |
|---|---|
| **ODIN** | *All-Father of the Gods* |
| **FREYA** | *Goddess of Love and Beauty* |
| **IDUNA** | *Protector of the Shining Apples* |
| **BRAGI** | *God of Poetry* |
| **FRIGGA** | *Queen of the Gods* |
| **SIF** | *Wife of Thor* |
| **THOR** | *God of Thunder* |
| **LOKI** | *Half-Giant Trickster* |
| **HEIMDALL** | *Watchman of the Gods* |
| **BALDER** | *Most Beloved of the Gods* |
| **THIAZI** | *Wind Giant* |

**NARRATOR:** In the midst of Asgard there grew a magnificent, golden orchard. Although it was breathtaking to behold, its object was not beauty, but the fruit it bore, for on the branches of the trees within budded shining apples with magical powers. These apples were tenderly cared for by the knowledgeable hands of the goddess, Iduna. It was her sole purpose to make sure the orchard continued to flourish. All the Æsir fed upon these apples daily, and this was the secret elixir that kept them eternally youthful.

**FREYA:** Hello, Iduna. I am here for another apple.

**IDUNA:** *(confused)* Another apple, Freya? You've already had one today.

**FREYA:** As you always say, an apple a day keeps the wrinkles away. But I was thinking, since one apple makes me look this good, if I ate *two* apples everyday, perhaps I could look even better. That is, if such a thing is possible. *(laugh)*

**IDUNA:** Oh dear. That would never work! If I picked two apples for you, the rest of the gods would want two. The trees would not have enough time to regenerate before the next day. Then where would we be?

**FREYA:** *(disappointed)* I never thought of that. *(sigh)* I guess I will just have to settle for *this level* of beauty. Hmmmm.

**NARRATOR:** Since Iduna's duty was so vital and demanding, she never left her orchard. The gods had a golden house built for her there below the boughs, so that she might always be pruning, watering, and pampering her beloved trees.

Iduna's husband, Bragi, lived there below the golden leaves with her. He was the god of poetry and spent his time plucking a harp, telling tales that stretched on from one day to the next.

**BRAGI:** *(slowly, dramatically)* And so the sun began to set—ever slowly—upon the pale plain of cool crystal lakes, and the tall trees—swaying so, so softly like dancing damsels—lost their leaves in the whisking, whisking wind, while the birds sang their chirp, chirp, chirp song that sounded like a—

**IDUNA:** Skip a bit, husband. Too much description tends to bore the listener.

**BRAGI:** *(pausing)* Of course, my sweet, sweet apple blossom. *(continuing)* And the tulips tiptoed and tapped their petaled heads upon the water, which rippled like a—

**IDUNA:** *(suddenly)* Enough! *(kindly)* I mean, let's take a break, dear.

**BRAGI:** But I was just getting to the good part.

**IDUNA:** *(annoyed)* You never get to the good part.

**NARRATOR:** Iduna smiled sadly at her confused husband.

**IDUNA:** Oh, Bragi. It's just that I seem so frustrated lately. I love my orchard and my shining apples. But I must tend them day and night. I often wonder what it would be like to lead a normal life. We never have adventures like the other gods. Haven't you ever wanted to have an adventure?

**BRAGI:** I feel it is far more fun to tell about the adventures of others—like Olaf the Bluetoothed. I believe his tale starts something like this… *(starts singing)*

**IDUNA:** *(suddenly)* No! *(calmly)* I love your stories, Bragi—although they are endless. They are like us gods—eternal. But what is eternity if you don't ever get to enjoy it? *(pause)* But wait. What am I saying? If I

didn't tend the apples, they would wither—and then so would we.

**BRAGI:** *(strangely)* Our ship would sail afar. Death. Nothingness. Or other worlds?

**IDUNA:** Yes, good point. What would it mean if the gods *died*?

**BRAGI:** No, it's not that, dear. It's the beginning of a song I was just remembering about Erik No-Ears. *(pause)* Or was it Gunther the One-Nostriled? Hmmm.

**IDUNA:** *(sigh)* Nevermind.

**NARRATOR:** Bragi's song droned on throughout the orchard, and Iduna returned to her work.

Meanwhile, in Valhalla at the long tables that filled the hall, hundreds of mortal warriors feasted on endless helpings of meat and ale. Having died valiantly in battle, they had been carried to Valhalla by the valkyries, the lovely but fierce shieldmaidens of Odin. There they spent the afterlife feasting and fighting.

Odin was slumped in his high seat, a look of supreme boredom on his face. Loki the trickster was seated by Odin's side watching the warriors' feast with disgust.

**ODIN:** *(sigh)* Ugh.

**LOKI:** I know. It's disgusting. You'd think their table manners would improve eventually.

**ODIN:** It's not that! I am discontent.

**LOKI:** Oh. That's not good. When Odin's not happy, nobody's happy. You know soon these warriors will start their daily battle. Would that cheer you up? Today my money is on Sven the Two-Toed. At the very least there'll be lots of blood and gore—maybe some severed heads.

**ODIN:** It's all pointless. The next day they'll be resurrected, and it will be the same old routine—feasting and fighting, feasting and fighting.

**LOKI:** Feasting and fighting. What else is there to life? Or in this case, the afterlife?

**ODIN:** From my high throne, I can see all of the Nine Worlds—all the wars of man, all the comings and goings of all the creatures in existence—but it's just not satisfying.

**LOKI:** Hmmm. It sounds like what you need is an adventure!

**ODIN:** An adventure? You can't be serious. Who would watch over Asgard?

**LOKI:** Watch over Asgard? Would you listen to yourself? Asgard can watch itself. You can't stay cooped up inside forever!

**ODIN:** Hmmm. Maybe you're right. But I'm Odin, All-Father. I can't just go parading around the Nine Worlds wearing my mighty crown. It would cause quite a scene.

**LOKI:** Then be like me and wear a disguise. Let's go see what's shakin' down in Midgard. Let's experience some of those earthly battles firsthand. It's got to be better than these.

**ODIN:** Then it's settled. We'll leave tonight.

**NARRATOR:** When darkness had fallen, Odin appeared at the gates of Asgard. He was wearing a wide-brimmed hat and a long blue cloak. In his hand he carried a walking staff. Loki soon appeared through the gloom.

**ODIN:** Loki!

**LOKI:** *(cry of fright)* Ah!

**ODIN:** It is I—Odin.

**LOKI:** Oh. Yeah. Good disguise. You about gave me a heart attack.

**ODIN:** *(proudly)* I thought of it myself. I tried to look like an average traveler.

**LOKI:** More like the Grim Reaper. But remember, you can't go around saying, "It is I—Odin." We are supposed to be simple travelers.

**ODIN:** Hmmm. Then I shall call myself Vegtam the Wanderer.

**LOKI:** *(not impressed)* Oh yeah. Good name.

**NARRATOR:** Loki and Odin passed down the Rainbow Bridge into Midgard. From there they wandered aimlessly, enjoying the simple hospitality of many humans who had no idea they hosted a pair of gods.

**ODIN:** This has been quite the adventure!

**LOKI:** *(grumbling)* You think? Each night we stay the night with some penniless farmer who talks his head off about his cows and goats. *Nothing* exciting has happened!

**ODIN:** I could do this for weeks!

**LOKI:** Weeks? *(groan)*

**NARRATOR:** As the pair continued to wander, the landscape began to grow barren and rocky.

**ODIN:** I can tell by the landscape that we're nearing Jotunheim. We should rest here for the evening. It's best not to go into the land of the giants when it is dark.

**LOKI:** Better not to go there at all! I've been in the land of the giants enough to last me a lifetime! I barely got out of there alive.

**ODIN:** *(booming laugh)* Oh, Loki! What do gods have to fear from giants?

**LOKI:** Plenty.

**ODIN:** I'm starving. I could eat a horse. Hmmm. But there are none of those to be seen here. Oh! There are some cattle grazing there not too far off. Why don't you fetch us one?

**LOKI:** Fine.

**NARRATOR:** Odin started a fire beneath a wide-spreading oak tree. Loki returned a few minutes later dragging a dead cow by the tail.

**LOKI:** Here's the beef!

**ODIN:** Throw the carcass in the ashes, and we'll have a fine dinner.

**LOKI:** Oh, no, no, no. Here's a fun fact about myself. On top of being the world's best trickster, I am also a gourmet cook. We will roast the meat on spits.

**ODIN:** Very well. Just roast it quickly!

**NARRATOR:** Loki produced a crooked dagger, flayed strips of meat from the cow, arranged them on spits, and laid them over the crackling fire.

**LOKI:** Now, to wait.

**NARRATOR:** After several minutes of cooking, Loki jerked the spits off the fire.

**LOKI:** This meat should be cooked to perfection now!

**NARRATOR:** Loki bit eagerly into the meat.

**LOKI:** Yuck! *(spitting sounds)* It's still raw! I can't believe it!

**ODIN:** Whatever the problem is, fix it, mister gourmet! I'm starving!

**NARRATOR:** Loki scratched his head in confusion and piled even more fuel on the fire. The meat cooked for some time over the blaze.

**LOKI:** Now it will be perfect. I promise!

**NARRATOR:** He handed a spit to Odin and took one for himself. The All-Father bit into his meat and quickly spit it out.

**ODIN:** *(angrily)* Loki! This meat still has not been cooked! This is no time for games! What kind of trick are you trying to play?

**LOKI:** It's not a trick! The meat should be cooked. *(to the fire)* Stupid fire! What's wrong with you? Cook! Cook, I say!

**NARRATOR:** Loki began to beat at the fire with his wooden spit.

**ODIN:** This is foolishness! I'm going for a walk. When I come back this meat had better be cooked—or I will not be happy!

NARRATOR: Odin stalked away into the darkness. Loki examined the fire with a wild look.

LOKI: Some magic must be at work here.

NARRATOR: He stared up into the dark branches of the oak tree above him. Just then, strange laughter boomed down at him.

THIAZI: *(loud laughter)* Ha-ha!

LOKI: *(yelling in fright)* Ah! Who's there?

THIAZI: I am the one working against your fire. I have stolen its heat.

NARRATOR: An eagle head materialized out of the gloom. The bird was so large that the mighty limbs of the oak sagged under its weight.

LOKI: What's the big idea?

THIAZI: With my mighty eagle breath, I have sucked the heat from your fire. That meat will never be cooked—until you allow me to eat my fill of it.

LOKI: Sharing, huh? I've never been fond of sharing.

THIAZI: Suit yourself. But I think your friend will be back soon, and he will not be happy if his dinner is not prepared.

LOKI: *(angrily)* Fine. Take your share. Congratulations on playing the lamest trick ever. I hope you choke on it.

NARRATOR: In a split second the eagle snatched up the bloody carcass of the cow and disappeared back into the darkness of the tree top.

THIAZI: *(loud smacking)* Gulp! Mmm.

LOKI: Gross. Didn't your mother teach you to chew with your beak shut?

THIAZI: Burp!

NARRATOR: The skeleton of the cow fell down to the ground—its bones picked completely clean.

LOKI: Hungry much? Whatever happened to eating like a bird?

THIAZI: I am not done yet.

NARRATOR: The eagle swooped down to Loki's fire and pecked at the meat cooking over it.

LOKI: *(shrieking)* Wait! That's mine! You promised you would cook it!

THIAZI: *(smacking sounds)* I did cook it. And it's delicious.

NARRATOR: Loki picked up Odin's walking staff and brandished it.

LOKI: All right, bird-brain! I'm going to teach you a lesson! Ah! *(battlecry)*

NARRATOR: Loki struck at the eagle with the staff. Then, to his horror, he realized two things simultaneously. His hands were firmly stuck to the staff. And the other end of the staff was clutched firmly in the eagle's talon.

LOKI: Hey! What's going on? Let me go! Let me go!

THIAZI: Time to go for a ride! Going up? *(booming laugh)* Ha-ha!

**NARRATOR:** The eagle spread its powerful wings.

**LOKI:** Uh-oh. This is going to be bad. *(screaming)* Ahhh-eeee!

**NARRATOR:** With an enormous thrust, the eagle shot into the air—Loki trailing behind at the end of the staff.

**LOKI:** *(cry of fright)* Ahhhhhh!

**NARRATOR:** The bird and his unwilling passenger disappeared into the night. It was not a minute later when Odin returned from his walk.

**ODIN:** Hmmm. I wonder where Loki has gotten off to. Oh well.

**NARRATOR:** He noticed the meat strips were lying near the fire.

**ODIN:** Oooh. Dinner's done.

**NARRATOR:** Meanwhile, the giant eagle was taking Loki for the ride of his life—and he hoped not his death—carrying him high over the mountains of Jotunheim.

**THIAZI:** Ha! You thought *you* were going to teach *me* a lesson. Me! Ha! But you are going to get the lesson today! And that lesson is—don't mess with Thiazi the mighty giant!

**LOKI:** Oh great. He's a giant. *(to himself)* Loki, why does this always happen to you?

**THIAZI:** So you are the famous Loki! I can't believe it. I always heard you were a great trickster. But I tricked you easily enough.

**LOKI:** You know me?

**THIAZI:** All giants know you, Loki. Once you escaped us, you became our enemy! We have long desired your death.

**LOKI:** Heh. Heh. Oh, let's let bygones be bygones. Can't we all just get along?

**THIAZI:** I will spare your life—but only if you aid me in a task.

**LOKI:** Help a giant? Are you crazy?

**NARRATOR:** The giant-eagle swooped low and dragged Loki through a forest of tall pines. *(branches breaking)*

**THIAZI:** Whoops. Silly me. I didn't fly high enough to clear the forest.

**LOKI:** *(cries of pain)* Oof! Ouch! Ow! I swear, if I ever get out of here alive I'll rip your beak off—Oof!

**NARRATOR:** The forest gave away to a deep valley surrounded by high mountains.

**LOKI:** You gutless piece of filth! Fight me fair and square!

**THIAZI:** Oh dear. Look at those high mountain peaks. I don't know if I'm flying high enough to clear those either. They look very sharp.

**LOKI:** Gulp!

*(loud thwacking sounds)*

**LOKI:** Ooof! Ow! Oof!

**THIAZI:** Oooh, look! A mountain lake. Fancy a swim?

**LOKI:** *(gurgling)* Noooo!

NARRATOR: When Thiazi pulled Loki up from the water, he was gasping for breath.

LOKI: Fine! Fine! I give up! I'll do whatever you want!

THIAZI: That's more like it.

NARRATOR: Thiazi drew up and landed on a mountain ledge. He snatched Loki up and squeezed him in his powerful talons.

LOKI: (hoarsely) That's a little tight. I thought we were friends now!

THIAZI: You promised to get me whatever I want. Well, let me tell you what I want. I want the golden apples of Iduna.

LOKI: Oh, you don't want those nasty, old things. They're so bitter. Plus, they leave a waxy build-up on your teeth. Are you going vegetarian on me? Better stick to red meat!

THIAZI: I want the apples, and I want the goddess herself as my prisoner.

LOKI: The last thing you want around here is some chatty goddess. Yakkity-yak all day long.

THIAZI: Stop making jokes! You made a promise, creature! You will honor it, or you will die!

NARRATOR: Loki saw the look in the bird's merciless eyes and the cruel curve of his beak.

LOKI: Gulp. Are you sure there's not a third option?

NARRATOR: The eagle-talons began to squeeze.

LOKI: All right! All right! I will bring you Iduna.

THIAZI: Seven days from now bring her down the Rainbow Bridge to Midgard. Do it, or I will find you, wherever you are, and slice you in half! Do we understand each other?

LOKI: Yeah, I got that. You're comin' through loud and clear.

THIAZI: Good. You just may be a giant-friend after all.

NARRATOR: When Loki finally limped down out of the mountains of Jotunheim, Odin was still sitting beneath the oak tree.

LOKI: Ah! Oh! Ow!

ODIN: There you are! Where have you been? I've been waiting here all morning!

LOKI: (sarcastically) Sorry to keep you waiting. I was just fighting for my life. No thanks to you, I might add.

ODIN: (ignoring him) I've been thinking, this adventuring is great fun, but we must get back to Asgard! Plus, I don't think this mountain air is agreeing with you. You look absolutely awful.

LOKI: Fine with me. The sooner, the better.

NARRATOR: As the gods turned back toward home, Loki saw the silhouette of the eagle watching him from atop the mountains.

Once back in Asgard, the trickster wasted no time. He went straight to Iduna's orchard. The gods were his friends—his sworn blood-brothers—but this giant meant business, and Loki's first priority was saving his own neck. He did not like the idea of being sliced to ribbons by a psychotic eagle.

**LOKI:**  Good morning, Iduna!

**NARRATOR:**    He found the goddess tending her shining apples as usual—a basket full of them looped about her arm.

**IDUNA:**  Loki, what brings you here? You do not eat the apples of the gods.

**LOKI:**  True. It's that giant blood I have in my veins. It keeps me naturally youthful and oh-so-handsome.

**IDUNA:**  Okay…

**LOKI:**  You know, I thought I'd find you here. Good old Iduna the homebody. You always know she'll be around.

**IDUNA:**  Well, I…

**LOKI:**  I came to tell you about a wonderful sight I saw while Odin and I were adventuring…but I'm afraid it might depress you.

**IDUNA:**  Why would a wonderful sight depress me?

**LOKI:**  You never leave your orchard, so me telling you about this great far-off thing might make you sad.

**IDUNA:**  It's not like I *can't* leave the orchard.

**LOKI:**  (*shocked*) Please, Iduna! Don't even joke! What would these apples do without you to watch them grow? In fact, Odin even told me specifically *not* to tell you.

**IDUNA:**  Why ever not?

**LOKI:**  He said, (*mimicking Odin*) "Don't put ideas about adventuring into Iduna's head! We need her here at all times. The last thing we need is her running off trying to enjoy herself! I forbid her to leave."

**IDUNA:**  What? I do this job because I want to! Nobody can order me around! Now, tell me—what did you see?

**NARRATOR:**    Loki leaned in and whispered.

**LOKI:**  (*whispering*) It was a shining tree. And it grew apples—just like these.

**NARRATOR:**  The eyes of Iduna widened.

**IDUNA:**  Just like mine? That can't be!

**LOKI:**  Oh, it's true. I thought you should know.

**IDUNA:**  What did its leaves look like? Was its trunk wide like the trees here?

**LOKI:**  You know, the details are all a bit hazy. Gee, I sure wish you could have a look-see yourself.

**IDUNA:**  I am not afraid to go. It's just…

**LOKI:**  You're right. You're right. Don't rock the boat. Besides, I'm sure someone has already discovered that tree. They're probably picking the apples right now. Oh! You know what I just realized?

**IDUNA:**  What? What?

**LOKI:**  If mortals pick apples from that tree, *they* might live forever. Hmmm. That wouldn't be good. A bunch of humans running around forever. Then they'd get all full of themselves and challenge the gods. Looks like all of Asgard is at stake here. But you have your boundaries. Oh well.

**IDUNA:** *(determined)* You know what? I have become a bit reclusive. It would be in the best interest of all the Æsir if I go see this tree and pick its apples for the gods.

**LOKI:** You're such a hero! But it's a dangerous world down there—especially for a female.

**IDUNA:** I'm not as fragile as you think. I will go! And I will take a basket of my own apples to compare to the others. Now tell me where you saw this tree again.

**LOKI:** Of course! But, you know, we might keep this between us. After all, we don't want it getting out that your apples aren't the only apples in town.

**IDUNA:** I never thought of that. I will slip away, have my adventure, and be back before anyone can miss me.

**LOKI:** A perfect plan!

**NARRATOR:** The next day, Bragi went among the gods, looking for his wife.

**BRAGI:** Has anyone seen Iduna? She did not return yesterday from her walk through the orchard.

**FRIGGA:** She must be in the orchard somewhere. Where else would she be?

**BRAGI:** No, I've searched it, and she cannot be found.

**FRIGGA:** Not in the orchard! We must go to Odin at once.

**NARRATOR:** The news of Iduna's disappearance troubled Odin.

**ODIN:** We must hope she will return—and soon. Without her care, the apples of youth will begin to wither.

**NARRATOR:** But for days and days, Iduna did not return, and, even though the goddesses of Asgard tried to tend the orchard themselves, it began to suffer without its mistress's masterful touch.

**FRIGGA:** I don't understand this. I have watered the trees every day, and yet they are looking sick.

**FREYA:** Don't ask me. I've never been good at growing things. I'm much better at being beautiful. In fact, I think I look more beautiful and younger than I ever have!

**SIF:** You've been picking two apples a day, haven't you? I knew it! We're only allowed one a day, you thief!

**FRIGGA:** Ladies! Ladies! Fewer and fewer branches are budding. Iduna must return soon, or we will run out of apples.

**FREYA:** *(in shock)* What? Are you serious?

**FRIGGA:** Yes!

**FREYA:** I will not allow my skin to wrinkle! I'll be hideous.

**NARRATOR:** News soon spread through Asgard that the apples were dwindling.

**ODIN:** Yes, the rumors are true. We are running out of apples.

*(muttering from the gods)*

**THOR:** Thor's wife, Sif, should be given the apples for sure. She has the greatest beauty in Asgard, and it must not be spoiled.

**FREYA:** I beg to differ! If she gets apples, I definitely get apples. I am the goddess of *beauty*.

**THOR:** And Sif is the goddess of the home!

**FREYA:** More like *homeliness!* There aren't enough apples in Asgard to help her looks!

**ODIN:** Beauty is not our main concern here. Thor and Tyr should have the remaining apples. They must keep their bodies strong and healthy in order to defend us from the giants.

**HEIMDALL:** I'm the Watchman of the Gods! If my eyes and ears get weak, then where will we be? Am I not important?

**BALDER:** I don't think that is what Father means, brother.

**FRIGGA:** Balder must have an apple! I won't see my baby boy growing old before my very eyes!

**ODIN:** Of course, Balder will have an apple.

**HEIMDALL:** You *would* favor him over the rest of us! Balder's always been the favorite!

*(arguing among the gods)*

**ODIN:** No one is allowed in the orchard of Iduna until further notice!

**FREYA:** You can't do that! You can't!

**FRIGGA:** Odin, this is not fair!

**NARRATOR:** Bragi walked slowly into the hall full of bickering gods.

**BRAGI:** It does not matter.

**ODIN:** Silence! Bragi, what do you mean?

**BRAGI:** The last of the trees have withered—their fruit hangs dead. My wife must be dead. She would never allow this to happen. There are no words to express it. It is just…

**ODIN:** Iduna has no apples, and Bragi has no words. We truly are doomed.

**NARRATOR:** The loss of Iduna's apples took its toll. Soon the bodies of the Æsir grew weak and infirm. Their joints began to ache, their muscles shrank and sagged, their teeth fell out, their hair lost its color. Only Loki retained his youth.

**FREYA:** *(old voice)* I can't believe this. I look horrible! My lips were once like cherries—now they're like prunes!

**BALDER:** *(old voice)* Did you say, "Prunes?" Yes, please. I'll take some.

**SIF:** *(old voice)* Odin! Odin! We have a crisis!

**NARRATOR:** Sif's cries woke Odin from one of his ever-more-frequent naps.

**ODIN:** *(old voice)* Wha—? What is it, Sif?

**SIF:** I have an emergency. Thor was taking his morning bath—

**ODIN:** Yes?

**SIF:** And, well, he's fallen, and he can't get up.

LOKI: *(cruel laughter)* Hee hee!

NARRATOR: The gods glared at Loki.

LOKI: What? It's funny.

NARRATOR: The hall-doors opened, and the bent form of Heimdall hobbled in—leaning heavily on his walking cane.

FREYA: Who is that?

SIF: I can't quite make him out.

NARRATOR: Ten minutes later Heimdall stood before the throne.

HEIMDALL: Odin!

ODIN: Wha—did I doze off again?

HEIMDALL: I've come to tell you about a new threat I've noticed in Midgard—a new group of humans—teenagers. They're between the age of thirteen and eighteen, and they are absolutely the worst!

FREYA: I agree!

HEIMDALL: Something must be done about them! Down in Midgard they're playing their music late into the night. I can't get any sleep!

LOKI: Hee hee!

BALDER: Well, I know exactly what we should do about that!

NARRATOR: The gods looked to Balder expectantly.

BALDER: Hmmm. Nope. I forgot it again.

NARRATOR: Thor entered the hall—holding his tender back.

THOR: *(groaning)* Thor has never felt such pain!

SIF: Honey, how did you get out of the bath?

THOR: I am Thor! Nothing can stop me! *(pause)* But this arthritis is coming pretty close.

LOKI: Hee hee.

FREYA: Respect your elders, young man!

LOKI: What? Can't a person laugh? C'mon. You have to think this is hilarious! Heimdall used to be the Watchman of the Gods, and now he can't see his hand in front of his face. Freya used to be the goddess of beauty, and now every part of her is heading south. And not one of you has enough teeth to eat solid meat.

ODIN: Loki, your attitude angers me beyond belief! And, furthermore—Zzzzzzzz.

NARRATOR: Odin's chin fell forward to his chest.

LOKI: Hey, I'm not the bad guy here. Iduna is the one who left you—not me.

HEIMDALL: Wait a minute. Something is coming back to me.

NARRATOR: Heimdall squinted his eyes as his rusty mind-wheels began to turn.

HEIMDALL: Right before all this started, I saw someone leading Iduna down the Rainbow Bridge. Now who was that?

**THOR:** Who was it? Tell us, Heimdall!

**HEIMDALL:** Oh, I can see his face. What's his name? Hokey—Poker—something like that—Wait a minute! Loki!

**NARRATOR:** Odin's aged head jerked up.

**ODIN:** What?

**NARRATOR:** In unison the gods turned toward Loki—their eyes narrowing into slits.

**LOKI:** Yikes. It's like the living dead.

**THOR:** Where is Iduna? Tell us the truth, you whippersnapper, or we'll beat it out of you!

**LOKI:** Easy, gramps. Don't break a hip there. I'm not afraid of you old fossils.

**NARRATOR:** Frigga, standing near her magical spinning wheel, touched it lightly with her hand, and the spindle began to whirr. *(whirring sound)* A gossamer line of thread shot out, winding itself around the body of Loki.

**LOKI:** Hey! What's this? Knitting tricks? No fair! No fair!

**NARRATOR:** Loki—completely cocooned by the thread—fell to the floor. The Æsir closed in.

**LOKI:** You don't have enough strength left to make *me* talk! Your bark is worse than your bite. What are you going to do? Gum me to death?

**ODIN:** No. We have a different weapon than force. *(to Bragi)* Oh, Bragi! Over here.

**NARRATOR:** The god of poetry shuffled over—harp in hand.

**LOKI:** *(suddenly afraid)* You wouldn't!

**ODIN:** Loki was hoping you would tell him that story that you love to tell—the long one—that saga about Olaf Bluetooth.

**BRAGI:** *(old voice)* Oooh. That's a good one. Well, it started a long, long, long time ago, when the world was a much different place. Times were hard then. The snow was colder, and the mountains were steeper, roads went uphill both ways, and gold went farther than it does now—

**LOKI:** No! Stop! All right. I give up! I thought his stories were horrible before! I'll tell you the truth! The giant Thiazi forced me to deliver Iduna to him, and I did.

**ODIN:** And now you're going to promise to get her back. Right?

**LOKI:** Ha! You are going senile. I'm not going into Jotunheim by myself.

**ODIN:** Bragi, continue.

**BRAGI:** Now, where was I? I can't quite remember. Well, I'll just start back at the beginning. The world was much different back then—

**LOKI:** You win! I'll go. Anything is better than this. Just let me out of this thread.

**NARRATOR:** Once freed, Loki stood and brushed himself off.

**LOKI:** I'll need Frigga's falcon cloak to fly to Jotunheim.

**FRIGGA:** *(old voice)* Of course, of course. Let me see. Now where did I put that? It was just here a minute ago. I swear, I'd lose my head if it wasn't attached.

**LOKI:** Oh brother.

**NARRATOR:** At last, Loki flew from Asgard in the skin of the falcon.

**LOKI:** Loki, do this. Loki, do that. Old age has made those gods even crankier than before!

**NARRATOR:** He steered his course toward Jotunheim, to the same mountain peak that the eagle-giant had taken him to before. Smoke came from a nearby cave. Loki landed, shedding the falcon skin, and crept toward the cave-mouth. Within a soot-stained figure huddled by the fire. He knew it had to be Iduna, but then he saw her face. It was a shriveled old crone.

**LOKI:** Psst. Old crone! Where is the giant who lives here? Does he hold one of the Æsir captive?

**IDUNA:** *(old voice)* You've got a lot of nerve coming here, sonny! Especially after what you did to me!

**LOKI:** Iduna? But you're so old!

**IDUNA:** I have to eat the apples to stay young just like everybody else! I have some here in my basket. I carried them all the way here. I've been gone from my orchard so long, I know they are the last ones. I'm saving them. Besides, my teeth fell out last week, and I couldn't eat them even if I wanted to.

**LOKI:** Where's Thiazi?

**IDUNA:** That giant brute snatched me up as soon as I came down the Rainbow Bridge, and I gave him a stern talking to. I said, "Young man, you put me down this instant!"

**LOKI:** Yeah. Yeah. But where is he?

**IDUNA:** His whole plan was to weaken us gods, and then the giants were going to launch a full-scale attack on Asgard. Can you believe that?

*(eagle screech)*

**LOKI:** Cut the chit-chat, granny. The eagle's back.

**NARRATOR:** Loki seized Iduna's withered hand and quickly uttered some magic runes—spells of changing.

**IDUNA:** What's that you're saying? Oh, you young people and your slang!

**NARRATOR:** The goddess shrank down, down into the tiny form of a nut.

**IDUNA:** *(growing smaller)* What's going on?

**NARRATOR:** Throwing the falcon skin around his shoulders, Loki snatched up the nut-form of Iduna and flew from the cave.

*(eagle screech)*

**THIAZI:** Wait! Intruder! Stay for lunch! You'll make a nice noonday meal for me!

**LOKI:** That's what you think, bird-brain!

**NARRATOR:** With the eagle screeching after him, Loki pumped his wings as hard as he could.

**IDUNA:** Slow down! Slow down! What is it with youngsters and going so fast these days?

**NARRATOR:** Jotunheim gave way to Midgard, and Loki could feel the savage beak of the eagle-giant tearing at his tail-feathers.

**THIAZI:** One more minute, fool, and I will have your bones as a snack!

**NARRATOR:** In a flash, Loki shot upward, over the Rainbow Bridge, and the eagle, too, changed direction, following him up into Asgard. Loki began to call out in his falcon cry. *(falcon cries)*

Back in Asgard, the Æsir were all seated in comfy chairs upon the wall—watching the sun go down. Frigga was lazily fanning herself.

**FRIGGA:** Do you hear something?

**ODIN:** I can't hear it thunder.

**THOR:** What?

**ODIN:** I said, I can't hear it thunder!

**THOR:** No, *Thor* is the God of Thunder.

**ODIN:** *(sigh)*

**NARRATOR:** Suddenly Odin leaned forward and squinted at the horizon.

**ODIN:** There's something way off there.

**HEIMDALL:** Maybe it's that fellow that left here not long ago. What was his name again? Pokey…

**ODIN:** Loki!

**HEIMDALL:** No, that's not it. It started with a *p* sound.

**ODIN:** It's Loki! And he's being chased! Quick!

**NARRATOR:** With great effort the gods raised from their seats.

**ODIN:** Something is chasing him. Everyone, fetch some firewood. Pile it here on the ramparts. Hurry!

**FRIGGA:** All right. All right. I'm going as fast I can!

**NARRATOR:** From afar off, Loki saw fire spring up on the walls of Asgard.

**LOKI:** Ha! Those old coots still have some gumption left!

**THIAZI:** Grrrrr.

**NARRATOR:** The claws of Thiazi shot out, and Loki dodged this way and that to avoid them.

**IDUNA:** What's going on up there? I'm going to talk to your mother about your flying!

**NARRATOR:** With one last burst of speed, Loki reached the walls, swooping down through the smoke of the god's fire.

**ODIN:** Now!

**NARRATOR:** The gods threw new fuel upon the fire. Loki shot past the flames, but Thiazi, swooping hot on Loki's heels, was caught in the new explosion of flame.

**THIAZI:** Ah! Argh! *(cries of pain)*

**NARRATOR:**   The giant's eagle form blazed as he crashed to the ground. He skidded across the turf and came to rest in a smoking heap.

**ODIN:**  He is dead!

**NARRATOR:**  Thiazi's feathers had burned away from his dead body to reveal his true form beneath—a gangly giant. Loki landed beside him and pulled the falcon skin from his shoulders.

**LOKI:**  All right! Let's hear it for the gods! They may be old, but they've still got it!

**ODIN:**   We'll celebrate later. Where is Iduna, Loki?

**NARRATOR:**  Loki held out his palm—the nut still clutched within it. He uttered the runes, and Iduna appeared before them.

**BRAGI:**  Iduna! *(pause)* You look so old!

**IDUNA:**  My friends! It's good to be home. I'm sorry for all the trouble I've caused you.

**ODIN:**  You? It was Loki who got you into this mess, I have no doubt!

**IDUNA:**  Well, yes, but I say we forgive the young lad. After all, he's taught me a valuable lesson. Never again will I desire to leave my orchard. It is my purpose and my place. And everyone needs a purpose.

**LOKI:**  Well said! Let bygones be bygones.

**ODIN:**  This doesn't get you off the hook, Loki!

**LOKI:**  Luckily, I can still run faster than you all.

**IDUNA:**  Not for long. Loki, help me with these apples.

**NARRATOR:**  Iduna ground the apples she still carried within her basket into an easy-to-swallow applesauce, and the Æsir happily partook. By the time they had finished their helping, all of the gods felt quickness and youth returning to their limbs.

**FREYA:**  My beauty is back!

**THOR:**  Yes, and Thor's strength!

**SIF:**  And your hearing thankfully!

**THOR:**  Father, true old age has taught me new wisdom.

**ODIN:**  And what is that, Thor?

**THOR:**  Youth is a treasure!

**ODIN:**  Well said!

*(cheers from the gods)*

**NARRATOR:**  With their youth restored the gods did not turn in early, which had become their custom, but celebrated late into the night.

## DISCUSSION QUESTIONS

- What would be the downside to never growing old?
- Did Loki have any other choice than the actions he took in helping Thiazi kidnap Iduna? Explain.
- Is Loki actually good or actually evil? What is his "true" nature? Explain.
- This version of the myth uses many stereotypes about old age for humorous

purposes. How is old age different in real life than it is presented here?

- What is different or even unique about the Norse concept of gods that can die?
- Loki doesn't stop to consider the effect of his actions. Do you know other people like this? What is the result of their thoughtless behavior?

# TREASURES OF THE GODS
## TEACHER GUIDE

## BACKGROUND

Treasures and trinkets were of great importance in Norse culture. Rings were a way for wealthy rulers to show favor to their subjects. Many of the artifacts from Norse cultures—everything from decorative broaches, intricate shields, and well-crafted swords—show highly-talented craftsmen demonstrating great skill. Metal was not the only medium explored by these craftsmen either. Expertly engineered and delicately carved ships have been unearthed. The Norse were a people of craftsmen, engineers, and inventors.

It's no wonder that the Norse culture developed the concept of dwarves—underground folk allergic to sunlight who spent their days forging amazing treasures. While the dwarves have much skill in craftsmanship, they also illustrate the negative side effect of too much gold. Their race is presented as greedy and self-serving. They use their riches to their own advantage instead of for the good of others.

In this myth the gods will gain some of their most famous treasures—including Odin's powerful spear and Mjolnir, Thor's mighty hammer. Unlike the dwarves, the gods will use these weapons for good—to fight the giants and keep the forces of evil at bay.

## SUMMARY

Hating to hear Thor bragging about Sif's golden hair, Loki cuts it off in the middle of the night. When the Æsir discover that Loki is behind this crime, they decide to punish him unless he can find some way to remedy the problem. Loki vows to go to Svartalfheim, the land of the dwarves, and find treasures that will compensate for his mischief.

Using his magical flying shoes, Loki travels to Svartalfheim and finds the forge of the dwarf, Dvalin. A great metalworker, Dvalin agrees to make treasures for the gods—in order to prove that his craft is the greatest among the dwarves. He makes a spear for Odin, a ship for Frey, and a golden wig to replace Sif's hair. Loki takes these items but realizes that he will need even more treasures to make up for what he's done. He goes to the forge of another dwarf-smith named Brokk. In order to get Brokk to make treasures for him, Loki declares that Dvalin is the greatest of the dwarf-smiths—stirring up Brokk's pride. Brokk is wiser than Loki thinks and agrees to make treasures only if Loki will wager his head in the deal. If Brokk's treasures are greater than Dvalin's, Loki will have to let Brokk chop his head off. Loki hastily agrees.

Brokk fashions three unparalleled treasures—a mechanical boar for Frey, a self-replicating arm ring for Odin, and the magical hammer, Mjolnir, for Thor. While the dwarf is fashioning these items, Loki turns into a stinging fly and stings at the dwarf, trying to force an error. His attempts fail.

Brokk accompanies Loki back to Asgard, where the gods judge that the treasures of Brokk are superior. Loki is infuriated. Brokk demands Loki's head as part of their deal, and the gods are powerless to help him. As the dwarf is about to cut off Loki's head, the trickster realizes a key legal point—Brokk is entitled to his head, but not his neck. Therefore, the dwarf cannot cut off his head. The gods applaud this witty turn-around, but Brokk is angry. He tells the gods about Loki trying to cheat in the contest by turning himself into a stinging fly. As a concession, Odin allows the dwarf to sew shut Loki's lips—teaching the trickster a lesson about deceit. The gods celebrate because they have a new set of fabulous treasures, but Loki sulks in his hall and begins to plot his revenge.

## ESSENTIAL QUESTIONS

- What things in life should be treasured?
- Should you always consider the consequences of your actions before you commit them?
- Can lies bring about good—or only evil?

## ANTICIPATORY QUESTIONS

- What are some of the things you treasure?
- What are some mean pranks people play on one another?
- What is a dwarf?
- What is a forge?

## CONNECT

**Days of the Week** The influence of the Norse gods is still seen today in the days of the week. Sunday and Monday are named for the sun (Sol) and moon (Mani) respectively. Tuesday (Tyr's day) is derived from the Norse god of single combat, Tyr. Odin—or as he was known in other parts of the world, Woden—lent his name to Wednesday (Woden's day). Thor is clearly seen in Thursday (Thor's day). Friday is probably named for either Frigga or Freya (Frigga's day or Freya's day). Saturday (known as "Washing Day" in early Europe) is the stand-out, named for the Roman god, Saturn.

**Artwork** Design a poster for each day of the week and feature its corresponding Norse god namesake in the design. Remember: The Norse viewed the female Sun and the male Moon as two gods driving light-emitting chariots across the skies. For Saturday you could pick any other god or goddess who has not been featured.

## TEACHABLE TERMS

- **Alliteration** The line "Sif's days were spent combing, coiffing, and curling..." on pg. 57 is an example of alliteration.
- **Wordplay** Loki's conversation with Sif and Thor on pg. 58 is an example of wordplay or verbal wit. Loki makes several verbal jokes off the gods' comments.
- **Anti-hero** For the first time this story focuses almost completely on Loki, making him the main character. Loki is an example of an anti-hero, a protagonist with less-than-desirable qualities.
- **Idioms** The act of Loki's lips being sewn shut on pg. 69 is an example of an idiom (a strange figure of speech) becoming a reality. The idioms "Zip your lip," "Button your lip," and "My lips are sealed" are just expressions, but Loki's punishment turns them into a reality.

## RECALL QUESTIONS

1. What does Loki do to Sif?
2. Where does Loki go looking for treasures?
3. How does Loki try to ruin some of the treasures as they are being made?
4. What does Loki wager in a bet?
5. How is Loki punished at the end of the myth?

# TREASURES OF THE GODS

## CAST

| | |
|---|---|
| **THOR** | *God of Thunder* |
| **SIF** | *Wife of Thor* |
| **LOKI** | *Trickster* |
| **SIGUNA** | *Wife of Loki* |
| **FRIGGA** | *Wife of Odin* |
| **FREYA** | *Goddess of Love* |
| **ODIN** | *All-Father of the Gods* |
| **FREY** | *Valiant God* |
| **DVALIN** | *Dwarf Craftsman* |
| **BROKK** | *Dwarf Craftsman* |
| **SINDRI** | *Dwarf Craftsman* |

**NARRATOR:** The goddess, Sif, had long, corn-golden hair, the most beautiful among all the goddesses of Asgard. Although the rest of her was very attractive, it was her hair that everyone took note of. Sif's days were spent combing, coiffing, and curling her golden cascade of hair. Some said it was her locks that allowed her to win the heart of the powerful thunder god, Thor.

**THOR:** Wouldn't you say the wife of Thor has the most beautiful, corn-golden hair?

**LOKI:** Eh.

**THOR:** *(angrily)* Say it! Or I will smite you!

**LOKI:** I'm supposed to blindly agree with whatever you say because you're three times my size?

**THOR:** *(growling)* Exactly.

**LOKI:** Then, yes. *(emotionlessly)* Your wife has beautiful, corn-golden hair.

**THOR:** I agree! I mean, look at the hair of *your* wife, Siguna. It's just not the same as Sif's.

**LOKI:** *(under his breath)* At least Siguna isn't a complete twit!

**THOR:** *(angrily)* What?

**LOKI:** I said, Sif's hair is more beautiful, isn't it?

**THOR:** Hey, that's what I think, too. *(calling out)* My dear! My dear!

**LOKI:** Yeesh.

**NARRATOR:** The young goddess, who stood conversing with the other Æsir, spun toward her husband—her hair twirling out behind her.

**THOR:** Darling, we were just talking about your hair. We were saying how beautiful it is!

**SIF:** Really? Tee hee. I have to admit, it is my crowning glory.

**LOKI:** *(under his breath)* Or your *only* glory.

**SIF:** I wake up each morning before the chariot of Sol has entered the sky. I comb my locks three thousand strokes before the morning meal.

**THOR:** It's true! *(hearty laugh)* Ha-ha! She is a—a—what do you call that?

**LOKI:** Narcissist? Flake? Psychopath?

**THOR:** Perfectionist!

**SIF:** Hair is my favorite pastime, but it's also my favorite topic of conversation. Can you think of any subject more exciting than hair?

**LOKI:** Death comes to mind.

**SIF:** *(confused)* You like to talk about death?

**LOKI:** No, it just came to mind. Wishful thinking.

**SIF:** What does *your* wife do to prepare her hair?

**THOR:** Apparently nothing. It looks like she has been using it to scrub her pots! *(hearty laugh)* Ha-ha!

**NARRATOR:** Loki sneered and looked to where his own wife, Siguna, was seated among the other Æsir. She was no beauty, a plain-looking goddess.

**THOR:** Do not be jealous of me, my friend! Not every man can have a wife like Sif!

**LOKI:** Or would want one.

**SIF:** *(lovey-dovey)* Oh, my darling! You say the most delightful things!

**NARRATOR:** The couple clasped hands and began to coo at one another.

**LOKI:** Excuse me. I'm going to go throw up now.

**NARRATOR:** Loki stalked away and seated himself by his wife.

**SIGUNA:** Hello, husband. What were Thor and Sif talking about?

**LOKI:** Themselves! What else? *(sudden idea)* You know somebody should teach them a lesson—show them the world isn't always sunshine and roses.

**SIGUNA:** Loki, I see a mischievous look in your eyes. Please do not cause any more trouble! The last time you played a trick, Odin barely forgave you for the trouble you caused.

**LOKI:** If I want a lecture, I'll let you know. Leave me alone.

**NARRATOR:** Loki returned to his chambers and began to plot some way to ruin the pride of Thor and Sif. Then—with the twisting and turning of his devious mind—he at last lit on an idea that tickled his fancy.

**LOKI:** Of course! Perfect! I can just see the look on her face! *(chuckling)* Hee hee!

**NARRATOR:** Loki was still laughing when Siguna returned from the feasting hall.

**SIGUNA:** *(sadly)* Oh, Loki. From your giggling, I can see you are hatching a trick.

**LOKI:** *(between chuckles)* Not just *a* trick. It'll be the best trick ever!

**SIGUNA:** But what trouble will it cause?

**LOKI:** Details. Details.

**NARRATOR:** Night fell upon Asgard, but the eyes of Loki could peer through the darkness like a cat. He took his crooked dagger into his hand.

**LOKI:** I think it's time to cut Sif down to size!

**NARRATOR:** The next morning Thor the thunder god awoke to a shock, and his cries filled his hall.

**THOR:** (crying out) No! My beautiful wife! Noooooo! Why? Why?

**NARRATOR:** His wailing awoke Sif, who lay by his side.

**SIF:** What is the matter, Thor? What has happened?

**THOR:** Someone has done something horrible! Look!

**NARRATOR:** Fallen locks of hair covered the bed.

**SIF:** Why that hair looks just like—(pause) No! It couldn't possibly be!

**NARRATOR:** Her trembling hands flew to her head—only to reveal the truth: She had been shorn. Stubble was all that remained of her former glory.

**SIF:** (screaming) Ahhh! Nooooo!

**NARRATOR:** Her screeches brought all of Asgard to Thor's hall. But try as they might, the other goddesses could not console Sif.

**SIF:** (enraged) What kind of monster would do such a thing? My hair was a work of art! This is not just an attack against me! It's an attack against the beauty of Asgard.

**FREYA:** Hmph. She definitely has a high opinion of herself.

**FRIGGA:** Now, Sif, dear. Let's not be overdramatic.

**SIF:** Overdramatic? If I am not Sif of the golden locks, I am nothing! I'm a joke!

(crashing noises)

**FRIGGA:** What is that horrible racket?

**SIF:** It's Thor. He's searching our house right now—examining every clue, making sure the villain is found!

**FREYA:** (sarcastically) Good idea. Who better than Thor to solve a baffling mystery?

**FRIGGA:** What will Thor do if (catching herself)—I mean, when—he figures out who committed the crime?

**SIF:** He has sworn to murder the criminal!

**FREYA:** (sarcastically) Well, that's certainly fair. A life for a pile of ratty hair.

**SIF:** He has no suspects yet. He cannot dream who would do such a thing!

**NARRATOR:** Freya and Frigga looked at one another knowingly.

**FRIGGA:** Isn't it obvious, dear? This has been done by Loki.

**SIF:** (gasp) What? What does Loki have against me?

**FRIGGA:** Nothing necessarily. He just likes to cause trouble.

**SIF:** Then Thor will grind him into cornmeal!

**FRIGGA:** That will be for Odin to decide.

**SIF:** If Odin won't give me justice, I'll take the law into my own hands!

**NARRATOR:** Thor burst into the chamber, his red beard bristling out on its ends.

**THOR:** Grrr! No sign of the devil! He has fled and left no clues behind!

**SIF:** Nevermind that, darling. We've cracked the case! Loki did this to me!

**THOR:** *(in shock)* Loki? Surely you must be mistaken. Loki is my friend. We adventure together.

**FRIGGA:** Yes, Loki is an excellent companion, but when there is not an adventure to be had, he is always causing mischief. It's just in his blood, I guess.

**THOR:** My friend has turned to a foe, eh? Hmmm. Very well. It's decided. *(yelling)* Thor will crush his skull!

**SIF:** *(happily)* That's my husband!

**NARRATOR:** With all the fury of a thunderstorm, Thor flew to the hall of Loki and pounded violently upon its door. *(loud knocking)*

**THOR:** *(yelling)* Loki! Loki! Thor demands you come forth!

**NARRATOR:** Loki answered the door nonchalantly.

**LOKI:** *(nonchalantly)* Yes? May I help you?

**THOR:** *(yelling)* You have gone too far this time, you weasely little weasel!

**LOKI:** Weasely weasel? Is that the best you can do?

**NARRATOR:** Thor gripped the trickster in his burly grip and started to drag him toward the hall of Odin.

**LOKI:** Hey!

**THOR:** Odin will give me justice!

**NARRATOR:** When Odin saw Thor dragging the kicking and screaming Loki behind, he sighed. These mischievous tricks of Loki were becoming a weekly occurrence.

**ODIN:** *(grumbling)* What now?

**THOR:** *(spluttering)* A crime almost too horrible to name! Loki has cut the golden hair of Sif, wife of Thor!

**ODIN:** *(annoyed)* I know who your wife is, Thor. Loki, what do you have to say for yourself?

**LOKI:** I don't know what this over-muscled moron is babbling about. I don't know who played this prank, but I applaud them.

**THOR:** *(sadly)* Sif's hair was like the golden wheat of summer! I used to call her my "golden one."

**LOKI:** I guess you'll just have to call her "baldy" now. Heh heh.

**SIGUNA:** Wait!

NARRATOR: It was Siguna, interrupting the gods' council.

SIGUNA: Please spare my husband! Spare him!

LOKI: (between his teeth) Go away!

ODIN: What is the meaning of this?

SIGUNA: Please! I told him not to cause anymore mischief, but he wouldn't listen to me.

LOKI: (through his teeth) Shhhhh!

ODIN: (coyly) Oh really. And what mischief has he caused?

SIGUNA: He snuck from our home last night into the hall of Thor and Sif and did something terrible! Spare him!

LOKI: (nervous laughter) She's crazy! Hallucinating! A bit too much mead with breakfast.

THOR: (roaring) I knew it! Argh!

NARRATOR: Thor raised his mighty fists to smash the skull of the trickster god, but Odin held up his hand for silence.

ODIN: (booming) Halt! No god may take the life of another here at Asgard!

THOR: He is no god! He's the offspring of a giant!

ODIN: We have adopted him into our court, and I say leave him alone!

NARRATOR: Thor lowered his fists, and Loki breathed a sigh of relief.

LOKI: Phew. (fake sadness) Awww. Tough luck, old buddy. Looks like Loki wins again.

THOR: Then let me vow before all the gods gathered here that I will grudgingly give Loki his life.

LOKI: (sarcastically) Why thank you! And I didn't get you anything.

THOR: But instead I will break every bone in his miserable little body!

ODIN: Sounds like a good compromise to me.

LOKI: (shocked) What?

NARRATOR: Thor wrapped his enormous arms around Loki's thin body and started to squeeze. (cracking noises)

LOKI: (choking) Help! Help! Wait! Stop! I'll get Sif's hair back for her. I'll get her hair even better than before!

THOR: (grunting) Impossible!

(more cracking sounds)

LOKI: (cry of pain) I'll get treasures—for all the gods! I swear it!

ODIN: Hmmm. What kind of treasures?

LOKI: (cries of pain) I don't know! I'll go to the dwarves! They can make all kinds of wonders!

ODIN: Very well. If you do this, Thor will spare your bones. (pause) Thor, unhand him.

NARRATOR: Thor released the trickster, who fell in a panting heap upon the floor.

**THOR:** But, Father!

**NARRATOR:** Odin gruffly waved him off.

**ODIN:** We'll see what treasures Loki can bring us from Svartalfheim. If he fails, you can have your revenge.

**THOR:** Loki, if you fail, don't show your face in Asgard again—or it will be the last mistake you ever make!

**NARRATOR:** Loki rose and hobbled from the hall of the gods.

**LOKI:** Those fools! I'll show them! I'll bring them treasures that will make their heads spin. Then they'll have to praise me! I'll make them eat their words. Now where did I put those sky-shoes?

**NARRATOR:** Loki put on his magical sky-shoes and flew from Asgard. He descended Bifrost, the Rainbow Bridge, down into Midgard and traveled toward Svartalfheim, the realm of the dwarves.

The dwarves were greedy, grubby, hairy beings with grotesque features and squat bodies. But in their underground workshops, they could craft the greatest wonders ever seen in all of the Nine Worlds.

Among the crags of the dark mountains, Loki spied a cave lit by forge-fires, and he made his way into its mouth. Two dwarves, their bodies black and grizzled by the fires, were hard at work in their forge. They took no notice of Loki.

**LOKI:** Ahem.

**DVALIN:** What do you want? We're busy—creating our treasures.

**NARRATOR:** Loki examined the pile of golden objects that were cooling from the forges of the dwarves' cave—gilded basins, cups, and pitchers.

**LOKI:** Actually I have come from Asgard to settle a bet. The gods say that the dwarves have lost their talents. They are no longer the craftsmen they used to be.

**DVALIN:** We don't have anything to prove to them. Our treasures speak for ourselves.

**LOKI:** You call these treasures? These are worthless knick-knacks! You need to do something with real skill—something impressive. Something like...making golden hair for a goddess.

**NARRATOR:** The two dwarves smirked at one another.

**DVALIN:** Okay, big-talker. What's in it for us? We dwarves do nothing *for* nothing.

**LOKI:** The favor of the gods!

**DVALIN:** And what if we don't?

**NARRATOR:** From a pack at his side, Loki drew forth his crooked dagger.

**LOKI:** I am Loki, the doer of good and the doer of evil. I am especially talented at the second part. Care to test me?

**NARRATOR:** The dwarf smith stopped pumping the bellows and turned to Loki unimpressed.

**DVALIN:** We know that Loki is full of wind because his father was a wind giant.

**LOKI:** *(angrily)* Why you—!

**DVALIN:** But we will create you some treasures. We will show the gods of Asgard what Dvalin the smith can do. Then they will say that there is no skill in all the Nine Worlds likened to that of the dwarves. *(to his partner)* Fetch me some gold!

**NARRATOR:** The dwarves pulled their current work from the forge-fire with tongs and threw it aside—where it rapidly dissolved into a molten puddle. *(hissing sound)*

The dwarves threw themselves into their new work. Loki took a seat and tried to appear indifferent, but as each new treasure passed from the forge of Dvalin, he could not contain his awe. When they were finished, the dwarves had completed three unparalleled treasures.

**DVALIN:** Here is the solid-gold wig you have requested. Not only will it attach to a goddess's head, but its strands will regenerate as actual hair does.

**NARRATOR:** The dwarf held up a wig made from woven strands of gold, so fine and delicate that they resembled the golden locks of Sif's head. To Loki's wonder, he realized the dwarves had forged something artificial that was even more breathtaking than the original. He put on a cool front though.

**LOKI:** Well, I guess this will do. But what else have you made?

**NARRATOR:** Dvalin smirked and held up a small, shining cube with intricate designs etched onto its sides.

**DVALIN:** This is Skidbladnir, the greatest ship ever created.

**LOKI:** That? Are you making a joke?

**DVALIN:** Behold.

*(clicking sounds)*

**NARRATOR:** Dvalin pressed a button on the side of the cube, and it began to unfold, section by section. When each section had unfurled, a life-sized, golden ship filled the cave. Loki, for once, was speechless.

**DVALIN:** It is large enough to hold the entire host of Asgard, yet can fold up small enough to fit inside your money purse. Its sails will always be filled with a fair wind.

**LOKI:** That's better—but still not as impressive as we were hoping. What else?

**NARRATOR:** Dvalin caused the ship to retract to its original size. Then he displayed a glistening spear with mystical runes glowing upon the finely crafted handle.

**DVALIN:** This is Gungnir, the mightiest spear ever made. It will always hit its mark—and always kill. *(pause)* Would you like a demonstration of this as well? *(chuckle)* Heh heh.

**NARRATOR:** Dvalin raised the spear at Loki.

**LOKI:** Ah! No! No, I think it will be fine.

**DVALIN:** Now be gone! Take these treasures back to Asgard, and never let the gods doubt Dvalin the dwarf smith again.

**LOKI:** Okay. I guess these will work.

**NARRATOR:** Loki gathered up the magical items and left the cave of Dvalin. He had planned to return directly to Asgard, but a new plan struck him.

**LOKI:**  These are truly wonders, and they will impress those foolish gods. But I want to really stun them. I want to come back with a boat-load of treasures. I want them to beg for my forgiveness! *(mocking voice)* How could we have ever doubted you, Loki? You're the best, Loki!

**NARRATOR:**  So instead of flying back to Asgard, Loki searched the black mountains for yet another dwarf-forge. Soon he found one.

**LOKI:**  *(happy voice)* Hellooooo! Helloooo!

**BROKK:**  What do you want?

**NARRATOR:**  Two dwarves were furiously working a forge—one holding a treasure within the fire and another pumping at the bellows to keep the fire hot.

**LOKI:**  Is this the workshop of Dvalin?

**BROKK:**  We don't speak that name around here, mister!

**LOKI:**  What? Why not? Dvalin is the greatest dwarf-smith who ever lived!

**BROKK:**  *(grumbling)* Grrr. That hack is nothing compared to Brokk!

**LOKI:**  Oh really? Look at all these treasures he just made for me. I was just going to track him down and say thanks again—for being the best.

**NARRATOR:**  The dwarf turned and spit upon the ground. *(spitting sound)*

**BROKK:**  Ha! You call those treasures? I've passed better treasures through my bowels!

**LOKI:**  Prove it! Only if you make me treasures that are better than these will I say that Brokk is the better craftsman.

**BROKK:**  No so fast, fancy-man. What will you do with these treasures? After I have won the contest, I mean.

**LOKI:**  Take them back to Asgard with me.

**BROKK:**  *(laugh)* Ha! You must think we are stupid! We know you, Loki the trickster. Dvalin is a fool, and he probably gave you those treasures in the name of his dwarf pride. But you won't get our treasures from us—not without something in return.

**LOKI:**  All right. Name your price, you grubby, little maggots!

**BROKK:**  If you take my treasures back to Asgard and the gods declare that my creations are superior to Dvalin's, I must win a prize.

**LOKI:**  What prize?

**BROKK:**  The opportunity to sever your scheming head from your scrawny neck. *(laugh)* Heh heh.

**NARRATOR:**  Brokk pulled a large, glittering axe from his belt.

**BROKK:**  This is one of my latest creations. It can split a hair.

**LOKI:**  If you chop off my head, what good will that do?

**BROKK:**  It will make me feel better for one thing. Plus, with you gone, there will be much less trouble in the Nine Worlds.

**NARRATOR:**  Loki smiled smugly.

LOKI:   Fine. Start forging! I'm confident that your treasures will be subpar!

BROKK:   Fetch me some more gold, Sindri. We have a head to claim.

NARRATOR:   The two dwarf brothers threw themselves into their work. Brokk fashioned the new treasures with cunning and skill, but Loki knew the most important part of their forging was when the objects were tempered with fire. If the temperature of the fire dropped, the treasures would be ruined.

LOKI:   (*yawn*) Mind if I take a walk?

BROKK:   Suit yourself!

NARRATOR:   Loki exited the cave, and once outside, shrank down into the form of a stinging fly.

LOKI:   Bzzzzz. (*small voice*) Time to swing the odds in my favor.

NARRATOR:   Buzzing back into the cave, Loki saw the dwarves had the first treasure already in the forge. Sindri was holding it within the flame, and Brokk was pumping the bellows with all his might. Loki brought out his stinger and dove directly toward the tender skin between Brokk's knuckles.

BROKK:   (*cry of pain*) Ah! Cursed fly!

NARRATOR:   Brokk swatted at Loki, but did not stop his pumping.

SINDRI:   Hold!

NARRATOR:   Sindri pulled the treasure from the fire. It was a golden boar. To Loki's astonishment, the creation began to move about the cave—its body parts and features all moving with life-like motion. (*squeal of a boar*)

BROKK:   A living battle-boar of gold! Let's see Dvalin top that! Put in the next treasure!

LOKI:   (*to himself*) Ah, who wants a stinky old pig? But I better make sure and ruin this next treasure. I'll hit him where it hurts!

BROKK:   Put in the next treasure!

NARRATOR:   The process began again. Loki dove toward Brokk's neck.

BROKK:   (*cry of pain*) Ah! Cursed fly!

NARRATOR:   The dwarf flinched at the pain, but once again, did not stop his work.

SINDRI:   Hold!

NARRATOR:   Sindri pulled the second treasure from the fires. It was a perfectly fashioned arm ring. Holding it aloft, Brokk shook it, and nine more rings—just as beautiful as the first—fell from it. (*metallic sounds*)

LOKI:   Uh-oh. That looks fancy.

BROKK:   Perfect! Put in the final treasure!

LOKI:   I have to stop him here! If I can't hurt him, I'll blind him.

NARRATOR:   The dwarf began to pump again, and Loki dove toward his face.

BROKK:   Be gone, accursed fly!

NARRATOR:   Loki landed between the dwarf's eyes, stinging left and right. Blood ran down the dwarf's face.

**LOKI:** That'll stop him!

**BROKK:** Argh!

**NARRATOR:** Brokk—blinded by the blood—stopped his pumping long enough to wipe the blood from his face.

**SINDRI:** No! Don't stop! It's almost finished!

**NARRATOR:** Laughing to himself, Loki flew back outside the cave and returned to his former shape.

**LOKI:** Heh heh.

**NARRATOR:** He sauntered back into the cave, where Brokk was still wiping blood from his forehead.

**LOKI:** Sorry about that. My walk took a bit longer than I expected. Done already?

**NARRATOR:** Brokk pointed an accusing finger in the trickster's face.

**BROKK:** I know it was you, you cheat! You tried to sting me into making an error! But you've lost—I tell you—lost!

**LOKI:** The gods will judge whether or not you've won, but I'm quite confident that I will be able to keep my head. After all, that last treasure was botched for sure.

**BROKK:** That's what you think! But we were able to save it! And it is the mightiest of the three!

**LOKI:** Ha! Impossible!

**NARRATOR:** The dwarf held up a still-smoking hammer.

**BROKK:** Behold! Mjolnir—the hammer of the gods! It is powerful enough to crack the skull of a giant.

**LOKI:** (*scoffing*) It's a little short in the handle. But look who I'm telling this to—the vertically challenged.

**SINDRI:** Why you—!

**BROKK:** Leave him be. This is his last defense. He knows he has lost. Now, we go to Asgard to display our treasures and claim the trickster's head.

**LOKI:** Lead the way, stubby.

**NARRATOR:** All of Asgard was abuzz with the news of the dwarves' arrival. The gods gathered in the meeting hall to see what treasures Loki had returned with. The trickster paraded grandly before the throne of Odin.

**LOKI:** Hello, chumps!

**ODIN:** Loki, I see you have returned.

**LOKI:** I have, All-Father, and true to my word, I have returned with treasures—treasures such as the gods have never seen. Prepare to be amazed! Where is the bald wife of Thor?

**NARRATOR:** Sif stood forward from the crowd—her eyes nearly puffed over from weeping.

**SIF:** (*through tears*) None of these treasures can bring my hair back!

**LOKI:** You have not seen the skill of Dvalin the dwarf-smith!

NARRATOR: Loki grandly displayed the golden wig, which by its own power, flew into the air and glided down gently upon the head of Sif. The golden filaments rooted themselves into her scalp and flowed down over her shoulders. Sif stood amazed.

THOR: Her hair is even more beautiful than before! I can't believe it!

SIF: This *is* amazing!

LOKI: No need to thank me.

THOR: Thank *you*? No need to thank *me* for not breaking every bone in your body.

LOKI: Ahem. The next treasure is for Frey, one of the noblest gods among us. It is the mighty ship Skidbladnir that he can carry inside his pocket.

*(clapping from the gods)*

NARRATOR: Loki demonstrated this treasure to the gods' amazement.

LOKI: And for illustrious Odin, wise beyond his years, gracious and merciful Lord of Asgard, who sees all and—

ODIN: Get on with it, Loki!

LOKI: I present to you, the mighty spear Gungnir, which never misses its mark.

*(gasping and clapping from the gods)*

NARRATOR: Loki handed the mystical spear to Odin.

LOKI: All three of these were created by Dvalin, the *greatest* of the dwarf smiths. I'm sure you all agree his craft is the greatest you have ever seen.

ALL: *(clapping and cheering)*

LOKI: All right. Looks like we're done here.

BROKK: Ahem.

NARRATOR: Brokk the dwarf stepped forward from in-between the gathered gods.

BROKK: Excuse me, All-Father, but we are not done. The trickster has made a wager with me. If my treasures are the better of Dvalin's treasures, then I am entitled to his head.

THOR: *(laugh)* Ha! Maybe we will see some entertainment after all!

ODIN: Loki, did you make such a bet?

LOKI: I did. But wait until you see these next three treasures, and you will see why I made it. They are trinkets. Doo-dads. Tacky knock-offs of the first three.

ODIN: Then show them to us, Loki.

NARRATOR: Loki reluctantly piled Brokk's treasures before the gods.

LOKI: *(bored)* Let's see. A golden boar for Frey—who needs that really? An arm ring for Odin. Watch out! It might turn your arm green. And a puny-handled hammer for Thor. Big whoop. It has some name, too, that I can barely pronounce.

NARRATOR: Brokk clapped his hands, and the treasures came to life. The golden boar sprang up and ran to Frey's side. The arm ring rose—dropping nine rings from itself—and attached to Odin's arm. The hammer spun upwards and settled down into the stunned grip of Thor.

**THOR:** A hammer for Thor? Magnificent!

**ODIN:** *(in shock)* By the Norns!

**FREY:** Wonder of wonders!

**LOKI:** I assume that you are talking about the first three treasures I gave you, and, yes, they are.

**ODIN:** No, Loki. I refer to the craft of Brokk. It is clearly superior.

**LOKI:** You can't be serious! Look at that! The gold is practically flaking off your arm ring. They probably picked these up at some dwarf flea market or something!

**THOR:** I agree with Father! These treasures are the greatest. Ha-ha! I will crush many giant skulls with this hammer.

**LOKI:** No! This can't be! You're all going to side with this mangy dwarf over me? You're willing to give up my life *to a dwarf?*

**ODIN:** Yep. That's right.

**ALL:** *(murmuring of agreement from the gods)*

**FREY:** It is not personal, Loki, but the second set of treasures is the better.

**LOKI:** I can't believe this! Betrayed! Right here in the hall of the gods!

**ODIN:** *You* made the bet.

**NARRATOR:** Brokk drew his glittering axe and pulled a hair from his beard. For effect he sliced the hair neatly in two.

**BROKK:** Trickster, my axe is prepared.

**NARRATOR:** Loki began to shy away from his approaching executioner.

**THOR:** Sif! Come here! Stop combing your new hair! You won't want to miss this.

**NARRATOR:** Loki turned imploringly to the gods.

**LOKI:** Help me! You're just going to sit there and let this happen? I just gave all of you gifts!

**BROKK:** Gifts? Those are treasures you stole from the dwarves with your lying tongue. Now I am going to end your lies forever.

**NARRATOR:** Loki turned to run. Two of the gods stepped forward and grabbed him, forcing him down upon his knees. Brokk advanced with axe raised.

**LOKI:** Odin! Help me!

**ODIN:** I'm sorry, Loki. The law is the law. *(pointedly)* You stuck your *neck* out and now you must pay with your *head.* I mean, you really risked your *neck* here. I thought you had a better *head* than that.

**LOKI:** Hey! That's it! Hold, dwarf! I only gave you the right to my *head.* No one ever said anything about my neck!

**BROKK:** What?

**LOKI:** Go ahead! Strike me! But only if you can take my head from my body without touching my neck. My neck is my own and must stay intact! Otherwise, you will be guilty of murdering a god.

**BROKK:** Preposterous! *(to Odin)* Will you stand for this, All-Father?

**ODIN:** Hmmmm. He does have a fine legal point, dwarf.

**THOR:** Ha-ha! Brilliant!

**BROKK:** Grrrr.

**NARRATOR:** Brokk slammed his axe into the floor of hall. Loki was released.

**LOKI:** Back off, chumps! Thanks for nothing!

**ODIN:** Now, Loki, don't be sore. We never doubted you would find a way out of such a scrape! You are quite clever—when you want to be.

**THOR:** That is why I say Loki makes for the best adventuring companion! Thank you for my new hammer!

**NARRATOR:** He clapped a hand on Loki's shoulder.

**LOKI:** *(sourly)* Don't mention it. And—don't touch me.

**NARRATOR:** But Brokk the dwarf was not finished. He tore at his beard in anger.

**BROKK:** No! No! This is not right! Why would you gods want to protect a lying cheat like him?

**ODIN:** A cheat? What do you mean?

**NARRATOR:** Then the dwarf explained how Loki had tried to ruin the contest and mar the forging of his treasures.

**LOKI:** You can't prove anything! It could have been any fly!

**THOR:** You tried to ruin my new hammer?

**LOKI:** You wouldn't have had it in the first place if it wasn't for me, you moron!

**ODIN:** Loki, this behavior is most displeasing!

**LOKI:** This coming from the people who were about to watch me get my head chopped off!

**BROKK:** I speak the truth, and he speaks only lies. *(pause)* Wait! I know!

**NARRATOR:** The dwarf pulled a spool of golden thread and an enormous needle from his belt.

**BROKK:** Let me sew up his evil lips, so he can tell no more lies!

**LOKI:** Never! You have no right! What proof is there?

**THOR:** Loki lied about Sif's hair!

**FREY:** Loki lied about tricking Iduna!

**FRIGGA:** Loki lies about everything!

**ODIN:** Loki, you have saved your head, but this might be a just punishment. Perhaps this will teach you not to cause mischief.

**LOKI:** This can't be happening!

**NARRATOR:** Loki was once again seized by the gods, and Brokk expertly sewed the trickster's lips together.

**LOKI:** *(cries of pain)* Oooh. Ahhh. Eee.

**NARRATOR:**  Brokk stepped back and admired his handiwork.

**BROKK:** Now try to tell your lies!

**LOKI:** *(muffled)* I curf yoo aw!

**ODIN:**  Brokk, thank you for your treasures. We will guard them well.

**BROKK:**  The dwarves do nothing for nothing. Our reward is knowing that Loki has learned his lesson.

**NARRATOR:** That night in the darkness of his hall Loki furiously ripped loose the dwarf's stitches. His smile, which had once been pleasant to behold, was now mangled by scars.

**LOKI:**  Hear me, darkness. Hear me, evil things of the world. I will have my revenge on those gods—on the whole pack of them—if it's the last thing I do.

**NARRATOR:**  So the trickster began to plot and harden his heart against the gods.

## DISCUSSION QUESTIONS

- Loki is called "the doer of good and the doer of evil." Is this a fitting title for him? Explain.
- Does Loki deserve to lose his head? Explain.
- Does Loki have a right to be angry with the gods? Explain.
- Which is the greatest treasure that the dwarves created? Explain.
- In this myth is Loki the hero or the villain—or both? Explain.
- In this myth what good comes from Loki's tricks?

# ODIN'S QUEST FOR WISDOM
## TEACHER GUIDE

## BACKGROUND

When the Norse people thought of Odin, their chief god, they did not think of a compassionate being. Odin was primarily a war god—one who coldly decided the fates of men in battle. He was also a grim god. In the great hall of Valhalla, he refuses to eat—simply throwing his portion of meat to the wolves at his feet. But in spite of his stoic nature, Odin was at times also a giving god. One of his gifts he gave to men was the knowledge of runes (or mystical writing symbols). Along with the other gods, he worked tirelessly to put off the inevitable Day of Doom, Ragnarok, which would mean destruction for the entire world and most of the immortals.

Odin was also a god of wisdom, and he paid a great price to receive it—one of his eyes. But it was not this price that made him so grim. It was the wisdom that he gained.

In this myth Odin sees the end of the world and how Ragnarok cannot be prevented, yet he vows to face that day boldly. It's interesting that the Norse people, who too often get stereotyped as thoughtless Viking invaders, knew that wisdom was important, but that it sometimes brings great sadness. "Ignorance is bliss" is the old saying. Grim Odin carries the burden of wisdom upon his shoulders.

## SUMMARY

Daily Hugin and Munin, Odin's two ravens, bring him news from the worlds below. Their news has become increasingly grimmer—evil is growing, and Odin's heart is troubled. He decides to visit the three Norns, mystical creatures who can tell him the future. Odin intends to visit the Norns by himself, but some of the other gods notice his departure and decide to tag along—much to his chagrin.

When the party reaches the Rainbow Bridge, Heimdall will not allow Thor to cross with his hammer. The weight of the hammer will cause Bifrost to collapse. Thor is forced to journey to the Norns through the rivers of cloud.

The gods make their way over the Rainbow Bridge and journey to the Well of Urda, where the Norns sit day after day. The Norns allow Odin to look into each of their eyes—for a glimpse of the past, present, and future. The future that Odin sees is grim—the gods and all the world will eventually be destroyed in a cataclysmic battle against the giants. Odin asks if there is any way that this future can be changed. The Norns tell him to consult with Mimir, the wise one. Mimir is the wisest creature in the world, and he always asks a steep price for a single drink from his pool of wisdom.

Odin leaves the rest of the gods behind and journeys to Mimir's Well. On his way, Odin encounters a giant riding on an enormous stag. The giant challenges Odin to a riddle game. The winner will get to cut off the loser's head. After Odin answers the giant's three tough questions, the giant realizes that Odin must be a god in disguise. Then Odin stumps the giant by asking, "What will be Odin's last words to his son, Balder?" Instead of slaying the stumped giant, Odin allows him to go free.

Odin finally reaches the Mimir's Well, and Mimir asks for one of Odin's eyes in return for a drink. Odin weighs his options and then agrees. He drinks from the well and sees that Ragnarok cannot be prevented. However, he also perceives that after the world is destroyed, it will be reborn and new gods will rule over it. Before he leaves, he plucks out one of his eyes, and it still lies at the bottom of Mimir's Well as a testament to the price that Odin paid for wisdom.

## ESSENTIAL QUESTIONS

- Why is wisdom important?
- Can knowledge sometimes bring you sadness? Is ignorance bliss?
- Can your fate be altered?
- Why is sacrifice sometimes necessary?

## ANTICIPATORY QUESTIONS

- What is wisdom? How is it different from intelligence?
- What price would you pay in order to know the future?
- If the future couldn't be changed, would you still want to know it?

## CONNECT

**Philosophy: Fatalism** Fatalism is the belief that future events are fixed in advance and no human effort can ever change them. An opposing viewpoint would be a belief in Free Will—or that your actions directly affect your changeable future. Think about how this myth demonstrates a belief in Fatalism. How would it be different if it was influenced by a belief in Free Will?

## TEACHABLE TERMS

- **Comedy Relief** The main events of this myth are grim—Odin foresees the doom of the gods and plucks out his own eye in order to gain wisdom—but some characters have been included to provide

a relief from the dramatic tension. Which characters serve this function?
- **Symbol** Mimir's Well, first appearing on pg. 81, is a symbol for wisdom. Wisdom is a drink. The Norse also had a myth about the Mead of Poetry, a drink that gave poetic abilities to those who drank it. Discuss these symbols. How are wisdom and poetic inspiration like a drink?
- **Theme** What theme does this myth have concerning wisdom? Consider the price that Odin paid for wisdom. What theme does this myth have concerning fate? Consider also that the gods cannot avoid their fate, but they can prolong it by noble actions.
- **Foreshadowing** Frigga's reaction after looking into the eyes of the Norns on pg. 78 foreshadows what for Balder? What do the revelations given to Odin foreshadow for the gods?

## RECALL QUESTIONS

1. What is the first well the gods visit?
2. Which god cannot cross over the Rainbow Bridge?
3. Odin encounters a giant riding on what type of animal?
4. What is Ragnarok?
5. What price does Mimir ask for a drink from his well of wisdom?

# ODIN'S QUEST FOR WISDOM

## CAST

| | |
|---|---|
| **ODIN** | *All-Father of the Gods* |
| **FRIGGA** | *Wife of Odin* |
| **THOR** | *God of Thunder* |
| **LOKI** | *Half-Giant Trickster* |
| **BALDER** | *Most Beloved of the Gods* |
| **HEIMDALL** | *Watchman of the Gods* |
| **URDA** | *One of the Norns* |
| **VERDANDI** | *One of the Norns* |
| **SKULD** | *One of the Norns* |
| **GIANT** | *Tricky Enemy* |
| **MIMIR** | *Wise God* |

**NARRATOR:** A dreary rain had been falling on Asgard, and menacing wisps of fog rose from the ground like lost spirits. Through the gloom flew two black specks. They were the ravens of Odin—Hugin and Munin. They soared over the thick wall of Asgard, darted among the high gables of the halls of the gods, and bore down upon Valhalla. There they found Odin the All-Father seated upon his throne with a pained expression on his face.

**ODIN:** *(somberly)* My messengers, you have returned at last. What news do you bring from Midgard?

**NARRATOR:** The two birds landed—one on each shoulder—and began to croak in their master's ear. *(croaking of ravens)* As they spoke, an even deeper sadness washed over Odin's features.

**ODIN:** *(sadly)* Then it is as I feared. Leave me. I must ponder these things.

**NARRATOR:** The god sat alone for many days—thinking. The Æsir had built a mighty fortress in Asgard. They had created the Nine Worlds. They had done all in their power to do good, yet somehow evil had crept into their creation—and that evil was slowly devouring it.

All the gods felt Odin's newfound depression, but it was Frigga, his queen, who was the first to speak to her lord of his depression.

**FRIGGA:** *(concerned)* Odin, what is wrong? Three days ago, while I was sitting at my spinning wheel, I saw the two birds of omen fly over. Since then you have not stirred from your throne. What news did they bring you?

**ODIN:** *(sigh)* Oh, Frigga. Do not ask me to burden you with my troubles.

**FRIGGA:** *(kindly)* Your troubles are my troubles. I am your wife. Tell me what is bothering you.

**ODIN:** It is useless, my love. All our efforts—all the work we have done—it will all come to nothing. Evil is in the world. The giants flourish. Men are wicked and cruel. One day it will become too much for us to control. There is no hope.

**NARRATOR:** Frigga bit her lip in thought.

**FRIGGA:** Perhaps if we consulted the three sisters? The three who keep the World Tree green and growing with their well. The Norns, Urda and her two sisters.

**ODIN:** What hope can they give me?

**NARRATOR:** Frigga took her husband's hand into her own.

**FRIGGA:** Maybe not hope, but at least the courage and wisdom to face whatever lies ahead.

**ODIN:** *(happier)* You speak wisely, wife. I shall do as you ask.

**FRIGGA:** Good. As you know, the Well of Urd lies beneath one of the roots of the World Tree. It will be a long journey. Won't you need companionship?

**ODIN:** *(urgently)* No, dear. The last thing I want is company on this journey. I must visit the three Norns alone.

**FRIGGA:** But every god here has seen your sadness. If you leave, they will wish to help. Your grief is our own.

**ODIN:** Then I will leave early tomorrow before Sol has begun her course across the sky. You may come with me if you wish, but I don't want any other companions.

**NARRATOR:** Frigga nodded, and she did not speak a word of it. But the gods of Asgard were perceptive and knew that a journey was about to be undertaken. They did not wish to leave their leader alone on such a quest.

In the grey mists of the morning, Odin and Frigga—heavily cloaked—made their way through the gates of Asgard. Within the shadows of the gate, a deeper shadow moved and stepped forward to reveal itself as Loki the trickster.

**LOKI:** *(coyly)* Going somewhere?

**ODIN:** *(surprised)* Ah! Oh, Loki, what are you doing lurking in the shadows?

**NARRATOR:** The trickster smirked.

**LOKI:** Lurking is what I do best. Leaving early in the morning, I see—wearing suspicious-looking hoods. I'd say someone is going for an adventure.

**ODIN:** *(irritated)* If I wanted a companion, I would have asked for one!

**FRIGGA:** *(sternly)* Odin wishes to visit the Norns alone.

**LOKI:** The Norns, eh? So that's where you're going! *(annoyed)* That means Balder was right. He's always right.

**ODIN:** *(sigh)* Balder knows about this? Don't tell me he is coming as well!

**FRIGGA:** *(suddenly afraid)* No! That won't do at all! He's not supposed to leave the safety of Asgard—for any reason.

**ODIN:** Please, Frigga! The boy is old enough to watch out for himself! *(realizing he's arguing against himself)* But in this case you're absolutely right!

**LOKI:** I make an excellent adventuring companion, but the rest of these fools—not so much. Maybe we should hurry before they get here.

**ODIN:** *(shocked)* They?

**LOKI:** Oh, yeah. Thor Thunder-brain overheard Balder and I talking. I'm surprised he could understand us. We were using pretty big words. Anyway, I told Balder to just lie about where we were going. But, of course, he didn't. Talk about a guy who needs to learn a little dishonesty.

**FRIGGA:** *(motherly)* Dishonesty. Hmph. My precious darling would never tell a lie!

**ODIN:** Perhaps if we leave quickly—

*(muffled footsteps and talking)*

**LOKI:** Too late.

**NARRATOR:** Two figures appeared through the mists. One was walking stately in perfect step. He had a handsome face and a perfectly glazed expression. He looked totally incapable of ever having a nasty thought or action. The other figure was huge and lumbering. His arms bulged with muscle, his face was overgrown with a red beard, and in his grip he carried an enormous hammer.

**LOKI:** *(hatefully)* Balder! I thought I told you to try to ditch Captain Thunder there!

**BALDER:** *(kindly)* I just couldn't leave him behind. His heart's in the right place.

**LOKI:** *(sigh)* His heart, yeah. But his brain? That's a different story.

**NARRATOR:** Thor raised his hammer in the air and shook it violently.

**THOR:** *(chuckling)* Foolish Loki! You cannot trick the mighty Thor!

**LOKI:** *(sudden shock)* Hey, look! Is that a giant over there?

**THOR:** *(insane rage)* Where? I will smite him!

**LOKI:** *(snicker)* Heh. Heh. Sucker.

**ODIN:** *(hissing)* Shhh! Would you be quiet! You three are bad enough. I don't want every god in Asgard tagging along! Now, let's go.

**NARRATOR:** Frigga began stroking Balder's head.

**FRIGGA:** *(whispering sound)* There. There.

**ODIN:** *(angrily)* By the Norns, woman! Leave the boy alone!

**FRIGGA:** *(frantically)* Just some traveling spells—for protection. You never know what can happen out on the open road.

**ODIN:** That boy will *never* get married at this rate.

**FRIGGA:** That's fine. No woman will ever be good enough for my Balder. Will they, sweetie?

**THOR:** Thor is married to the beautiful Sif, a goddess with lovely golden hair.

**LOKI:** *(sarcastically)* Very good, Thor. Now, if you could only learn your address.

**ODIN:** I knew I should have gone on horseback.

**NARRATOR:** Odin stalked away through the gloom. The others ran to catch up—that is, all except Balder. Frigga insisted that he walk.

Odin was the first to reach Bifrost the Rainbow Bridge. The watchman, Heimdall, flashed his golden smile and greeted him grandly.

**HEIMDALL:** *(formally)* Hail, Odin, All-Father of the Gods!

**ODIN:** Shhh!

**NARRATOR:** The All-Father looked back behind him. There was no sign of his unwanted companions.

**ODIN:** *(hopefully)* Maybe I lost them.

**HEIMDALL:** *(whispering)* Are you traveling in secret, my lord?

**ODIN:** *(quietly)* Yes, I'm on sort of a secret mission.

**HEIMDALL:** *(quietly)* Oh, I see. *(startled)* Hark! Four figures come through the mists! Quickly! Or they will learn of your secret!

**ODIN:** *(sigh)* No, they already know. It's kind of a *group* secret.

**NARRATOR:** The rest of the god's party blundered up.

**HEIMDALL:** *(grandly)* Hail, Loki the trickster!

**LOKI:** *(sarcastically)* Hail, Heimdall, the lame-brained.

**HEIMDALL:** Hail, Thor, God of Thunder!

**THOR:** Hail, Heimdall, the Watchman of the Gods!

**HEIMDALL:** Hail, Balder, Beloved One!

**BALDER:** Hail, Heimdall the Golden-teethed—I mean, toothed.

**ODIN:** *(annoyed)* Enough! Enough! We don't have time for all of this.

**HEIMDALL:** Aw. That's my favorite part. There's so little chance for chit-chat out here. Well, on to my speech then. *(reciting)* I, Heimdall the Watchman of the Gods, give you, Odin the All-Father, leave to cross the great Rainbow Bridge. Thou shall pass—

**ODIN:** *(hurriedly)* Thank you! Thank you!

**HEIMDALL:** *(feebly)* But I wasn't finished.

**ODIN:** No time! No time! The fate of the world may be at stake here!

**HEIMDALL:** What do you hope to find in the world of men?

**ODIN:** We're not going to Midgard! If you must know, we're going to Urda's well.

**HEIMDALL:** Oh, then you'll want to hang a right before you get to the land of the dwarves.

**ODIN:** *(sarcastically)* Thank you. I think I know my way around the Nine Worlds. I did create the World Tree, you know.

**NARRATOR:** Heimdall moved aside and let the gods shuffle by. As Thor started to pass, Heimdall barred his way.

HEIMDALL: (shocked) Wait a minute! You can't take that hammer on the Rainbow Bridge!

NARRATOR: The thunder god looked at him blankly.

THOR: What do you mean? I am Thor, enemy of giants. This is my mighty hammer! I take my mighty hammer everywhere I go!

HEIMDALL: (angrily) Not on this bridge, you don't. The bridge is not as sturdy as it used to be. No offense, my friend, but you and your hammer weigh a bit more than you probably think.

THOR: I can't believe this!

LOKI: Now that he mentions it. You have put on a pound or two. You're kinda getting a mead-gut.

FRIGGA: Thor, you've always been a bit—husky.

THOR: So I can't cross the bridge?

LOKI: How many times does he have to say it?

HEIMDALL: (insistently) You will break the bridge! You must leave the hammer with me, or you cannot pass!

THOR: I will not leave my hammer!

LOKI: Oh well, too bad. I hate to see you go, Thor-boy, but that's life.

ODIN: The bridge is not the only way to Urda's well. You could ford across those two cloud rivers there. The rivers are a perilous path to take, as they are suffocating and deep—

LOKI: Yeah, good idea. Go that way!

NARRATOR: The thunder god looked confused. He stood silently for several seconds. Then—without a word—he dove over the edge of the bridge into the surging waves of clouds.

THOR: (fading out) Thor away!

BALDER: (distantly) Perhaps I should go that way, too. I feel sorry for him being by himself.

LOKI: Oh, shut up.

FRIGGA: (motherly) Don't you even think about it, mister! You're going to stay right here by your mother!

NARRATOR: The company descended the Rainbow Bridge and followed the secret paths to the root of the World Tree where Urda's well bubbled up from the earth. There eternally sit the Three Norns—weird sisters, older than time, that water the root of Yggdrasil, keeping it healthy.

ODIN: (quietly) Say nothing to offend the Norns! They are stingy enough with their information as it is.

NARRATOR: The gods nodded their heads in agreement. Soon the giant, gnarled root of the World Tree appeared, and where it penetrated the earth sprang up a crystal pool. Three female creatures hunched around it. One was old, stooped, and haggard beyond time. One was youthful and radiant. The third could barely be seen—faded out around the edges as if maybe she were not really there at all.

The hag-like Norn raised her gaze from the well and pointed a warty finger at the company.

**URDA:** *(crone-voice)* Halt! Visitors from above, what seek ye with Urda and her sisters?

**ODIN:** I am Odin the All-Father.

**ALL NORNS:** We know.

**ODIN:** I have come from Asgard to seek information.

**ALL NORNS:** We know.

**ODIN:** *(annoyed)* Then why did you ask? As you already know apparently, I seek knowledge of the future!

**VERDANDI:** What is the future without present or past?

**ODIN:** I don't have time for riddles! I need to know how to save the world from the evil that infests it.

**SKULD:** *(cackle)* Well, then. The answer is easy enough. The world will *not* be saved. Ragnarok, the Day of Doom, will come—no matter what is done.

**URDA:** Ragnarok—the end of all things.

**ODIN:** There must be some way to stop it!

**SKULD:** The enemies of the Æsir will overcome them.

**VERDANDI:** Fire will destroy the World Tree.

**URDA:** All of you—will *die!* *(cackle)*

**NARRATOR:** This news hit the gathered gods like a blow. At last, Odin spoke.

**ODIN:** But can it be delayed?

**URDA:** We cannot give you all the answers, god of above. Our answers only raise more questions, more fears. You may each look into our eyes. In mine, you shall see the past. In my fair sister's, you shall see the present. In my faded sister's, you shall see the future. Little hope will it bring you. You have been warned.

**NARRATOR:** Odin first stepped forward to peer into the eyes of each of the Norns. Afterward, his face was grim.

**FRIGGA:** Husband, what did you see?

**ODIN:** *(grimly)* The same doom that I heard from Hugin and Munin. I saw the fires of Ragnarok. But now I know what I must do next. Something I have put off for many years.

**FRIGGA:** What?

**ODIN:** My wisdom is not enough to see a way past this problem. I must seek another well—the well of Mimir, the Wise One.

**FRIGGA:** You must go then—and this time alone.

**URDA:** *(pointedly)* Queen of the Æsir, it is your turn to look!

**NARRATOR:** Frigga turned to confront the Norns. She looked into the eyes of the faded Norn first and then cried out.

**FRIGGA:** *(crazily)* Balder! My son! No! *(weeping)*

NARRATOR: Frigga ran weeping to Balder and threw her arms about him.

BALDER:  What is it, Mother? (tearing up) You know that when you cry—it—it makes me cry, too.

NARRATOR:  At that moment from a thick wall of cloud near the well, Thor burst forth—swinging Mjolnir high above his head.

THOR: (booming) Argh! Thor the mighty has traveled through the perilous cloud rivers!

LOKI: (dryly) Great.

NARRATOR: Balder raised his head from his mother's grasping arms.

BALDER: Wait a minute. Where is our father?

FRIGGA: (sniffling) He has gone—to seek wisdom. (hurriedly) But enough of that! We have work to do. We've got to protect Balder here—at any cost. He's a very special boy, and we're not going to let anything happen to him!

NARRATOR:  As the remaining gods departed, the three Norns turned back to their well.

Meanwhile, Odin was beginning a second journey to Mimir's Well, which lay in Jotunheim the land of the giants.

ODIN: I will have to disguise myself.

NARRATOR: Odin's form began to change. His strong stature was replaced with the body of an old, bent man. His regal winged crown and cape turned into a worn traveling cloak and a wide-brimmed hat.

When he once again reached the outpost of Heimdall, the watchman did not recognize him.

HEIMDALL: (sternly) Halt, mortal! You shall not pass!

ODIN: (old voice) Heimdall! It is I, Odin!

HEIMDALL: (snort) Nice try, low-life! I know the lord of Asgard when I see him. He just passed by a few hours ago.

ODIN: (annoyed) I am in disguise. I am Odin no longer, but Vegtam the Wanderer.

HEIMDALL: Sure you are, buddy. Move along before I smite you for trying to impersonate the all-powerful sky-god.

NARRATOR: Odin sighed, and raising his arms above his head, he summoned an enormous rain-cloud. (storm sounds) The cloud sailed right above the confused bridge-keeper, stopped, and began to spill its innards upon him. (rain noises)

HEIMDALL: Yep. It's you, Odin. Sorry about the mix-up.

NARRATOR: Odin traveled on for several days. Never once did he summon rich food or drink or use his godly powers to ease his journey. The burdens of man were his own. At night he slept on the cold earth without a shield from the elements, and images of Ragnarok drifted through his mind.

ODIN: (tiredly) I have traveled many days, and I know that I draw close to Jotunheim.

NARRATOR: The ground became broken, and a jagged line of mountains rose before him. This was the wall that separated Midgard from Jotunheim. Odin struggled to the heights of the mountains and crossed into the land of the giants.

Once he reached the far side of the mountains, Odin saw a creature approaching on the valley-path. It was a giant riding on a humongous stag as one would ride a horse. Odin sat down by the side of the road and waited for the giant to draw nearer.

**GIANT:** (*growling*) Trespasser! Who are you and what do you want in the land of the giants?

**ODIN:** I am Vegtam the Wanderer, and I seek wisdom here in your land. Who are you?

**GIANT:** My name is not important, but know this—I am the wisest giant that ever lived, and I will kill you for passing this way.

**ODIN:** Is that a fact? If you are so intelligent, perhaps we should have a battle of wits?

**GIANT:** Fine! I will ask three questions, and then you may ask three. If you cannot answer even one of them, I win, and I shall cut off your head. If you win, you may cut off mine.

**ODIN:** (*sarcastically*) What a civilized game. Fair enough.

**GIANT:** You are either very brave or very foolish. I have taken many heads in my day. I have wagered my own skull in many contests, but I have never lost it.

**ODIN:** I see that. I understand the risk, and I will play your game.

**NARRATOR:** The giant dismounted, the stag was left to graze, and the two sat beneath a tree. Before the giant spoke, his knotty features assumed a cunning look.

**GIANT:** First question. Tell me, human— what is the name of the river that divides Asgard from Jotunheim?

**ODIN:** (*nonchalantly*) Easy. Ifling is the name of that river.

**GIANT:** (*in shock*) What? You possess great knowledge for a mortal. Very well. I underestimated you. My next question will be more difficult. What are the names of the horses that are harnessed to the chariots of the sun and moon?

**ODIN:** Well, that is simple. Skinfaxe and Hrimfaxe.

**NARRATOR:** The giant growled.

**GIANT:** (*angrily*) What? No mortal could know that! Fine. I will ask you a question about the future. What is the name of the plain on which the final battle between the giants and the gods will be fought?

**NARRATOR:** Odin thought back to what he had seen reflected in the eyes of the Norns.

**ODIN:** The plain of Vigard.

**GIANT:** (*angrily*) What? I paid dearly for that knowledge! The Norns have given you a bit of their wisdom, I see! It is your turn to ask, but I am not afraid. I know everything!

**ODIN:** (*coyly*) Then answer my question, wisest of giants. What are the last words that Odin will speak into the ears of his dying son, Balder?

**NARRATOR:** The giant's eyes grew wide, and he jumped up.

**GIANT:** (*growling*) Only Odin would know the answer to that question! You are not a mortal at all! You are Odin! Argh.

**NARRATOR:** The giant roared with anger and ripped the tree up by the roots. Odin remained calmly seated.

**ODIN:** Please. Calm yourself. Can you answer the question or not?

**GIANT:** (*angrily*) Argh! I can't! You have won!

**NARRATOR:** The giant dropped the tree and re-seated himself, with tears welling up in his eyes.

**GIANT:** (*crying*) Now, you can cut off my brilliant head.

**ODIN:** (*calmly*) I do not want your ugly head. I merely want to pass in peace.

**GIANT:** What? What business does Odin have in the land of the giants?

**ODIN:** I must drink from Mimir's Well.

**GIANT:** Mimir's well! How we giants hate it! You gods were the ones who put Mimir there to guard over it—to keep us from drinking from it!

**ODIN:** Any creature can drink from it, if they pay Mimir's price. Even I must pay a price to drink. But until now, I had not been willing to make such a sacrifice.

**GIANT:** Many giants have gone to Mimir's Well, but he has always asked more than

we are willing to sacrifice. Wisdom is not more important than our own selfishness.

**ODIN:** A good observation. You are the wisest of a foolish race.

**GIANT:** Thank you. (*realizing*) Wait a minute! Grrrr. Well, you may have beaten me in a battle of wits, but I see that you are truly the greater fool. Even Mimir's wisdom will do you no good! Our day will come! (*laughter*)

**NARRATOR:** The giant climbed onto his stag and rode away. Odin stood, stretched, and continued his journey. He mused as he walked.

**ODIN:** (*to himself*) What if Mimir asks for something that I cannot give? There is no shame in turning back. I can easily return to Asgard, and no one will think the lesser of me.

**NARRATOR:** Then he thought of the Day of Doom and the death and destruction he had seen there.

**ODIN:** If I do not succeed, no one will.

**NARRATOR:** Soon his plodding feet brought him to the second massive root of the World Tree. Beneath it flowed the Well of Wisdom. Odin raised his arms and called out in a loud voice.

**ODIN:** I summon you, Mimir, guardian of the Waters of Wisdom!

**NARRATOR:** The waters began to churn, and up from them floated an aged head—its long beard dangling below it.

**MIMIR:** Hail, Odin! Or should I say Vegtam the Wanderer? Many years ago, I died in the war between the Æsir and the Vanir. You took my head and placed it here to guard this Well of Wisdom against all who were undeserving of it. You did not drink then because you had no cause to sacrifice so much. Now, you return—to drink.

**ODIN:** You have grown wise, Mimir.

**MIMIR:** These waters have made me wise. But there is little happiness in wisdom. It will not ease your sorrows. Because of what I see, what I know, my tears mingle daily with this pool. The world's sorrows are my own. Odin, you should have let me die. Oblivion would have been better than this.

**ODIN:** You are the guardian. Without you, any could drink.

**MIMIR:** Many have come—but they have not been ready to pay the price. Are you?

**ODIN:** I will pay the price like any other.

**MIMIR:** I know your heart. I am the only one in all of creation who knows your sorrow. I know you will pay this price—but it will be for nothing. Wisdom cannot prevent the inevitable. Wisdom cannot change the future or even the past. Wisdom cannot stop death—your death, the death of others, the death of the world. Ignorance is much better. It dulls the mind against reality. It allows happiness to exist where it has no place.

**NARRATOR:** Mimir's sad eyes bore into Odin's.

**ODIN:** (*grandly*) I know I cannot change the final outcome. I cannot stop Ragnarok. The World Tree will burn no matter how hard I try. But at the very least, I can strive to put

off that day as long as I can. And I can see that all that exists up until that point is the best that it can be.

**MIMIR:** Brave words, Eldest of the Gods. For those, I will let you drink. This well will give you wisdom that not even death can diminish. But for all the sight these waters will give you, you must give them a portion of your own.

**ODIN:** What is your price?

**MIMIR:** Your eye.

**NARRATOR:** The god paused.

**MIMIR:** Oh, I know what you are thinking. You are the ruler of Asgard. What good will wisdom do you if you are half-blind? Wisdom will not help you hurl a spear or defend your home. You will see the future, but without your eye, you will miss half the present.

**ODIN:** It is my choice to make, and I choose wisdom.

**MIMIR:** Then drink.

**NARRATOR:** A drinking horn—filled with the well's waters—lifted from the pool and floated into Odin's hands. Odin stared at it for a second and then drank deeply.

**MIMIR:** Inside these waters are all the sorrows of men, all the sorrows of the gods, of yesterday, of today, of tomorrow.

**NARRATOR:** As the god drank, visions crept into the corners of his mind—paintings of sadness and pain, the torturous end of time. It was almost too much for him to bear, but he continued to drink.

At the end of the draught, when it

seemed that things could become no more bitter, Odin tasted a sudden sweetness. He saw through the sorrows. He saw why they must be borne and how through them, great good would be accomplished.

He saw that while everything would one day be destroyed, from those ashes would spring a new tree, a new world, ruled by new gods. And as the last drop touched his godly tongue, peace that he had never before felt came into his heart.

**MIMIR:** You have drunk well, Eldest of the Gods.

**NARRATOR:** Odin lowered the drinking-horn into the pool. Then reaching his hand to his face, he calmly plucked out his eye. He made no sound as he did so. He held it out to the head of Mimir, which bowed before him.

**MIMIR:** (*grandly*) Even I, the wisest who ever lived, have learned something from you this day. Place this eye within the pool. It will lie there until the end of time, so that all might see the price that Odin, Lord of Asgard, paid for wisdom.

**ODIN:** Farewell.

**NARRATOR:** Without another word Odin turned and disappeared into the gathering gloom.

## DISCUSSION QUESTIONS

- What sets the Norse gods apart from deities from other mythologies is their knowledge of their own doom. The Norse gods know that they will not live forever, and for this reason, they are often gloomier than the carefree gods of other cultures. Does this make them more or less likeable? Does this make them more human? Explain.
- Is wisdom important? Explain.
- Should the leader of a group always be its wisest member? Explain.
- What's the difference between being "wise" and being "smart"?
- Why do you think Odin sacrifices an eye in this myth—instead of something else? What makes the eye so important?
- Can wisdom bring both joy and sorrow? Explain.
- The Norse believed in persevering even in the face of inevitable defeat. How is that attitude reflected in this myth?

# FREYA THE BRIDE
## TEACHER GUIDE

## BACKGROUND

Masculinity and all the attitudes that went with it—rigid honor, bravery, perseverance—were revered in Norse society. Even women determined their own value by their husband's masculinity. If a woman were married to a cowardly husband, she made it her job to prod him into acts of bravery.

On the other hand, it was incredibly dishonorable for men to engage in feminine practices such as wearing women's clothes. Loki the trickster frequently takes on the disguise of a woman—in the first myth, he disguised himself as a female horse. These weren't mere surface-level transformations either. According to one myth, Loki actually gave birth to the mighty steed, Sleipnir. But these actions were considered incredibly inappropriate and labeled him even more firmly as a villain.

So it's quite a surprise when Thor, manliest of the gods, agrees to cross-dress in this myth in order to get back his magical hammer. What can be determined from this? Was Thor actually *not* the epitome of manliness in Norse culture? More than likely, it shows that even the Norse—with their rigid gender guidelines—still had a sense of humor and enjoyed a good laugh at Thor's expense.

## SUMMARY

Freya, the goddess of beauty, is easily distracted by jewels. Although she has a wondrous treasury, she decides to journey into Svartalfheim, the land of the dwarves, in search of even greater treasures.

Meanwhile, a tribe of dwarves called the Dark Dwarves, have just finished their crowning achievement—a golden necklace that has no equal. Their goal for creating the necklace is to bribe a woman into marrying them. Freya happens along and spies the necklace, but the dwarves refuse to give it to her—unless she agrees to marry each of them for one day. The power of the necklace is too much for Freya, and she agrees.

When she returns to Asgard, she realizes that she cannot wear the necklace, as the other gods will ask where or how she got it. She only wears it in the secrecy of her own garden. But rumors of her dwarf-marriages soon surface, and Loki brings these accusations before Odin. The All-Father is reluctant to accuse Freya of dishonor without proof, so he commands Loki to bring him the necklace.

Transforming himself into a flea, Loki goes into Freya's garden while she is asleep. He bites at her cheek until she turns so that he can get the necklace off her. He brings the necklace before Odin, and Freya is officially accused of ruining the reputation of the gods. The goddess can deny nothing, and as a punishment, Odin commands her to wander through the land of men and giants for a period of six months, living as a mortal, and doing all the good she can.

Six months pass, and when Freya returns, she is reformed—having learned true humility and kindness.

After a night of feasting to celebrate Freya's return, the gods realize that Thor's hammer has been stolen. Loki is immediately accused but points out giant footprints sneaking into and out of the hall of the gods. Loki borrows Freya's falcon-skin and flies to Jotunheim to find out more information. A giant named Thrym is waiting for Loki on a mountain peak. He has stolen Thor's hammer and buried it miles underground. The only way he will give it back is if the gods will give him Freya as his bride. (He caught sight of her while she wandered the earth.) Loki returns to Asgard with this news.

The gods refuse to give Freya as a bride, but they desperately need Thor's hammer for protection. They light upon a brilliant idea—disguising Thor as Freya long enough for him to retrieve his hammer. The plan is put into action.

All the gods travel to Jotunheim for the wedding. Thrym is fooled by his bride, and he presents "her" with his wedding present, Thor's hammer. Thor immediately grabs the hammer and kills Thrym and all the giants present. The gods celebrate their victory.

## ESSENTIAL QUESTIONS

- How important are possessions in life?
- How can certain trying events cause people to mature?

## ANTICIPATORY QUESTIONS

- What would happen if Thor lost his mighty hammer?
- Which of the gods or goddesses do you think will get married in this story?
- Who is the manliest of the gods?

## CONNECT

*Thor* (2011) Based on the popular Marvel Comics series *The Mighty Thor*, this film adaptation transports the world of Norse Mythology to a science-fiction setting. Thor, who is more superhero than god, is banished to earth by Odin and must try to stop his adopted brother, Loki, from taking over Asgard. Many of the Norse gods are represented in the film but have major differences from their mythological counter-parts. One plot point does involve Thor temporarily losing his hammer (a similarity to this myth). Watch the film. Then compare and contrast Thor in the film with Thor from Norse mythology.

## TEACHABLE TERMS

- **Dramatic Irony** To achieve part of its humor his myth uses dramatic irony, a situation where the reader knows something a character in the story does not. Thrym the giant does not know that Thor is posing as his bride, but the reader does. This helps generate the humor in his reactions to Thor's appearance.
- **Characterization**  Why didn't Thrym the giant try to kill the gods while he was in Asgard? Why is he interested in marrying Freya? Is he really as bad as the gods make him out to be? Explain.
- **Plot Hole** Defined as a weak spot in a story or an event that doesn't seem plausible, plot holes can be found in many stories. Does this story have any plot holes?
- **Title** Does the title "Freya the Bride" have new meaning after reading the story? Is the title misleading? Is it intended to be ironic?

## RECALL QUESTIONS

1. What new treasure do the dwarves create?
2. What form does Loki take in order to steal from Freya?
3. What has been stolen from Asgard?
4. Where has Thrym the giant hidden this item?
5. What is the true identity of Thrym's bride?

# FREYA THE BRIDE

**CAST**

| | |
|---|---|
| **FREYA** | *Goddess of Beauty* |
| **ODIN** | *All-Father of the Gods* |
| **LOKI** | *Half-Giant Trickster* |
| **HEIMDALL** | *Watchman of the Gods* |
| **TYR** | *God of Battle* |
| **FRIGGA** | *Wife of Odin* |
| **THOR** | *God of Thunder* |
| **DVALIN** | *Leader of the Dark Dwarves* |
| **DWARF** | *Henchman of Dvalin* |
| **THRYM** | *Giant of Jotunheim* |

**NARRATOR:** Of all the gods Freya had always been the most dazzling, and her collection of fine jewels, with which she adorned her body, could not be rivaled. Her jewelry boxes were overflowing with all kinds of sparkling wonders. But as she amassed more and more of these trinkets, they left her vaguely unsatisfied.

**FREYA:** I am the most beautiful goddess of all, and I have the greatest jewel collection in Asgard. Why can't I be happy?

**NARRATOR:** It was then that she remembered the dwarves who lived down in Svartalfheim. Not only did they harvest jewels from the earth, but they were also craftsmen capable of creating new wonders—perhaps even a wonder that could stir her heart anew.

**FREYA:** The dwarves don't live so far away! They will surely make me a treasure when they see my beauty.

**NARRATOR:** Freya's vibrant eyes began to flit back and forth as thoughts of glorious treasures bounced through her head.

**FREYA:** I'll go at once! Maybe they will make me a jeweled dress or a jeweled crown! *(gasp)* Or even a bathtub to fill with jewels!

**NARRATOR:** Not even bothering to put on a cloak, she dashed from Asgard. She neared Bifrost, the Rainbow Bridge that leads to the world below. Heimdall, the Watchman of the Gods, stood there at his post.

**HEIMDALL:** Hail, Freya! Where are you going this fine day?

**FREYA:** *(musically)* No time for small talk, Heimdall. I'm going jewel-hunting in Svartalfheim.

**HEIMDALL:** *(shocked)* My lady, surely you are not headed down into the land of the dwarves!

**FREYA:** Of course!

**HEIMDALL:** All by yourself? The dwarves can be a tricky lot. Their minds are as warped as their bodies, and they use their treasures to lure folks into mischief.

**FREYA:** I think I can handle a bunch of little men, thank you very much. Now, good day!

**NARRATOR:** It happened that the dark dwarves of Svartalfheim had just finished their greatest creation—the most glorious piece of jewelry ever forged—the legendary necklace, Brisingamen. Deep under the mountain, the dwarves gathered around the glowing forge to survey their completed work.

**DVALIN:** *(greedy voice)* Gentle-dwarves, our work is done. We have forged the great necklace! Now, we must use it for its special purpose.

*(loud dwarvish cheering)*

**DWARF:** *(dumb voice)* Will we sell it?

**DVALIN:** We're not going to sell it, you simpleton! We're going to use it as bait.

**DWARF:** Bait for what?

**DVALIN:** What do you think? Women!

**DWARF:** *(confused)* Women?

**DVALIN:** Look in the mirror, chump! We're hideous, hairy creatures! The only way we're going to get a woman is by tricking one.

**DWARF:** Oh, I see.

**DVALIN:** Now, take the necklace up to the entrance of the cave and leave it there.

We'll wait for some fair, young maiden to come along and be completely enchanted by its brilliance!

**NARRATOR:** The dwarves rubbed their grubby hands together as the trap was laid.

Soon the frazzled form of Freya appeared upon the bleak landscape. She was extremely upset. She had been in the land of the dwarves for hours and so far had found no jewels. Then her eye spotted something glinting upon the ground.

**FREYA:** *(gasp)* At last!

**NARRATOR:** There lying next to a dank hole in the ground was a flawless amulet of gold—a sheen emanating from the milk-white stones upon it.

**FREYA:** *(stunned)* By the Norns! It's the most gorgeous thing I have ever seen!

**NARRATOR:** Mesmerized, Freya moved toward the necklace, her hand outstretched.

**DVALIN:** *(clears throat)* Ahem!

**NARRATOR:** Freya snapped out of her trance and nearly jumped. Standing on the rock beside her was the dirtiest creature she had ever seen.

**DVALIN:** Ah—ah—ah! Not so fast, my lady.

**FREYA:** *(hatefully)* What do *you* want?

**DVALIN:** I am Dvalin. I am the leader of the dark dwarves, the makers of this necklace. It is not yours for the taking.

**NARRATOR:** Three other grimy dwarves appeared from the hole in the ground and murmured their agreement. *(Dwarven grumbling)*

**FREYA:** *(forcefully)* I must have it! I am Freya, the most beautiful of the goddesses—as you can see. I desire this necklace. Now give it to me!

**DVALIN:** Ah! And we would be happy to give it to you, *but* we ask something in return.

**FREYA:** *(happily)* Oh! I see. No need to ask. Yes, you may gaze upon my radiant beauty! No charge! But do hurry. I'm ready to try on that gorgeous necklace.

**NARRATOR:** The dwarf stared at her blankly.

**DVALIN:** That is not what we desire.

**FREYA:** Fine. Fine. What *do* you want? A lock of my hair? I get that request a lot.

**DVALIN:** *(annoyed)* Listen very carefully, goddess. We are dwarves. We live in a dirty hole. We have no hope of ever having a wife of our own.

**FREYA:** *(thinking)* Well, I could play matchmaker, I guess. I have several single friends. But I'm afraid you all are horribly hideous. None of my friends are quite that desperate.

**DVALIN:** We want *you* to be our wife!

**FREYA:** *(completely scandalized)* That's totally out of the question! I'm a desirable goddess! I'm not going to marry a disgusting dwarf! I have my pride to think about! I'd rather marry a giant!

**DVALIN:** It would only be for one day, and then you would be released from the commitment.

**NARRATOR:** This caused the goddess to pause.

**FREYA:** Only one day? And then I would have the necklace?

**DVALIN:** Yes, but you see, more than one of us contributed to the necklace. You'd have to be married to each of us for one day, and then the necklace would be yours.

**FREYA:** What? All four of you?

**NARRATOR:** Dvalin stepped in front of the necklace and crossed his arms.

**DVALIN:** *That* is our price.

*(dwarvish laughter)*

**NARRATOR:** Freya looked helpless. The necklace was glimmering up at her—asking her to take it. It filled her mind. It made her forget Asgard, her status as a goddess, her honor. She feebly complied.

**FREYA:** *(weakly)* I shall do it.

**NARRATOR:** Four days later Freya made her way back up to Asgard. She was clinging to her new necklace, but she had realized that she was too afraid to wear it. What if someone asked her where she obtained such a treasure? Then she would have to admit to her four dwarf-marriages.

**FREYA:** Four dwarf marriages! I'd be the laughing stock of Asgard!

**NARRATOR:** So Freya hid the necklace away and only wore it in her garden, where no one else ever went. But it did not take long for the rumor of Freya's dwarf-marriages to spread throughout the Nine Worlds and finally reach the ears of Loki. It seemed that he was a magnet for bad news and loved nothing more than passing it along. He went immediately before Odin.

**LOKI:** Odin, I hate to be the bearer of bad news.

**ODIN:** Do you? You can barely keep that smile off your face.

**LOKI:** It concerns our darling goddess, Freya. Apparently, there has been a little secret matrimony going on behind our backs.

**ODIN:** Freya? Married? She has never taken a husband!

**LOKI:** Oh, she's taken a few actually. And they're not exactly what you could call "catches" either.

**ODIN:** What do you mean?

**LOKI:** She's acquired a new piece of jewelry—a necklace—that she wears only in the confines of her own home. It cost her dearly.

**ODIN:** Explain yourself.

**LOKI:** Four dwarves made the necklace, and in return for it, Freya agreed to marry each of them for one day.

**ODIN:** Loki, this is a serious accusation! It is unacceptable for a noble goddess of Asgard to be linked with a bunch of scummy dwarves!

**LOKI:** It is true, and I can prove it to you!

**ODIN:** Just a second. Why do you care? What business is it of yours?

**LOKI:** She's dishonored us all with her actions. *(pause)* Plus, just for once, I want to see someone else get the bad rap—instead of me!

**ODIN:** *(hatefully)* Fine. Bring me this necklace you speak of, and you shall have proved your words.

**LOKI:** With pleasure.

**NARRATOR:** Loki headed for the hall of Freya and peered over the walls of her garden. In the midst the goddess was asleep on a clump of heather, and there about her neck was her secret treasure.

**LOKI:** Bingo! Heh! Heh! It's showtime!

**NARRATOR:** The trickster crept silently over the wall and snuck close to the slumbering goddess. He saw that the clasp of the necklace was trapped beneath her white neck. He could not undo it without waking her.

**LOKI:** *(to himself)* Not a problem.

**NARRATOR:** Loki's form shrunk down, down, down into the form of a flea. He hopped onto her cheek and sunk his pinchers into her flesh.

**FREYA:** *(in her sleep)* Ungh.

**NARRATOR:** Freya fidgeted, swiped at her face, and turned upon her side, but did not wake. Now the clasp was exposed. Loki laughed silently, quickly transformed, and removed the dwarf treasure from her neck. In a flash he was back in Odin's throne room—the necklace dangling from his open hand.

**ODIN:** I had still hoped that you were mistaken, Loki. Or at least that this was one of your tricks. The truth is much worse.

**LOKI:** When Freya wakes and sees her necklace gone, she'll know she's been found out. She can't deny it now. Bring her here and ask her yourself. She'll have to tell the truth!

**ODIN:** And then what will happen? She will be publicly shamed. What good will that do anyone?

**LOKI:** It will do *me* good to see it.

**ODIN:** Very well.

**NARRATOR:** Freya's summons drew the attention of the other gods, and they gathered to watch the spectacle. When the goddess mournfully came before the throne of Odin, her eyes were red with tears. She saw her precious necklace laid at his feet.

**ODIN:** *(sadly)* Freya, we have heard rumors about your actions, and we hope they are not true.

**NARRATOR:** Freya lowered her eyes to the floor.

**FREYA:** It's all true, my lord.

*(collective gasp)*

**ODIN:** I can't believe it!

**FREYA:** I have betrayed the honor of the gods—all for a worthless band of gold. All I want now is forgiveness.

**NARRATOR:** Odin furrowed his brow and thought for a moment.

**ODIN:** Then I decree that you should wander in the worlds below for a span of six months and do good works to any you find there. Then—and only then—will you be allowed to return.

**FREYA:** I accept your decree.

**ODIN:** Now here is your necklace.

**FREYA:** *(hatefully)* I refuse to wear that necklace any longer! I hate it! It has caused me so much dishonor!

**ODIN:** But you must always wear it to remind you of your sorrow and your shame. That is also part of my decree.

**FREYA:** *(sadly)* Yes, my lord.

**NARRATOR:** So the goddess of beauty set out on her journey, traveling through the world of men and giants. She did not walk haughtily as she did before, and the tears she cried turned into rich, red gold. Everywhere she went, she taught man and beast alike the meaning of humility, and the world in turn loved her. Brisingamen was always about her neck, but it was forgotten and unnoticed. The goddess herself now outshone it in beauty and worth.

**ODIN:** Freya has been gone for many months now. My ravens tell me that she has done much good in the world, and they have gone to summon her home.

**NARRATOR:** In Asgard a celebration was announced to welcome home the wandering goddess. When she appeared, there was an explosion of applause. *(applause)*

**ODIN:** Welcome home, beautiful goddess!

**FREYA:** Thank you! Thank you!

**ODIN:** Have you learned your lesson, Freya?

**FREYA:** Yes. I have learned that the beauty within is greater than the beauty without.

**ODIN:** Then let us celebrate your return!

*(cheers from the gods)*

**NARRATOR:** The gods feasted in the hall of the gods until they could feast no more. They celebrated the fact that all was well in Asgard. But it did not take long for that to change again.

The following morning, new trouble was already brewing. Thor's cries filled Valhalla.

**THOR:** *(shouting)* Thor's hammer! Thor's hammer has been stolen!

**ODIN:** *(waking up)* What? Did you take it home with you last night?

**THOR:** I slept here last night. Thor takes his mighty hammer everywhere. I even sleep with it—to keep it safe! Now it is nowhere to be found.

**ODIN:** Wait a minute. Where is Loki? I haven't seen him since Freya returned yesterday.

**TYR:** He'll be behind this, I'm sure!

**HEIMDALL:** I saw him heading down the Rainbow Bridge yesterday—before the great feast began. I've learned it's always best to keep an eye on Loki. I watched him for many miles. I know exactly where he is!

**NARRATOR:** All the gods looked to Heimdall expectantly.

**HEIMDALL:** What?

**ODIN:** *(annoyed)* Well, go after him!

**HEIMDALL:** Oh right!

**NARRATOR:** When Heimdall finally returned, he was carrying a slippery seal in his arms. *(seal noises)*

**HEIMDALL:** *(grunting)* Stop squirming, you blasted creature!

**THOR:** *(angrily)* We sent you to find Loki— not some strange sea-mammal!

**HEIMDALL:** This *is* Loki! He saw me coming after him and leapt into the sea to escape me! But you can't outswim Heimdall!

**NARRATOR:** He plopped the seal down in front of Odin's throne. The air flickered, and Loki appeared in the seal's place, drenched by salt water.

**ODIN:** *(smugly)* Trying to escape, were you?

**LOKI:** *(slyly)* Of course not. You know I love fresh fish. *(hiccup)*

**NARRATOR:** A fish fell from Loki's mouth and flopped about on the floor.

**LOKI:** Metal-mouth here just interrupted my weekly fishing trip.

**ODIN:** Nevermind your stories! What have you done with Thor's hammer?

**LOKI:** I don't know what you're talking about. From the question though, I guess old Thunder-brain has lost his hammer?

**THOR:** *(yelling loudly)* Thor's hammer is gone! Gone!

**LOKI:** I love that you automatically assume that *I* have stolen it. What would I want with his stupid hammer?

**TYR:** Well, you are part-giant.

**NARRATOR:** Loki sneered at Tyr.

**LOKI:** I am also part-god.

**TYR:** That means you're *half* trustworthy.

**ODIN:** Stop bickering! Well, Loki, if you didn't steal it, who did? You must help us find the culprit.

**LOKI:** I see how it is. One minute I'm the bad guy. The next minute I'm the only person smart enough to help you out of this mess.

**THOR:** Loki, please help us! Without Thor's hammer, Asgard will be lost!

**LOKI:** *(sigh)* Well, for starters, nobody has noticed the large set of footprints that lead into this hall and then disappear out the side door.

**NARRATOR:** Loki pointed to the floor, and, sure enough, giant tracks were there.

**THOR:** *(in shock)* Giants! Here in Asgard?

**LOKI:** *(sarcastically)* He's catching on. Logically, we have to deduce this—a giant snuck in here last night and stole Thor Thick-skull's favorite toy.

**TYR:** But the giants have been peaceful for many months. We've heard nothing from Jotunheim.

**LOKI:** Exactly. They were just lulling you into a false sense of security before they struck.

**TYR:** Leave it to you to think like a giant!

**ODIN:** Loki, your words make sense. Thor's hammer must have fallen into the hands of the giants.

**LOKI:** *(pause)* You all can apologize at any time now for suspecting me.

**THOR:** *(bellowing)* Thor will get his hammer back! I leave for the land of the giants at once! Who's with me?

**ODIN:** Silence! *You're* not going anywhere. We're no match for the giants without Mjolnir. We know that, and they know that. That's why they have stolen it. We cannot attack them. We must try to solve this diplomatically.

**TYR:** There's no way to negotiate with a bunch of hotheaded giants. They only want to see Asgard destroyed—and nothing more!

**ODIN:** Loki, you must go to them and see if we can retrieve Thor's hammer peacefully.

**LOKI:** Me? Why me?

**ODIN:** None of the rest of us can venture there and return alive.

**LOKI:** Fine! But no more of this looking-down-on-Loki business! I am one of you—your equal. Or—dare I say it?—your better!

I can do things that none of the rest of you can.

**NARRATOR:** The gods eyed Loki in stony silence.

**LOKI:** If I go, Freya must give me her magical falcon cloak. It's the only thing that can insure I won't get my brains bashed out.

**ODIN:** That is for Freya to decide.

**NARRATOR:** Freya stepped forward and looked intently at the one who had previously caused her so much grief.

**FREYA:** I know it was you who brought me so much pain, Loki. But the gods have given me forgiveness, and I must do the same for you.

**LOKI:** Whatever.

**FREYA:** Here. Take this falcon cloak and find Thor's hammer.

**NARRATOR:** A long cape of woven feathers appeared within her arms. Loki snatched it away and threw it about his shoulders. It attached itself there, and with several thrusts from his now-winged arms, he flew from the hall.

**LOKI:** *(bird sounds)* Farewell. Farewell.

**NARRATOR:** As the bird flies, Jotunheim was not a long journey, and Loki—amid his grumblings—spied a snow-covered peak. But as he drew nearer, he saw that it was in fact a snow-covered frost giant, wearing a very smug look on his face. Loki pulled up and hovered before him.

**THRYM:** *(booming, smugly)* Hello, birdy.

**NARRATOR:** The giant's icy breath caused crystals to form on Loki's wings.

**LOKI:** Stop that!

**THRYM:** Huh. A bird that speaks. You must be one of the gods.

**LOKI:** More or less. I don't suppose you've seen an enchanted hammer around here anywhere, have you? It answers to the name of Mjolnir.

**THRYM:** Of course, I have. I am Thrym the giant. I used my magic to sneak into your god-hall last night and steal Thor's hammer! I've been waiting for you to come. I expected you to come much sooner.

**LOKI:** *(sarcastically)* Sorry to keep you waiting. Now, tell me where it is so I can be getting back home!

**NARRATOR:** The giant chuckled, and his breath nearly froze Loki in mid-air.

**THRYM:** I have hidden it. It is down at the roots of this mountain—eight miles beneath the earth to be exact.

**LOKI:** That's a bit excessive, don't you think? You've certainly done a thorough job of hiding it.

**THRYM:** Yes, and only *I* can retrieve it.

**LOKI:** I suppose you want something in return for it. What's your price? Thor's head served up on a platter? The riches of Asgard?

**THRYM:** No, no, no. The giant-slayer and jewels do not concern me. I am looking for a bride. I desire one of the gods for my wife.

**LOKI:** Oh, Norns. A giant in love.

**THRYM:** Many days ago, I saw the beautiful goddess Freya wandering through our land, and I desired her.

**LOKI:** I don't know how to break this to you, but she has a shady past.

**THRYM:** She is the desire of my heart.

**LOKI:** It probably wouldn't work out. You're as big as a mountain peak. She's into dwarves.

**NARRATOR:** The giant glared at the hovering trickster.

**THRYM:** Grrrr. Ever been an icicle before?

**LOKI:** *(sigh)* I'll tell her, but she's not into strange creatures. Trust me. I've tried. *(pause)* But recently she has been slumming a bit.

**THRYM:** Bring her here to marry me! Or I will not give you back the hammer!

**NARRATOR:** The giant plucked Loki out of the air, packed him tightly into a ball of snow, and hurled him high, high into the sky—all the way back to Asgard. *(whistling noise)*

**LOKI:** *(screaming)* Ah!

**NARRATOR:** The snowball impacted upon the magical walls of Asgard, and Loki dragged his aching body loose from the slush. He limped before the assembled gods and told them the frost giant's demand.

**FREYA:** Me? Why would he want me? Can't he find a wife among the giants?

**LOKI:** Have you ever seen giant-women?

**FREYA:** *(sadly)* This is all my fault.

**LOKI:** Well, I did offer Thor to the giant, but he didn't want *him*.

**FRIGGA:** *(sudden idea)* Wait a minute, Loki. That's it! There is a way to get Mjolnir back and save Freya from an unwanted marriage.

**LOKI:** Eh. What's one more marriage to her?

**FRIGGA:** We'll give the giant his bride!

**NARRATOR:** Frigga snapped her fingers and armfuls of pastel fabric appeared.

**FRIGGA:** Help me, goddesses. Gather around Thor here.

**THOR:** I am confused by this!

**LOKI:** What *doesn't* confuse you?

**NARRATOR:** The goddesses draped layer after layer of cloth over the burly god.

**ODIN:** I understand your plan!

**FRIGGA:** See?

**NARRATOR:** Thor was now dressed in the clothing of a goddess.

**FRIGGA:** Thor can marry the giant!

**THOR:** *(enraged)* Thor will not!

**ODIN:** Son, you won't actually marry the giant. All you have to do is get close enough to ambush him.

**LOKI:** This is never going to work! There's absolutely nothing feminine about Thor.

**ODIN:** Giants are poor judges of beauty.

**FREYA:** I believe this plan could work.

**THOR:** (*grumbling*) This disguise does not befit the manliest of the gods.

**ODIN:** Even better. They would never suspect you.

**NARRATOR:** As Thor sulked the goddesses combed out his long, red-gold hair. Then they made him a veil that carefully concealed his face.

**LOKI:** No matter how he looks, he's never going to be able to act the part. He refers to himself in the third person all the time!

**THOR:** (*angrily*) Thor does not.

**ODIN:** All right, ladies. Is our bride ready?

**NARRATOR:** The crowd parted, and there stood Thor. His face had been painted, and apart from his bulging biceps and beard, he did look slightly womanish.

**ODIN:** It will have to do. Hopefully, it will work long enough to get the hammer back.

**NARRATOR:** Sporting their banners of celebration, all the gods of Asgard began the long procession to Jotunheim. Their heavily veiled "bride" rode in a gilded chariot pulled by Odin's eight-legged horse, Sleipnir. Even Freya, disguised as a maidservant, came along to watch the show.

From his mountain peak Thrym the Giant saw the gods coming and blew a note upon a large horn. (*horn sound*) Then he came bounding down the mountainside to meet them.

**THRYM:** (*overjoyed*) My bride! My bride is here!

**NARRATOR:** The frost giant towered over the gods.

**THRYM:** Greetings, gods. Now we will have a wedding! Where is my bride?

**ODIN:** (*sadly*) You have beaten us, giant. We humbly offer up the goddess Freya to be your bride. (*pause*) Freya? (*pause*) Ahem.

**NARRATOR:** Odin gave Thor a sharp nudge.

**THOR:** Oh!

**NARRATOR:** In his disguise the hulking god strode forward. Thrym squinted down trying to see through Thor's thick veil.

**THRYM:** (*breathlessly*) Ah! She is even more beautiful than I remembered! And beefier, too! I like that in a woman!

**NARRATOR:** Loki—who had been hastily disguised as a bridesmaid—stood next to Thor. Thrym eyed Loki coldly.

**LOKI:** (*female voice*) Hi there!

**THRYM:** It is a good thing that I am not marrying this hideous she-creature. Her looks leave much to be desired. And she is far too scrawny!

**LOKI:** Oh, go on! Tee hee.

**NARRATOR:** The blast on the giant's horn had summoned other giants, and they appeared from the mountains, bearing all the provisions necessary for a wedding. A feast was laid out, and the guests, gods and giants, seated themselves for the celebration.

**THRYM:** Sit here by me, sweetie!

**THOR:** *(grumbling)* How much longer must Thor endure this disguise?

**LOKI:** *(whispering)* Shut up, you dumbbell! We don't have the hammer yet! Now, eat your meat! They'll get suspicious!

**NARRATOR:** The thunder god began to poke down large hunks of goat meat.

**THOR:** *(burp)* Brap! More meat! More ale!

**NARRATOR:** After many helpings, Thrym began to look at his bride suspiciously.

**THRYM:** *(suspiciously)* Hmmm. Freya has eaten fifteen goats and drank ten gallons of ale. I do not remember any goddess ever being able to eat that much.

**THOR:** Errrrr...

**LOKI:** Tee hee. Since Freya has been so excited about her wedding, she has not eaten for eight days. She's terribly hungry. Normally she just nibbles.

**THRYM:** Hmmm. Remove her veil. I want to see her face.

**NARRATOR:** Thor and Loki looked at each other helplessly.

**LOKI:** Well, just a peek. It's not proper to get too close a look before the wedding!

**NARRATOR:** Loki raised Thor's veil.

**THOR:** Grrrrrrr.

**THRYM:** *(cry of surprise)* Ah!

**NARRATOR:** Thrym drew back, and Loki lowered the veil back into place.

**THRYM:** Her eyes glow with a fire! A fire like lightning! I don't remember them looking like that before.

**LOKI:** Ermm—well—Freya has not slept a wink these past days. Her eyes are terribly bloodshot.

**THRYM:** Hmmm. Oh well! She is so beautiful it does not matter!

**NARRATOR:** Thrym stood and clapped his hands for the attention of his guests.

**THRYM:** Now, the time has come for me to present my bride with her wedding present.

**NARRATOR:** The giant uttered some mysterious words, and the ground beneath them began to rumble. *(rumbling)* Mjolnir rose from the rocky ground, spinning— spraying gravel in all directions.

**THRYM:** *(grandly)* Behold! Mjolnir! The hammer of Thor! I am only sorry that the foolish Thor is not here to see me give away his precious weapon.

**THOR:** *(battlecry)* Ahhhh!

**NARRATOR:** Much to Thrym's surprise, his beautiful bride hitched up her dress and bounded over the wedding table—spilling its spread and seizing the hammer in her not-so-dainty grip. *(crashing sounds)* Thor rounded upon the giant—brandishing his hammer.

**THRYM:** (*complete surprise*) What?

**THOR:** Thor will not get married this day!

**NARRATOR:** Thor sprang high into the air and brought Mjolnir down upon Thrym's head. (*shazam*) The force of the blow drove the giant down into the ground so far he could no longer be seen.

**THOR:** (*battlecry*) Rar!

**LOKI:** Now look who's eight miles down! Looks like the honeymoon's over!

**THOR:** Who's next?

**NARRATOR:** The thunder god ripped off his disguise, and the mouths of the giants fell open. Thor attacked them—his hammer gleaming and swinging. (*screaming of the giants*) The other gods sat back and watched as Thor singlehandedly thrashed the mob. Frost giants flew through the air in all directions.

**TYR:** I think Thor likes his wedding present.

**HEIMDALL:** It is a treat to watch the master at work! Pass the goat-meat please.

**LOKI:** Well, Odin. So much for your diplomatic solution. Maybe Thor misunderstood when you said, "Make peace with the giants." He thought you meant "make pieces of the giants." Heh heh.

**ODIN:** One thing is for sure. The giants won't be sneaking into Asgard again anytime soon!

**FRIGGA:** They won't be sneaking anywhere!

**NARRATOR:** All the giants, who did not flee back into the mountains, were killed. Thor stood upon a pile of bodies, his hammer raised in triumph.

**ODIN:** Let's hear it for Thor!

**NARRATOR:** The gods threw up their hands and cheered. (*shouts of "Huzzah!"*)

**LOKI:** And let's hear it for Loki!

(*sound of crickets*)

**ODIN:** Today has been a mighty victory for the dwellers of Asgard! Many evil giants have been slain, Mjolnir is safe again, and Freya is preserved!

**FREYA:** Thor, thank you for keeping me from being a giant's bride.

**NARRATOR:** Freya kissed Thor upon the cheek, and the god immediately reddened. Sif, Thor's wife, crossed her arms angrily.

**LOKI:** Ahem.

**NARRATOR:** Loki drew near Freya and pointed to his own cheek, but the goddess ducked quickly past him.

**THOR:** In the future Thor shall keep a better eye on his hammer! It is one thing that a blushing bride should never be without!

(*merry laugh from all*)

## DISCUSSION QUESTIONS

- What is the tone of this myth? How can you tell it's not completely serious?

- What lesson does the goddess Freya learn about possessions?
- In this myth how is Thor an object of humor?
- For once it is not Loki causing problems for the Æsir. Is it fair that they automatically assume that he is behind the theft of Thor's hammer? Explain.

# IN THE LAND OF THE GIANTS
## TEACHER GUIDE

## BACKGROUND

*J*otuns in the Norse myths are called "giants" by many translations. But since the tales give little physical description, the question still remains: Were the "giants" actually giant? In some stories they tower over the treetops. In others "giants" look so much like the Æsir that the gods do not recognize them for what they are. Some gods even intermarry with the giants.

Enormous or not, there is no question of the giants' evil nature. They are the personification of all the forces that threatened to destroy the Norse people—starvation, wild animals, and the unforgiving elements. They are named *wind* giants and *frost* giants for that reason. The giants' only desire is to destroy. As the giants represent the chaos of nature, the Æsir represent order and society, and they struggle to keep the giants at bay. The day the giants overpower the gods will be Ragnarok, the end of the world.

In this story the giants, who are often shown as unintelligent and barbaric, have a resident wit as their king—a giant who can outsmart the gods. In the original tale his name is Utgard-Loki, which means he is the Loki of the giants. He is a much more formidable opponent since he has a giant intellect to match his gigantic size.

## SUMMARY

*G*iants are Thor's mortal enemies, but he often enjoys venturing into their land just so he can give battle. Thor enlists Loki (against his will) to accompany him on his latest adventure. As they pass through Midgard, Thor picks up one of his mortal servants, a tall boy named Thialfi who has incredible speed.

As they pass into Jotunheim, darkness catches the travelers without a place to stay until they spot a strange hall. The hall has five passageways, but none of them leads anywhere. They spend the night within, but a horrible roaring shakes the hall. In the morning, they see an enormous giant stretched out on the ground beside the hall. His snoring was the roaring they heard throughout the night. They also realize that what they thought was a hall was actually the giant's glove.

The giant awakes, introduces himself as Skrymir, and challenges the gods to accompany him back to Utgard, the fortress of the giants. Thor accepts the giant's invitation as he plans to slay him. The travelers follow the giant all day. When the giant makes camp and falls asleep once again, Thor tries three times to crack his skull with Mjolnir, but three times the blow has no effect on the giant. Enraged, Thor vows to follow the giant until he slays him.

The next day Skrymir leads them to Utgard, where they are taken before the giant king. The giant king challenges them to a series of contests. He puts Thialfi in a race and Loki in an eating contest. Both lose to their giant opponents (much to their shock). Then Thor is put to the test. He is asked to lift the king's giant cat, drink from a drinking-horn, and wrestle the king's grandmother. Thor, cockily assured of his victory, is flabbergasted when he fails in all his events.

At last it is revealed that the king is actually Skrymir, and he has been using his magic to frustrate the gods. Previously, each time Thor struck at him with the hammer, the giant had magically moved a hill in-between the strike and his skull. The giant-opponents who faced against Thialfi and Loki were actually the wind, who can run faster than anything else, and wildfire, who can devour things faster than anything else. The true nature of Thor's opponents are revealed as well—the Midgard Serpent, which he did manage to lift a tiny bit, the sea, which he did manage to drain to a dangerous level, and Old Age, whom he did make go down on one knee as he wrestled. Before Thor's rage can be unleashed, Skrymir and the rest of the giants disappear. The gods return home in defeat.

## ESSENTIAL QUESTIONS

- Should you ever take yourself too seriously?
- What is stronger—the mind or the body?
- Is all fair in love and war?

## ANTICIPATORY QUESTIONS

- What do you think Jotunheim, the land of the giants, is like?
- Are the giants dumb or intelligent?
- If the gods and the giants created an Olympic event, what would it be?
- How are the Norse gods similar to superheroes? What powers do they have?

## CONNECT

*Odd and the Frost Giants* by Neil Gaiman This young adult novel uses Norse mythology as a background for adventure. Odd is a half-orphaned Norse boy with a lame leg. One day he discovers a fox, an eagle, and a bear—who are actually Loki, Odin, and Thor trapped by a frost giant's evil spell. The giants have taken control of Asgard, using the magic of Thor's hammer, and are sentencing the world to eternal winter. Read this novel and then examine the elements of Norse mythology

found within it. How are the characters and events different or similar from how they appear in the Norse myths?

## TEACHABLE TERMS

- **Everyman** Thor is not overly intelligent, but he is strong and true. In Norse culture Odin was recognized as a regal god for kings and wealthy rulers. Thor was the everyman, the "average Joe" character that most Norsemen could identify with.
- **Personification** This myth personifies many abstract elements by giving them physical shape and characteristics. Wildfire, the wind, and old age all assume physical forms and act as characters in this story.
- **Situational Irony** When Thor fails at his various physical tests, humor is created through situational irony (or outcomes contrary to what is expected).
- **Setting** How is the land of the giants different from Asgard? What new challenges does it pose to the gods? Why is setting important in this story?

## RECALL QUESTIONS

1. For what is Thialfi, Thor's mortal servant, known?
2. Where do Thor, Loki, and Thialfi spend the night?
3. In Utgard what is Thor asked to lift off the ground?
4. In what kind of contest did Loki compete?
5. Unknown to him, Thor is actually wrestling whom or what?

# IN THE LAND OF THE GIANTS

## CAST

| | |
|---|---|
| **THOR** | *Thunder God* |
| **LOKI** | *Trickster* |
| **THIALFI** | *Mortal Boy* |
| **SKRYMIR** | *Crafty Giant* |
| **KING** | *Giant Ruler of Utgard* |
| **LOGI** | *Skinny Giant* |
| **ELLI** | *Old She-Giant* |
| **GUARD** | *Giant Guard* |

**NARRATOR:** Loki was lurking in the courtyard of Asgard when he saw Thor, the thunder god, approaching.

**LOKI:** Oh great.

**NARRATOR:** The trickster tried to slink away, but Thor hailed him.

**THOR:** Hail, Loki!

**LOKI:** Why me? *(half-heartedly)* Hail, Thor.

**THOR:** It is time for Thor to go adventuring again! *(loud laugh)* Ha-ha!

**LOKI:** Still talking in third-person, I see.

**THOR:** Yes—I think. So will you come with me or not?

**LOKI:** Well, I'd rather stab my eyes out.

**THOR:** Ha-ha! I love your strange sense of humor! Let's be off!

**LOKI:** *(sigh)* Fine. I have nothing better to do.

**THOR:** I am off to Jotunheim to kill some giants.

**LOKI:** Good thing this whole giant-hunting thing isn't awkward for me or anything. I mean, my father was a wind giant.

**THOR:** *(ignoring him)* Ha-ha! You know what I always say, don't you?

**LOKI:** Yes, unfortunately.

**THOR:** The only good giant is a dead giant. Now let Thor bid his beautiful wife, Sif, farewell!

**NARRATOR:** Thor enthusiastically kissed Sif goodbye.

**LOKI:** Yuck! Get a room.

**NARRATOR:** The two gods departed Asgard and made their way down the Rainbow Bridge.

**THOR:** As we travel through Midgard, we must pick up my human servant, Thialfi.

**LOKI:** We're taking a human along on this journey? I hate humans.

**THOR:** Is there a creature you *don't* hate?

**LOKI:** Good point.

**THOR:** Yes, we might need Thialfi on our journey. He's the fastest human alive.

**NARRATOR:** In Midgard they stopped before a small hut, and a peasant family came out to greet them. One long-legged boy was two feet taller than the rest of his family.

**LOKI:** *(sarcastically)* Hmmm. I wonder which one he is.

**THOR:** *(not understanding)* He is the tall lad on the right.

**LOKI:** *(grumble)* Nevermind.

**THOR:** Hail, Thialfi!

**THIALFI:** Hail, Thor! Hail, Loki!

**LOKI:** *(sourly)* Hail yourself.

**THOR:** Are you ready to adventure with us?

**THIALFI:** Of course, my lord!

**NARRATOR:** The three companions continued toward the land of the giants. Thialfi, taking huge strides, kept a swift pace.

**LOKI:** *(huffing/puffing)* Mind slowing down a bit? Some of us *aren't* long-legged freaks!

**THOR:** What is the matter, Loki? Can't keep up? *(loud laugh)* Ha-ha!

**LOKI:** *(sarcastically)* Your wit amazes me.

**THOR:** Soon we will cross the boundary between the world of men and the land of the giants. *(poetically)* The lamp of heaven is falling low in the sky. Twilight nears. I fear it will soon be dark.

**LOKI:** *(sarcastically)* I fear you will keep talking like that. Tell me, Hammer-Head— have you thought about where we are going to sleep?

**THOR:** Hmmm.

**NARRATOR:** The thunder god squinted through the dusk.

**THOR:** Hark! There is a hall ahead— nestled up against that ridge! I can barely make it out. We'll see if anyone is there.

**LOKI:** With any luck they'll be hostile and put us out of our misery.

**NARRATOR:** By the time they reached the hall, darkness had fallen.

**LOKI:** Doesn't look like anyone is around. We might as well let ourselves in.

**NARRATOR:** The three companions went into the open doorway.

**LOKI:** I can't see a thing! Don't they believe in torches around here?

**NARRATOR:** Mjolnir began to glow in the darkness—giving them a bit of light.

**THOR:** Thor's hammer will guide the way. See? There are a few hallways branching off here. Let's split up and search for sleeping quarters.

LOKI: Split up? I thought you'd never ask.

NARRATOR:   The travelers dispersed down the various hallways, but each passageway abruptly ended in a blank wall. They regrouped.

THOR:   Hmmm. What kind of hall has five passageways that lead to nowhere?

LOKI:   Is this some kind of riddle? Who cares? Let's just sleep right here. This place gives me the creeps.

NARRATOR:   They did as Loki suggested. Around midnight, they were awakened by a deafening roar. *(deafening roar)* The entire hall was shaking on its foundations.

THOR:   *(gasp)* The hall is moving!

LOKI:   *(sarcastically)* You think?

THOR:   Let's get out of here!

LOKI:   Are you crazy? Don't you hear that roaring out there? It's obviously some kind of monster. We better just stay here until it's gone.

THOR:   Then we will stand our ground here and wait for morning.

NARRATOR:   The roaring and shaking continued all through the night. When morning broke, Thor turned to his sleep-deprived companions.

THOR:   We must now venture forth and perchance determine the source of this noise. Perchance the maiden sun will shed her light on this dark riddle.

LOKI:   Perchance you'll stop talking like that.

THOR:   Come!

NARRATOR:   They crept forth, and in the light of day the mystery of the strange roaring was quickly solved.

THOR:   By the Norns!

NARRATOR:   What they had thought was a ridge of rock the night before was actually the side of a sleeping giant.

THOR:   I have never seen a giant so huge!

LOKI:   I'll be darned. Now let's get out of here!

NARRATOR:   The giant's mouth opened, and the tremendous roaring sound they had heard previously escaped from it. *(roaring snore)*

LOKI:   Whoa. He's a heavy sleeper.

THOR:   Grrrr. Let's wake him—and end his life!

LOKI:   He looks tired.   The poor thing probably needs his beauty rest.   You know what they say—let sleeping giants lie.

NARRATOR:   Just then the giant sat up.

SKRYMIR:   *(yawning and stretching noises)*

THIALFI:   My heart grows cold with fear!

THOR:   Hmph. It will take more than that to intimidate me!

NARRATOR:   The giant caught sight of the three companions.

LOKI:   He's seen us!

**SKRYMIR:** Hello there, small ones.

**THOR:** Ha! Who is this fool calling small?

**LOKI:** I think us. Look at him! He can call us anything he wants!

**SKRYMIR:** My name is Skrymir.

**THOR:** *(laughing)* Skrymir. That is a dumb name. If I had a dog, I would give it that name.

**LOKI:** *(gritting his teeth)* Bad idea.

**SKRYMIR:** Heh.  Heh.  You do not need to tell me *your* name.  Only the god Thor could be so bold. But do not worry.  I will not break the peace. I am traveling to Utgard, one of the many giant strongholds. Would you care to join me?

**LOKI:** *(sarcastically)* Hmmm. A trip into a giant stronghold? Gee. That sounds like fun.

**THOR:** Of course! That is where we are headed as well.

**LOKI:** *(under his breath)* What—are—you—doing?

**THOR:** *(whispering)* Thor will find a way to slay this giant!

**LOKI:** What are you going to do? Kick him in the shin?  He almost hit his head *on the sky*!

**THOR:** You are too cowardly, Loki. He's not *that* big!

**SKRYMIR:** Hmmm. Where did I put my glove? Oh! There it is!

**NARRATOR:** The giant's glove was lying upon the ground before them. It was huge—as big as a building.  In fact, it was the hall they had just spent the night in.

**LOKI:** Not that big, huh?

**SKRYMIR:** Ha-ha! So you spent the night in my glove, huh? How cute you small creatures are!

**THOR:** Grrrrrr.

**NARRATOR:** Skrymir picked up his glove and shoved it upon his hand.

**SKRYMIR:** Now, my miniature friends, we will go. Try to keep up.

**NARRATOR:** The giant stood, took three steps, and was nearly out of their sight.

**THOR:** Gah! No time to lose! After him! Thialfi, we must keep up!

**LOKI:** Oh great!

**NARRATOR:** There was no telling how many miles the three companions covered. Each time they would manage to catch sight of the giant, he was once again lost over the horizon. At last they saw the giant had stopped and prepared a camp for the evening.

**SKRYMIR:** I must say you small ones are rather slow.  I've been sitting here for hours.

**THOR:** *(huffing and puffing)* You...will... not...escape us...so easily.

**SKRYMIR:** Well, good night.

**NARRATOR:** With an earthshaking jolt the giant flopped onto his side and immediately began to snore. *(loud snoring)*

**THOR:** *(shouting over the snoring)* Now I will strike my blow!

**LOKI:** What?

**NARRATOR:** Thor shimmied up a tree and found a branch that was about level with the giant's head. He drew Mjolnir up to his full height.

**THOR:** Strike, Hammer of the Gods! *(battlecry)* Argh!

**NARRATOR:** He brought the hammer down full force. *(CLANG)* The mighty weapon only rebounded off the giant's skull, and the force of the blow sent Thor shooting backward out of the tree.

**THOR:** Ah!

*(crashing sounds)*

**NARRATOR:** The giant rose and looked around him.

**SKRYMIR:** What was that? Did a leaf fall on my head? *(pause)* Oh well.

**NARRATOR:** He flopped back onto the ground and continued his sleep. *(snoring)* Thor appeared from the underbrush.

**THOR:** *(stunned)* I—I don't believe it. Mjolnir has never failed before.

**LOKI:** Don't take yourself so seriously. C'mon. Let's get some sleep.

**NARRATOR:** The companions bedded down, but the giant's raucous snoring kept them from any hope of sleep.

**THOR:** This is intolerable! Thor cannot sleep with such racket. I'll put an end to this. Last time I must not have struck with my full force.

**NARRATOR:** Thor once again grabbed his hammer and climbed up the rocky rise near the sleeping giant's head. He raised the hammer up to his full height and brought it swiftly down. *(CLANG)* Once again the shock of the blow threw Thor backward off the hill of rocks. *(crashing sounds)*

**SKRYMIR:** Wha—what? Did an acorn fall on my head? *(pause)* Oh well. Back to sleep.

**NARRATOR:** Thor appeared over the hillside—red and shaking.

**THOR:** He compares the power of the almighty Thor to—to—an acorn!

**LOKI:** I don't know what's worse—your ranting or his snoring!

**THOR:** There is some mistake! My strike hit home! I felt it!

**LOKI:** Go try to kill him again. Maybe this time he'll figure out what's happening and rip you in half. At least then I won't hear your whining anymore.

**NARRATOR:** Thor climbed to a high spot to attack once again. This time he leapt into the air toward the giant's head.

**THOR:** *(battlecry)* Ahhh!

**NARRATOR:** The hammer sizzled as it cut through the air and hit home with all the fiery force of a thunderbolt. *(Shazam!)* Sparks flew everywhere.

**THIALFI:** By the gods!

**SKRYMIR:** Huh? Okay. I really felt something that time. A bird must have flown over and laid a little present on my head.

**NARRATOR:** The giant returned to sleep. Thor—singed and smoking—lay on the ground where he had fallen. A look of complete and utter confusion was on his face.

**THOR:** *(weakly)* It's not possible…

**SKRYMIR:** *(waking up)* Well, my rest is completed. My tiny friends, you can find your way from here. You can see Utgard away there on the horizon. I wish you happy, *little* lives.

**NARRATOR:** The giant rose and sauntered into the distance.

**LOKI:** Sooo, Thor, old buddy—ready to give up yet?

**THOR:** No! No! No! There must be some explanation!

**LOKI:** So we're still going to the giant city? Even though your hammer seems to be virtually worthless? Yep. Good idea.

**THOR:** Mjolnir will strike again, and this time it will kill! Rarr!

**NARRATOR:** Thor jumped up from the ground with a furious snarl and ran toward the far-off giant-city. Thialfi took quick pursuit behind him.

**LOKI:** Oh great. More running.

**NARRATOR:** When the three companions reached the giant stronghold, they saw it was carved from a mountain whose top was lost amongst the clouds and had gates as tall as trees. Thor pounded his hammer ferociously upon door. *(boom, boom, boom)*

**THOR:** Open these doors! Visitors from Asgard are here!

**LOKI:** Well, looks like nobody's home. At least we tried.

**NARRATOR:** The trickster tried to slink away, but the thunder god caught him up by his collar.

**THOR:** These enemies might be crafty, Loki. We will need your tricks more than ever.

**LOKI:** I need my life more than ever!

**NARRATOR:** Just then the doors swung open, and two enormous giant-at-arms, the guardians of the gate, grinned down at them.

**GUARD:** Ah! The puny thunder god and his creature-friend. Skrymir told us to expect you. In fact, he has told the King of Utgard about your coming as well. The king is dying to meet you.

**THOR:** He *will be* dying when he meets me! Isn't that right, Loki?

**LOKI:** Leave me out of this.

**NARRATOR:** Thor strode boldly between the legs of the giant guards and into the fortress. The guards pulled Thialfi and Loki inside.

**LOKI:**   Easy, fellas! I'm half-giant, you know. We're probably related.

**NARRATOR:**   They arrived in the throne room of the giant king, who had a face so grotesque, fearsome, and ugly that it would cause many to die of fright. His nose nearly touched his chest. But Thor, of course, was undaunted.

**THOR:**   I am Thor! Who might you be?

**KING:**   I am the king.

**THOR:**   King of what? King of this dung hill? I'm surprised you claim it.

**KING:**   *(chuckle)* Big talk will get you nowhere around here, godling. That is why we have arranged a little contest for you.

**THOR:**   A challenge! I gladly accept! I'll show you once and for all that the gods are the superiors of the giants.

**KING:**   We shall see.

**THOR:**   Come, come. What is the challenge?

**KING:**   The contest is not for you alone. It will also involve your diminutive companions.

**THOR:**   Did you hear that, Loki? He called you *dim*!

**LOKI:**   That's not what that means, you muscle-head!

**KING:**   Loki, huh? Even here we have heard tales of you. You're a half-breed, correct?

**LOKI:**   *(groveling)* Oh, I'm *at least* three-fourths giant—thankfully!

**KING:**   Butt-kissing will not be part of the contest, Loki. What else do you do well?

**THOR:**   He is a mighty eater! No one in Asgard can out-eat him.

**KING:**   Really? I believe there is someone here in Utgard who could beat him.

**LOKI:**   Oh really? Then bring them forward! I've never been beaten at eating.

**KING:**   Logi, come forth!

**NARRATOR:**   The giant king clapped his hands, and a gray, bone-thin giant was brought forward.

**LOKI:**   Kind of skinny, isn't he?

**NARRATOR:**   Two enormous troughs of food were laid out before Loki and his opponent.

**LOKI:**   Give that guy a sandwich! He'll starve before the contest begins. This *isn't* a fair fight—just the way I like it.

**KING:**   Eat!

**NARRATOR:**   Loki's jaws went into motion, and he devoured the food with a wolf-like appetite. *(gobbling and smacking sounds)* The trough was enormous, but he had cleared it of all its contents in a matter of seconds. Gorged and groggy, Loki held up his arms, sure of his victory.

**LOKI:**   There! I have won! *(burp)*

**NARRATOR:** To his shock, Loki realized that the food in his opponent's trough was also gone—in fact, so was the trough.

**LOKI:** What the—? Where's the trough?

**THIALFI:** He snapped up the food in a second, and then he ate the trough as well.

**LOGI:** *(burping)* Brap!

**NARRATOR:** The thin giant belched and bits of sawdust flew from his mouth.

**LOKI:** That guy beat me? I think I'm going to be sick! *(gurgling)*

**THOR:** You might have beaten Loki, but my other companion here is the fastest creature who has ever lived!

**KING:** Is that so? We'll just see about that.

**NARRATOR:** The giant king clapped his hands again. This time a second giant appeared—one with long, flowing hair.

**KING:** You two shall race around the perimeter of this fortress. The one who returns here before me first will be declared the winner.

**THOR:** Don't fail me, boy!

**THIALFI:** No problem!

**KING:** Go!

**NARRATOR:** Thialfi sped away. As for the long-haired giant, there was a blur in the air, and then he reappeared as if he had never left. A few seconds passed, and Thialfi returned to the throne room—winded and completely shocked that he had not won the contest.

**THIALFI:** *(out of breath)* I don't believe it!

**KING:** *(loud laughing)* Well, *mighty* Thor, can you do any better than your friends?

**NARRATOR:** Seething with anger, Thor spewed forth his answer.

**THOR:** You bet I can! And once I have proved myself, I am coming for your head, giant king!

**KING:** Very well. Three tests I set before you, most boastful of the gods. The first is a wrestling match.

**THOR:** A contest which I have never lost! Thor wears a magical belt that doubles his strength.

**KING:** Good. You will need it when you wrestle with the most formidable opponent known to Jotunheim—my grandmother!

**LOKI:** Huh?

**NARRATOR:** An old, crippled giantess hobbled forward. Her back so crooked that she stood no higher than Thor did.

**THOR:** How dare you giants mock me!

**KING:** It is no joke. Grandmother Elli is the best wrestler in Jotunheim.

**ELLI:** *(old woman voice)* C'mon, sonny. Show me your stuff.

**LOKI:** What are you waiting for, Thor? Even *I* could take her!

**THOR:** Very well.

**NARRATOR:** Thor flew forward, expecting to throttle his elderly opponent immediately, but the old woman's gnarled arms flew out and stopped him in his tracks.

THOR: Huh? *(grunting)*

NARRATOR: To Thor's surprise, he could not overpower her. He tried every move he knew, but nothing could throw the old woman from her feet. The giants who watched roared with laughter. *(laughter from the giants)*

LOKI: *(laughing)* Thor beaten by an old grandma! It's too rich!

THOR: Gar!

NARRATOR: Thor at last forced the old giant woman to one knee, but his strength had all but left him.

KING: Enough! The match is over. We'll call it a draw.

LOKI: Yeah, Thor. You and granny can share the booby prize.

ELLI: Better luck next time, sonny boy.

THOR: *(panting)* Impossible! There is some kind of trick here! Bring on the next contest.

KING: Next you will face yet another fearsome opponent, a creature so hideous few men have been able to tame it. Yes, I am talking about—my cat!

THOR: What? What do you want me to do to your cat?

KING: All you have to do is lift it off the ground.

LOKI: Hopefully, the cat's not as good a wrestler as Granny was! *(laughter)*

NARRATOR: A humongous cat sauntered forward, eyed Thor coldly, and plopped down in the midst of the throne room. *(purring)*

THOR: *(battlecry)* Ahhh!

NARRATOR: Thor ran forward and seized up the cat by its enormous belly—thrusting it as high as he could into the air. *(meowing and hissing)* Yet as he did so, the cat's four legs stretched out to their full length—keeping its paws firmly planted upon the ground.

THOR: *(grunting)* This—can't—be—happening!

NARRATOR: Thor pushed the cat higher and higher, but it continued to arch its back—hissing fiercely. *(hissing)* *(laughter from all the giants)* At last it lifted one paw from the ground, but Thor's strength was spent. He released the cat and gave it a mean-spirited kick. *(cat hiss)* It disappeared into the shadows of the hall.

THOR: *(panting)* There is trickery in this, and I will stand it no longer!

KING: Maybe strength is not the best contest for you.

THOR: I am Thor! The strongest of the gods!

KING: Are you known for anything other than your strength?

LOKI: Well, there's his dazzling intellect!

KING: Perhaps a drinking contest.

**THOR:**  Fine! I have never been beaten in one of those. I have an enormous thirst.

**KING:**    Very well.    Bring forward a drinking horn, and we shall see how thirsty the god can be.  All you must do is drain this tiny horn.

**NARRATOR:**    A drinking horn was brought forward and Thor examined it suspiciously.  It was just like those in Asgard—the hollowed-out horn of a bull. The giants filled it with mead, and he raised it above his head.

**THOR:**    I drink to your defeat, giants! Bottoms up!

**NARRATOR:** Thor's Adam's apple bobbed up and down as he gulped and gulped. (*gulping sounds*) He gulped for minutes on end, but the horn did not empty.

**THIALFI:**  What is happening?

**NARRATOR:**    Thor began to sweat. His face grew red, then blue, then finally purple.  The mead's level had lowered—but only slightly.    At last Thor let loose his breath, and mead flew in all directions.

**THOR:**  (*spewing sound*) Ahh!

**NARRATOR:** The thunder god fell to the ground, gasping for breath.

**KING:**  Beaten again!  I say, Thor, you are not the mighty warrior we giants thought you to be.

**THOR:**  (*breathlessly*) I don't understand.  I don't understand.

**NARRATOR:**  The giant king smiled good-naturedly.

**KING:**    Perhaps this will explain things. Behold!

**NARRATOR:** The giant king's appearance began to change.    His face melted and shifted. He now appeared in his true form— Skrymir, the giant they had met in the countryside.

**THOR:** You!

**SKRYMIR:** Yes, me! And I must admit you did much better at these contests than I thought you might have.  The old grandmother you wrestled was actually old age herself.  Even the strongest man or god cannot keep old age from beating him. But you at least got her down on one knee. And my cat. Well, that was no cat. It was an enormous serpent who lives in the Iron Wood—a serpent a mile long.    You struggled with it—and you did what no other person has ever done, you nearly lifted him out of the forest where he lives. And the other end of the horn of mead you drank from was attached to the wide ocean. The sailors of the world were in shock today when they saw the sea shrinking around them.  Thank goodness you could not drink it all!

**THOR:**  (*angrily*) Magic!  Magic!

**SKRYMIR:**  Of course, magic!

**LOKI:**  And who did I face off against?

**SKRYMIR:**  Logi or wildfire—the eater that gobbles up everything in his path.  No one could expect to beat him.

**THIALFI:**  And me?

**SKRYMIR:**  You raced against the speed of my mind.  Do not mourn that you lost in such a race! As soon as I imagined him to return to his starting point, he was there.

**THOR:** You *trickster!* I should have killed you when I had the chance.

**SKRYMIR:** You almost did! No giant could have lived through the blows you tried to deal me. But I was too clever for you. Each time you swung, I used my magic to put a hill in between your hammer and my skull. On your way back through Jotunheim you will see three valleys—each deeper than the last—all made from those terrible hammer-strokes of yours.

**LOKI:** Clever! But why? Why all these tricks?

**SKRYMIR:** We giants are not all fools. You are supposed to know your enemy, right? You have learned a valuable lesson today.

**THOR:** And *you* will not live to see tomorrow! *(battlecry)*

**NARRATOR:** Thor flew into the air, brandishing his hammer, but before he could strike, Skrymir disappeared in a puff of smoke.

**SKRYMIR:** *(bodiless voice)* Ha ha. I see someone did not learn his lesson today. Until our next meeting, godlings…

**NARRATOR:** Around them the fortress of the giants melted into a fog and was whisked away by the breeze. The three traveling companions found themselves sitting on a barren hilltop.

**THOR:** *(cry of rage)* No! Come back here and fight!

**NARRATOR:** For the longest time Thor could not be persuaded to move from that spot. He sat sadly—staring into space.

**THOR:** Thor has lost his honor here today.

**LOKI:** Big deal. Life makes the best of us look like chumps.

**THOR:** I will never again let a giant get the better of me. I swear this upon the sanctity of my own hammer!

**LOKI:** Well, at least we escaped with our heads intact. We have lost, but we live on to fight another day.

**THOR:** In that you speak the truth, my friend.

**NARRATOR:** With that the three companions began the trek home—turning their backs upon the land of the giants.

## DISCUSSION QUESTIONS

- What is a lesson that can be learned from this myth?
- Why does Skrymir not kill Thor, Loki, and Thialfi?
- What events of this story did you find surprising?
- The King of Utgard (Skrymir's disguise) is often given the name Utgard-Loki, meaning the Loki of Utgard. What is the significance of this name? How are Loki and the giant king similar?
- Thor is the Norse epitome of virility and manly strength. How does this myth poke fun at him?
- Does this story have a villain? If so, who is it?

# THE CHILDREN OF LOKI
## TEACHER GUIDE

## BACKGROUND

Loki is Norse mythology's most interesting character. He is both the gods' greatest ally and their greatest enemy. He is the trickster that is common in so many mythologies—the one who causes trouble, but whose ingenuity is able to solve many problems.

As a half-giant, Loki is also an outsider. On the inside he is continually struggling against his giant nature—his desire to destroy. At last this spirit of destruction is unleashed, and Loki turns against the gods, deciding instead to ally himself with the giants of Jotunheim.

Unlike the gods of Greek mythology, the Norse gods can die. This makes their struggle against the giants, Loki, and his children much nobler. In the end the gods will give their lives to defeat Loki and his children. Through this—their sacrificial deaths—they become much more worthy of admiration.

## SUMMARY

Evil is growing in the worlds below, and Odin can feel it. He spends his days seated on his high throne, scanning the world below for some sign of the evil he feels. He often casts his eye upon Jarnvid, the Iron Wood of Jotunheim. He recalls how once before, a creature came out of those woods—a monster-woman whose body was half-living and half-dead. Her name was Hela, and she was a witch. Odin condemned her to Niflheim to watch over the dead who come there. Now he fears another monster has been born in the Iron Wood. He takes Thor and Loki along to investigate.

Once they reach the tangled wood, Odin sends Loki ahead to scout out a path, but Loki does not return. Odin and Thor go in after him, only to be attacked by a giant serpent. After battling the serpent, Thor finally seizes it by the tail and flings it high over the trees. Loki reappears, having conveniently missed the battle.

The spirit of Hela appears before the gods, telling them that she has come to speak to her mother—a giant-witch who lives within the wood. She cryptically mentions that she did not expect to see her father there as well. Odin and Thor wonder what she means. Hela disappears, and they realize that Loki has disappeared again. They return to Asgard alone.

When Loki has not returned to Asgard, Odin takes to his throne to search for the trickster. Odin spies Loki leaving the Iron Wood with a monstrous creature—a giant wolf. He summons Loki to him at once. Odin accuses Loki of treachery. Loki has been visiting the witch who lives in the forest and is actually the father of Hela and the giant snake. Odin commands that Loki must help the gods destroy his latest child—the giant wolf—or he will no longer be a part of Asgard. Loki reluctantly agrees.

Fenrir, the giant wolf, is brought to Asgard. The gods learn that the beast's hide can never be pierced by iron, and like his serpentine brother, the wolf will continue growing until he is large enough to consume the whole world. The gods decide that Fenrir must be chained. Angered by their treatment of Fenrir, Loki finally shows his true colors. He declares that he is no longer the friend of the gods and vows to join the giants in a war against them. He leaves Asgard—presumably for good.

The gods try desperately to chain Fenrir,

but the beast breaks each chain they try. To keep Fenrir from running, the gods bribe him with food, but they soon realize that they do not have enough food to satisfy his large appetite for long. Odin goes to the dwarves and asks them to make a chain strong enough to bind Fenrir. Meanwhile, Fenrir eats all the food put before him. Once the food is gone, he will be free to run again. The god Tyr, knowing that Odin has just returned with the dwarves' chain, volunteers to place his sword-hand within the wolf's mouth. This is the only way Fenrir will agree to be chained.  The dwarf-chain holds, but Fenrir bites through Tyr's wrist. Fenrir howls violently at having been chained, and Tyr swears to have his revenge on Loki at any cost.

## ESSENTIAL QUESTIONS

- What causes someone to become evil?
- What happens when a friend becomes an enemy?
- Are evil people right in their own eyes?

## ANTICIPATORY QUESTIONS

- Do you think Loki will always be the gods' ally? What are some of the evil acts Loki has committed?
- Based on the title, "The Children of Loki," what do you think will happen in this story? What type of children would Loki have?
- What is the most frightening type of animal you can imagine?

## CONNECT

**Etymology** The term *hell* (used to define an afterlife of eternal punishment) is connected to *Hela*, the name of Loki's corpse-like daughter who rules over the dead of Niflheim. Unlike the typical concept of hell (a place of fire and brimstone), Niflheim is a frozen wasteland.

## TEACHABLE TERMS

- **Mood** This myth has a darker mood than those preceding it. While the previous myths were mostly lighthearted, in this story Loki completely embraces his evil nature, becoming the enemy of the gods. Events, such as the loss of Tyr's hand, make for a darker mood.
- **Character Development** Loki's character has come full circle from his first appearance in Norse mythology. Once he was a helpful trickster. Now he has become the embodiment of evil. What events have led to his descent into darkness? Could this process be reversed? Could he become good again? Explain.
- **Culture**  Think about Tyr's loss of his sword-hand. How do you think the Norse people viewed acts of sacrifice? Think about Valhalla, the heaven-like hall where only the bravest of warriors are allowed to go when they die. What can you tell about Norse culture from these details?

## RECALL QUESTIONS

1. Who is Hela?
2. What type of creature fights against Thor and Odin in the forest?
3. What type of creature is Fenrir?
4. What do the gods need from the dwarves?
5. What does Tyr sacrifice in order to trap Fenrir?

# THE CHILDREN OF LOKI

## CAST

| | |
|---|---|
| **ODIN** | *All-Father of the Gods* |
| **LOKI** | *Trickster* |
| **SIGUNA** | *Wife of Loki* |
| **TYR** | *God of Battle* |
| **BALDER** | *Most Beloved of the Gods* |
| **HELA** | *Evil, Half-Dead Witch* |
| **FENRIR** | *Gigantic Wolf* |
| **FREYA** | *Goddess of Love and Beauty* |
| **THOR** | *Thunder God* |
| **DWARF** | *Dwarf Craftsman* |

**NARRATOR:** The high throne of Odin was ornately carved from the trunk of a tree, and mystical runes glowed out from it. When the All-Father sat upon his throne, he was given new vision—the power to look down into any of the worlds below. But, lately, he had been searching for something—an unseen evil that he felt like a pressure upon his heart.

His single, wise eye flew over the mountains, the seas, the forests, the swamps—searching for signs of evil. He felt that evil was growing below, but as much as he searched, he could not discover its source. His gaze brushed across the Iron Wood.

Odin kept an especially close watch on Jarnvid, the Iron Wood of Jotunheim. Dark things lived there—things that should never be spoken of. Once, years before, something had slunk out from the Iron Wood—a corpselike being, the type of phantom that nightmares are made of. One half of it lived. The other half rotted on the bone.

Odin shuddered as he recalled it and stood from his throne. The far-vision faded.

**ODIN:** *(shouting)* Thor! Thor!

**NARRATOR:** There was a flash of lightning, and the thunder god appeared before him.

**THOR:** All-Father, Thor has come to do thy bidding!

**ODIN:** I feel that we must travel to the Iron Wood. Some trouble is brewing there.

**NARRATOR:** Thor grinned and wielded his hammer high.

**THOR:** We should take the creature, Loki, with us.

**ODIN:** Hmmm. Loki has been acting strangely lately. He is even more withdrawn than normal. I don't understand it.

**THOR:** I don't try to understand such creatures, Father. They are all strange to me.

**ODIN:**   We will bring Loki along if you wish.

**NARRATOR:**  When Loki arrived in Odin's hall, the All-Father had assumed his earthly disguise, Vegtam the Wanderer.

**LOKI:**  Vegtam rides again, I see. Off on another oh-so-exciting adventure?

**ODIN:**   Yes, and we would like you to come along.

**LOKI:**  Why? So I can get you out of all your scrapes? I'd rather have a tooth pulled.

**THOR:**  *(loud laughing)* Ha-ha! I'd rather have a tooth pulled! The creature cracks me up!

**LOKI:**  Gee. It makes me feel so much like an actual person when you call me "the creature." It sounds like some re-animated corpse.

**ODIN:**  It is funny that you mention that. We are traveling to the Iron Wood.

**NARRATOR:**   A look of sudden nervousness passed over Loki's face.

**LOKI:**  Oh. What's going on there?

**ODIN:**  That's what we want to find out. It has been many years since we last fought a monster there—a corpse-like hag. Remember?  Now I have the same feeling as then—a foreboding. We must investigate.

**THOR:**   Whatever type of monster it is, Thor will smash its brains out with one hit from his hammer!

**ODIN:**  I hope the problem is that easily solved. This evil feels deeper—and closer. An evil we have never known.

**THOR:**  Then I will hit it—*really hard!*

**LOKI:**  It's always hitting with you! Your mother never hugged you as a child, did she?

**ODIN:** Let's go!

**NARRATOR:**  The Iron Wood was like no other forest in creation. Its iron-tough, spike-covered trees grew snakily, coiling around another like a thicket of briars. It was nearly impenetrable.

**LOKI:**  Here we are. Now what?

**ODIN:**  We must go in there.

**THOR:**  Hmmm. Let's send the creature in.

**LOKI:**  Me?

**ODIN:**  Find a path, Loki, and then lead us in. We must find the source of this evil.

**LOKI:**  *(under his breath)* Oh, I'll find a path all right… *(grumbling)*

**NARRATOR:**  The trickster eased toward the tangled branches of the forest, sliding his bony body easy through them, and disappeared into the darkness. Time passed.

**THOR:**  The creature has been gone for a long time now. Do you think he's coming back?

**ODIN:**  I don't know. Something may have happened to him. Maybe we should go in after him.

THOR: Thor will clear the way.

NARRATOR: The thunder god barreled forward, slashing at the thick trees with his hammer. *(clanging noises)* But the twisted trunks were as tough as iron.

THOR: *(panting)* I think I'm making some headway!

ODIN: *(sigh)* They call this the Iron Wood for a reason.

NARRATOR: Hours later they had made their way into the tangled forest, and a thin path at last presented itself.

ODIN: Loki better have a good excuse for abandoning us—or he'll have to answer to me.

THOR: So this was the same forest where we mighty gods defeated that hag?

ODIN: She was more of a monster. If you'll remember, half of her was living and half was dead.

THOR: She had powerful magic, but we defeated her. What happened to her again?

ODIN: Hela was her name. I sent her down to Niflheim to watch over the dead. But let us not speak of such things here. I fear something worse awaits us.

NARRATOR: The trees grew tighter, and the light grew fainter. Finally, though their eyes told them nothing, they could feel a space had opened around them. Odin held up his staff, and the runes upon it began to glow. A briar dome arched high above their heads.

ODIN: Get ready, Thor. Something evil approaches.

NARRATOR: Thor raised his hammer and stepped forward. It was then that something lunged from the underbrush. *(loud hiss)* The creature struck at Odin, and his staff fell to the ground—plunging them into darkness again.

THOR: Die, monster, die! Argh!

*(sounds of a scuffle)*

NARRATOR: Odin snatched up his staff. When it relit, he saw the monster that was attacking Thor. It was a giant serpent—its many coils looped around the god—trying to squeeze the life from him. Thor's arms were pinned, and his face was red from struggling.

THOR: Argh! *(struggling noises)*

NARRATOR: Odin raised his staff, and it transformed into his mighty spear, Gungnir.

ODIN: Unhand that god, serpent! This is Gungnir, the spear that does not miss.

*(hissing from the snake)*

NARRATOR: The snake's yellow eyes moved from the god to the fierce tip of his spear. It began to loosen its coils.

ODIN: A wise choice, snake!

NARRATOR: But instead of releasing Thor, the snake struck again—its poisonous fangs aimed for Odin this time. *(snake hiss)* The All-Father dove to the side, and the snake's fangs lodged into the trunk of a tree behind. *(clang)* As the snake thrashed, trying to free itself, Odin rose to hurl his spear. But Thor—finally free of its coils—seized the serpent by the tail. (*hissing from the snake*)

**THOR:**    (*grunting*) Thor—hates—snakes! Ah!

**NARRATOR:**  With an enormous tug Thor yanked the snake loose from the tree and swung it above his head. Around and around, he swung it. The serpent thrashed wildly—spewing its green venom into the air.

**THOR:** Argh!

**NARRATOR:** With a final thrust Thor sent the snake rocketing up through the branches above. (*crashing and whistling sound*)

**THOR:**   That will teach him to challenge Thor!

**LOKI:**   (*slow clapping*) Bravo. Very nice. Very nice.

**NARRATOR:**      The gods—breathing heavily—looked upward. Loki was there, lurking in the shadowy tree branches.

**LOKI:**   Nice distance, Thor-boy. I bet you hurled that snake all the way to Midgard. But, you know, I think he'll be back.

**ODIN:**  What was that beast?

**LOKI:** Jormungand, the great serpent—one of the newest residents of this wood. He's just a newborn. Otherwise, he would have been much larger and fiercer.

**ODIN:**   You seem to know a great deal about these dark creatures.

**LOKI:** We *creatures* have to stick together.

**NARRATOR:**   A blue mist started to rise from the ground beneath their feet. Odin and Thor stepped quickly aside. The form of an emaciated woman stood within it. Half of her flesh was living. The other half was decayed with death.

**ODIN:**  Hela! What are you doing here? I condemned you to Niflheim.

**HELA:**   Relax, All-Father. What you see before you is only a projection of my spirit. I have come to this wood to speak to my mother.

**ODIN:**  Your mother?

**HELA:**  She resides here in the Iron Wood. She is a giant—a witch, you would call her. She gave birth to me, and she gave birth to my brother, Jormungand, that you just met. And she will birth again—soon.

**ODIN:**  Go back to the dead, Hela!

**HELA:**  I came to see my mother, but I had not expected to see my father here as well.

**THOR:**  What are you babbling about, you hideous, half-dead hag?

**HELA:**  It is a mystery, I guess. Farewell, gods. I descend.

**NARRATOR:**   The blue flame of Hela flickered and went out.

**THOR:**  Let's be done with this vile place. Wait! Where is Loki? Gone again?

**ODIN:** Nevermind. This experience has left me more troubled than before.

NARRATOR: When Thor and Odin returned to Asgard alone, the goddess Siguna approached them, looking for Loki.

SIGUNA: Where is my husband? Didn't he leave with you?

ODIN: He has not returned here?

SIGUNA: I haven't seen him. But I don't see much of him these days. He's always off on some mission—and then leaving again as soon as he returns.

ODIN: Where could he be going?

SIGUNA: I don't know. He has changed.

NARRATOR: Odin went at once to his throne—sending his far-vision out toward the Iron Wood.

ODIN: Something doesn't make sense.

NARRATOR: Even Odin's enhanced sight could not see into the darkness of Jarnvid. But Loki soon appeared on the fringes of the wood—creeping stealthily out from under its branches.

ODIN: (to himself) Loki.

NARRATOR: What Odin saw next caused his heart to freeze. A black creature slunk out of the wood behind Loki.

ODIN: No! Assemble the gods in the meeting hall! When Loki returns to Asgard, bring him before me at once!

NARRATOR: When Loki at long last returned to Asgard, he was brought immediately before Odin.

LOKI: (coldly) You rang?

ODIN: (slowly) Loki, we have accepted you here as a friend, so I will give you a chance to explain yourself. What dealings have you had with the witch who lives in the Iron Wood?

LOKI: I don't know what you're talking about.

ODIN: First, it was Hela the hag, and we marveled how such a creature came into existence. But we dispatched her.

LOKI: Mistress of the dead. Not the worst job a person could have.

ODIN: If you could call her a person. Then came Jormungand the serpent.

THOR: Thor hurled him to the ends of the earth!

LOKI: Brilliant move, by the way. You threw him into the sea, and there he will grow larger and larger. By the time he's fully grown, he will surround the entire world.

THOR: Oh.

LOKI: Luckily, that's not my problem. But it might be yours someday, Thor-boy. But I'm still trying to see what all this has to do with me.

ODIN: Those two monsters were birthed by the she-giant witch who lives in the Iron Wood.

LOKI: Well, duh.

NARRATOR: Odin leveled his stern gaze at the trickster.

**ODIN:** (angrily) I saw you, Loki! I saw you leaving the Iron Wood today! How long have you been visiting the she-giant that lives there? And don't you dare deny it!

**LOKI:** You caught me. So what?

**NARRATOR:** Siguna, finally realizing Loki's crime, began to weep.

**ODIN:** All these years, we had no idea! But it was *you* all along who fathered those monsters!

**LOKI:** Why should I deny it?

**ODIN:** And now the she-giant has given birth to another monster—the worst of the three! A giant wolf with an appetite large enough to devour the world! How dare you, Loki! How dare you!

**NARRATOR:** Loki's eyes glittered with sudden hatred.

**LOKI:** So what?

**ODIN:** We gave you a wife from among the gods! Was she not good enough for you? Now look at the evil you have produced!

**LOKI:** Evil is in the eye of the beholder.

**ODIN:** It is only my eye that matters, and I say these acts are evil! This wolf must be subdued—just like his siblings. I am giving you a choice. Either you aid us in subduing this newest child of yours—or you will be destroyed along with him!

**NARRATOR:** Loki clenched his pointed teeth.

**LOKI:** (coldly) So it's come to this? After all we've been through—all the tight spots I've gotten you out of? (pause) I guess I have no choice but to obey.

**ODIN:** Go! Bring your wolf-son here quickly—before I decide *not* to spare you!

**NARRATOR:** After Loki had departed, the gods talked hurriedly among themselves. What did it all mean?

**FREYA:** I can barely believe it! All these years, Loki has been breeding evil against us.

**TYR:** Believe it! I always knew that half-breed would betray us!

**THOR:** But Loki has been a good companion to me. He's gotten me out of many scrapes.

**TYR:** Yes, but how many of those scrapes did he get you *into*?

**THOR:** Good point.

**BALDER:** There is still good in Loki.

**ODIN:** For years he's been nursing a secret hatred toward us, and these monsters are the product of that hatred.

**NARRATOR:** Just then Loki re-entered the hall. Behind him walked a wolf so large it had to duck to pass through the doors. (loud gasping from the gods) In spots the wolf's hide was bare and covered in oozing sores. His eyes glittered with hatred, and his serpentine tongue flicked from side to side.

**THOR:** A giant wolf!

LOKI:  No fooling you, thunder-brain. Yes, this is Fenrir. And I am not ashamed to admit it—he is my son.

NARRATOR:  Hearing this, Siguna could bear no more and rushed from the hall. The wolf let out a little hissing laugh.

FENRIR:  *(hissing laugh)*

FREYA:  Loki, aren't you going to comfort your wife?

LOKI:  She'll be fine. I have business to settle here.

ODIN:  So this *creature* is your latest abomination?

LOKI:  Easy now. Monsters have feelings, too.

TYR:  You *would* defend this…thing!

LOKI:  *(angrily)* You gods! You can't accept anything that's different than you, can you? There's no reason Fenrir couldn't live with us here—in harmony.

BALDER:  Maybe Loki is right.

TYR:  Ha! The first time we turned our backs, we'd be dead in our beds!

LOKI:  Wouldn't that be a shame!

THOR:  Thor says that wolf is a freak of nature!

LOKI:  *(hatefully)* Look who's talking!

FREYA:  This wolf is horrible, but what he stands for is worse! How could you betray Siguna?

LOKI:  I don't think *you* should be lecturing *me* about morals! We all know how you came by that necklace you wear around your neck! How many dwarf-marriages did that take again?

FREYA:  Why you, little—!

ODIN:  Enough! We must decide what to do with this monster!

LOKI:  Well, he would make a formidable enemy. You can obviously see his strength in his rippling muscles. He has a powerful hunger—a great desire to devour. He has also inherited his father's cunning mind.

TYR:  I don't think a beast can be cunning.

FENRIR:  *(wolf growl)* Grrrr. Is that so, little man?

TYR:  It speaks! It truly is evil! Let's destroy it at once!

FENRIR:  I thank you for inviting me here—because that means you cannot destroy me. Odin has declared that no blood can be spilled in this holy hall.

LOKI:  A fine point, son. Odin, looks like you have a new pet. What do you say to that?

ODIN:  I say that it is time we muzzle this overgrown dog!

FENRIR:  Grrrrr.

NARRATOR:  The gods glanced at the snarling beast uneasily.

LOKI:  *(snicker)* Easier said than done. Fenrir is fast—and strong! And as you can see, his teeth are as sharp as swords.

**ODIN:** Then all the more reason he should be chained!

**FENRIR:** *(evil laugh)* I am strong enough to break any fetter known to man.

**ODIN:** *(yelling)* We'll see about that! Bring me a chain! Ready the blacksmiths! Begin forging at once! We must bind this cur!

**NARRATOR:** A cold gleam appeared in the red eyes of Fenrir. The anticipation of a chase was growing there.

**ODIN:** Loki, restrain your wolf-son! You have created this mess, and you are going to help fix it!

**LOKI:** You know what, *All-Father*? I decided something just now. I'm through helping. I've helped you all since the beginning, and where has it gotten me? Nowhere! You can deal with Fenrir on your own!

**ODIN:** *(yelling)* Loki! I'm warning you!

**LOKI:** Rage all you want! I'm done! Do you hear me? I am through with you all! All you hypocrites—all you preening fools! You don't have a tenth of the brains I have. You'd be helpless without me!

**BALDER:** Loki, no! There is still hope. Let us still be friends.

**LOKI:** I've seen how you hypocrites treat "friends"!

**BALDER:** Don't say such things! Don't let yourself be ruled by your hatred!

**LOKI:** *(mock kindness)* Oh, Balder—you and your goodness. *(angrily)* Don't you know? I hate *you* most of all!

**NARRATOR:** Pain appeared in Balder's eyes.

**ODIN:** Loki, if you leave Asgard now, you will break our blood-bond and become our sworn enemy—no better than a filthy *giant*.

**LOKI:** That's the key, isn't it? You've never given me a fair chance! Well, you know what? If I can't be one of the gods, I'll become one of the giants. They threw me out once, but I know they'll take me back now! I have a weapon! I know the in's and out's of Asgard. I know the cracks in your invincible fortress. We'll see how long Asgard will stand without Loki!

**ODIN:** Is that a threat?

**LOKI:** You heard me, old man! Now, Fenrir! Run!

**FENRIR:** *(roaring)* Grrrr! Catch me if you can, puny gods!

**NARRATOR:** Fenrir's enormous haunches flew into motion, and he burst through the wall as easily as if it had been made of paper. *(crashing)*

**ODIN:** *(yelling)* After him!

**LOKI:** Whoops. I think he is getting away. *(snicker)* Heh! Heh! Farewell, fools!

**THOR:** Argh!

**NARRATOR:** Tyr and Thor dashed after the gigantic wolf. Loki chuckled to himself and sauntered from the hall. Odin remained upon his throne—looking completely bewildered.

A great series of catacombs existed below Asgard. Fenrir found his way into these tunnels—leading Thor and Tyr deep into the earth. The giant wolf twisted his way through the labyrinth of tunnels—turning and snapping at the two gods with his enormous jaws.

**FENRIR:** *(snarling)* Don't think I run because I'm afraid of you godlings. It's just good sport! Besides my hide is so thick that no steel can pierce it.

**THOR:** *(booming)* Thor will destroy you anyway!

**FENRIR:** You'll have to catch me first!

**TYR:** *(out-of-breath)* Wait! Wait! Hear me, wolf! You said before that no steel can pierce you, but still you run. Are you a wolf—or a frightened *lamb?* You are as much a coward as your father!

**NARRATOR:** At this, the beast hissed.

**FENRIR:** I'll bite you in half for those words! I am *not* a coward. Fine. This chase is boring me. Do your worst.

**NARRATOR:** The beast settled onto his haunches and bared its razor-sharp teeth.

**FENRIR:** I'm hungry, and I am no dainty eater. Find me all the food you can, and I will sit and eat until all that food is gone.

**TYR:** Done! Now, Thor, go and get our guest something to eat. And tell the blacksmiths to forge us a chain at once.

**THOR:** I will return. Take care, brother!

**NARRATOR:** Thor disappeared into the darkness.

**FENRIR:** A chain? Heh heh. I can break any chain. I am like my brother, the serpent.

The power inside of me will continue to grow. I will grow larger and larger until I will be too powerful to contain—then I will slay all you gods.

**TYR:** I see you are your father's son.

**NARRATOR:** Servants from above soon appeared—carrying load after load of foods from the larder of Valhalla. They approached the wolf timidly and heaped the foodstuffs before him.

**FENRIR:** Now I feast—for a time.

**NARRATOR:** Fenrir began to eat greedily. *(wolfish snapping sounds)*

**FENRIR:** *(smacking)* When this food has run out, tiny one, I shall eat *you.*

**TYR:** *(confidently)* That time will not come. When we are finished, you will be chained—trapped forever.

**NARRATOR:** Thor appeared from the darkness.

**THOR:** The smiths are forging a chain as we speak.

**NARRATOR:** He stared in shock at the rapidly disappearing pile of food.

**THOR:** Has he eaten so much? *(yelling)* More food! Bring more food!

**NARRATOR:** The smiths of Asgard worked quickly—forging a mighty chain in their fires. They carried it down to where the wolf lay. Thor and Tyr crisscrossed it across the wolf's body and bolted it into the rock.

**FENRIR:** *(through a mouthful of food)* Stupid gods, I have told you—no chain can hold me.

**NARRATOR:** No sooner had they secured the chain, Fenrir flexed his feral muscles against it—and the chain snapped. *(tinkle sound)*

**FENRIR:**  Too easy! Now bring me more food, or our chase will begin again.

**TYR:** Quick! More food and another chain!

**NARRATOR:**  More and more food was brought and added to the pile, but it still quickly dwindled under Fenrir's monstrous appetite.   The smiths forged chain after chain, but the wolf-beast snapped each.

**FENRIR:**  Soon this food will be gone, too, and I will still be free.

**TYR:** *(concerned)* Thor, our workmanship is not strong enough!

**THOR:**  The All-Father has gone himself to the land of the dwarves to beg them to forge a chain for us.

**FENRIR:**    *(laughing)* Look, gods. Notice anything?

**NARRATOR:**  Tyr's heart grew cold. As the wolf had devoured each pile of food, he had become larger and larger. Now he almost filled the underground cavern.

**FENRIR:**  With each helping of food I am growing stronger. There is no chain in all the Nine Worlds that can hold me. Your search is futile.

**NARRATOR:**  Meanwhile, Odin, carried by Sleipnir, his eight-legged steed, had reached the land of the dwarves.

**ODIN:**  Quickly, dwarves! Forge us a chain that can bind the greatest monster ever born!

**DWARF:** *(grumbling)* Leave us be! We have our own treasures to complete!

**ODIN:**  Listen to me! If we do not chain this wolf-beast, he will devour the world—gods, dwarves, elves, and all! Now forge and forge quickly! Your lives depend on it!

**NARRATOR:**  The dwarves knew of Odin's wisdom and flew at once to their work. At last from their glowing forge, they drew forth a line of shimmering metal—a chain that was so finely wrought that it was as thin as a hair.

**ODIN:** Is this some kind of joke? This chain is too thin! I come to you for aid, and you give me *this*?

**DWARF:**  This chain is the strongest ever forged. It is Gleipnir! Not even the great Midgard Serpent could break this chain.

**ODIN:**  It is light as a feather!

**DWARF:**  Do not question our skill! That chain will hold!

**ODIN:**   It better, or we will all be wolf-meat!

**NARRATOR:**  Odin spurred Sleipnir back to Asgard.   When Odin appeared, Tyr looked up with tired, hopeful eyes.

**TYR:** *(weakly)* Odin, the wolf is finishing the last of the food.  We have emptied

Asgard's larders. We can hold him no longer.

**ODIN:** I have here our final hope: a chain—made by the dwarves.

**NARRATOR:** He placed it into Tyr's hands.

**TYR:** *(surprised)* This is far too weak! I can barely feel it!

**ODIN:** It is our only hope.

**NARRATOR:** Tyr slowly turned to face the grinning jaws of Fenrir.

**FENRIR:** Puny god, I have finished your feast. I see that you have another chain to try. It looks thin—thin enough to break without lifting a paw.

**TYR:** This is the final chain. If you break this one, you may go free. You will be free to destroy as you like.

**NARRATOR:** Tyr began to bind the wolf.

**FENRIR:** Ah, ah, ah. Not so fast. You have forgotten our agreement. I am out of food.

**NARRATOR:** The beast was right. He had devoured the last of the food.

**FENRIR:** Farewell.

**TYR:** *(panicked)* You *must* stay!

**FENRIR:** *(wolf laugh)* Perhaps if you gave me something else to eat…

**TYR:** *(solemnly)* We have emptied Asgard of its foodstuffs. What is it that you want?

**NARRATOR:** The wolf licked his cracked lips, and his red eyes danced.

**FENRIR:** No food left, huh? What a pity! Then give me your hand, warrior-god! It looks especially juicy.

**NARRATOR:** Tyr's face hardened.

**ODIN:** Don't do it, Tyr!

**TYR:** Why not? You gave your eye for wisdom. This beast must be stopped. The least I can do is forfeit my hand.

**FENRIR:** *(chuckling)* Place your hand into my mouth and then bind me with your puny chain! When I have snapped this chain, I shall eat the rest of you godlings!

**TYR:** Very well.

**NARRATOR:** The beast opened his gigantic pink mouth, and a blast of foul breath escaped. Tyr bravely placed his left hand inside.

**FENRIR:** Ah, ah, ah. Not that hand. It wouldn't be much of a loss for a warrior to lose his left hand. Your sword-hand is what I desire.

**THOR:** Without your sword-hand, you will be useless to us, Tyr! We need your sword to fight against the giants!

**TYR:** None of us will be able to conquer this beast if he is allowed to go free.

**FENRIR:** I'm waiting…

**NARRATOR:** Tyr shot the wolf a cold glance and placed his right hand within his jaws.

**TYR:**  Now!

**NARRATOR:**  Odin and Thor threw the chain into the air, and Fenrir's sharp teeth clamped down upon Tyr's wrist.

**TYR:**  Ah!

**NARRATOR:**  The dwarf chain took on a life of its own, coiling around Fenrir's limbs, and cinching him down tightly to the ground. Fire shot from the wolf's eyes. His teeth sliced through Tyr's wrist—rending flesh and bone. Tyr pulled his arm free, leaving his hand behind.

**TYR:**  *(in intense pain)* Argh!

**NARRATOR:**  Fenrir thrashed against the chain, but he could not break it.

**FENRIR:**  What is this? *(snarling)* It can't be! It can't be! Curses upon Tyr the One-Handed!  Curses upon the gods of Asgard! I have been tricked!

**NARRATOR:**  Wearily, Tyr tucked the bloody end of his arm within his cloak.

**TYR:**  *(weakly)*  I may be the One-Handed…but I have chained you, dog.

**ODIN:**  Come away from this place, Tyr. Leave the beast to his madness.

**FENRIR:**  *(grimly)* You may have won this battle, but I have taken your sword-skill from you.  No one will ever fear Tyr the Cripple!

**TYR:**  Give me my sword.

**NARRATOR:**  Thor drew Tyr's sword for him and placed it into his left hand.

**FENRIR:**  No steel can kill me! No steel can pierce my hide!

**TYR:**  Then I'll teach you to keep your mouth shut!

**NARRATOR:** Tyr drove his sword into the mouth of the raging wolf.

**FENRIR:** *(raging cry of pain)*

**NARRATOR:**  Foam and blood ran forth, and Fenrir howled in pain.

**FENRIR:** *(howling) My father* will come for me and free me from this magic trap.  Then I will rise and destroy you all!

**TYR:** We will be ready.

**NARRATOR:**  With the rabid cries of the wolf echoing behind them, the gods navigated the passageways back to Asgard above.  When the other gods beheld Tyr's wound, they mourned.

**ODIN:**  The son of Loki has been chained below—but for a high price.

**NARRATOR:** Balder—a look of sadness in his eyes—drew near to Tyr. He looked painfully at the god's wound.

**BALDER:**  This wound is like the one I feel in my heart. I fear there is no hope for peace. I fear our brother Loki has left us forever.

**TYR:** *(angrily) Brother* Loki? *(grandly)* Hear me, gods of Asgard.

**NARRATOR:** Tyr raised his remaining hand.

**TYR:** I will train this sword-hand to be as skillful as the last. Then I will find Loki. I will track him down. And I will drive my blade into his heart!

**NARRATOR:** Peace had been torn from Asgard as surely as the hand had been torn from Tyr.

## DISCUSSION QUESTIONS

- Why does Loki make a formidable enemy?
- Do you feel sorry for Siguna, Loki's wife?
- Fenrir will remain chained underground until the fateful battle of Ragnarok, when he will fight against Odin himself. How do you think this battle will end?
- Loki's children are the personification of what? Explain.
- How do you think Loki will strike back at the gods?
- What type of creatures did the Norse people consider to be evil? How can you tell from this story?

# THE DEATH OF BALDER

## TEACHER GUIDE

## BACKGROUND

Ragnarok, the Day of Doom, is rapidly approaching for the gods. Fate has declared that many of the gods must die in this ultimate battle, but the magnitude of this does not sink in until the most beloved of the gods, the peace-loving Balder, is murdered right in the midst of Asgard. Only then do the gods see the true power of the evil that they face. Balder's death is the ultimate tragedy of Norse mythology.

Even though Ragnarok will spell the demise of the world, it will not be the end. The Norse believed that while the World Tree would burn in the flames of war, a new tree would grow from the ashes, and new gods and new humans would reside within it. As a final symbol of this perfected world, Balder would rise from Niflheim and use his goodness to rule over the newly-created world.

## SUMMARY

Balder, the most beloved of the gods, has been plagued by strange dreams that suggest he will soon die. When his mother, Frigga, discovers that this has been happening, she sets out on a mission to make sure her beloved son will never be harmed. She casts protective spells over him and sends messengers to every living or non-living thing that resides in the Nine Worlds—asking all of creation to swear never to harm Balder. She receives promises from all creatures and substances—including even rock, iron, and wood. The

only thing that will not respond is mistletoe, but Frigga deems this too small a plant to worry about. She declares her mission a success and invites all the creatures of the Nine Worlds to a celebration in Asgard.

Balder has a long-forgotten twin brother named Hodur, who is blind. Although every other creature bears Balder no grudge, Hodur is jealous of his brother's privileged life. At the celebration Frigga makes a game of casting weapons at Balder, just to show how powerful her spell is. He is attacked with axes, boulders, massive clubs, but nothing is able to harm him.

An old crone comes to Frigga to ask about the festivities and learns from her that only mistletoe has not sworn an oath of protection. The crone then goes to blind Hodur and convinces him to join in the game. Using her magic, the crone crafts a spear from a sprig of mistletoe and gives it to the blind god. The crone is, of course, the exiled Loki in disguise.

Hodur hurls his mistletoe spear at Balder, and everyone is horrified when the weapon strikes and Balder falls down dead. Death, even the death of a criminal, is not allowed in Asgard, so the terrified Hodur is banished. His punishment will come later.

Odin immediately sends word to Hela in Niflheim to release Balder's spirit back to Asgard, but the Queen of Death says that she will only release him if every creature upon the earth sheds a tear for Balder. Odin sends out the gods to tell all the world that Balder has died. Every creature sheds a tear, except for an old woman who refuses (Loki in disguise). The trickster flees before the gods can capture him, but the damage has been done—Balder must remain in Niflheim.

Balder is placed on a burial ship, and gods, dwarves, and even some giants arrive to attend his funeral. During the ceremony, Balder's wife, Nanna, dies of grief and is laid alongside him in the ship. Then a giantess pushes the burning ship out into the sea.

The gods go in search of Loki to punish him for what he has done. The trickster tries to escape the gods by transforming into a fish, but the gods catch him up in a net. Because they have sworn oaths of brotherhood with him, they cannot kill him outright. Instead they take him to a deep cavern and chain him to a rock. Above him they secure a poisonous snake, whose fangs leak acid. The venom drips down onto Loki, causing him extreme pain. There the gods leave him. Siguna, Loki's wife, hears of his fate and comes to soothe her husband's suffering by catching the snake's venom in a dish. Yet when she turns aside to dump out the bowl, a drop falls onto Loki, and his raging causes the earth to shake.

## ESSENTIAL QUESTIONS

- Is there such a thing as fate?
- Can you outwit or outmaneuver fate?
- What events in life are tragic?

## ANTICIPATORY QUESTIONS

- Do you know someone who has no enemies? What is he or she like?
- How can a god die?
- What has happened to Loki? Do you think he will try to take revenge?
- Who would ever want to kill Balder?

## CONNECT

**"The Descent of Odin: An Ode" by Thomas Gray** This 18th-century poem uses vivid imagery to re-tell Odin's journey into Niflheim to consult with the spirit of the giantess, Angerboda.

## TEACHABLE TERMS

- **Foreshadowing**    Balder's dreams mentioned at the beginning of the play are an example of foreshadowing as they prefigure his fate.
- **Foil**  Many of Hodur's attributes are the opposite of Balder's, making him a dramatic foil for his brother.
- **Personification**    Frigga requests that every substance in existence promise not to harm Balder. When water, rock, and plant-life speak on pg. 136, this is an example of personification.
- **Myth Motif**    A motif is a repeated situation or event in multiple myths. In many different mythologies from around the world, characters are required to journey into the afterlife or the underworld, just as Odin does in this story. In Greek Mythology Orpheus travels into the Underworld to retrieve the spirit of his deceased wife. In Roman mythology Aeneas travels to the Underworld to speak with the spirit of his deceased father.

## RECALL QUESTIONS

1. Why does Odin travel to Niflheim?
2. What does Frigga ask everything in the world to promise?
3. What is the one plant that does not agree to her promise?
4. Who is Hodur?
5. How is Loki punished at the end of the myth?

# THE DEATH OF BALDER

## CAST

| | |
|---|---|
| **ODIN** | *All-Father of the Gods* |
| **FRIGGA** | *Wife of Odin* |
| **BALDER** | *Most Beloved of the Gods* |
| **THOR** | *God of Thunder* |
| **NANNA** | *Wife of Balder* |
| **LOKI** | *Exiled Trickster* |
| **TYR** | *God of Battle* |
| **WATER** | *Bubbling stream* |
| **ROCK** | *Large Boulder* |
| **PLANT** | *Creeping Vine* |
| **GIANT** | *Guest from Jotunheim* |
| **HELA** | *Ruler of the Dead* |
| **HODUR** | *Blind Brother of Balder* |
| **HERMOD** | *Servant to Odin* |
| **ANGERBODA** | *Deceased Witch* |
| **HYRROKIN** | *Giantess* |

**NARRATOR:** The eight hooves of Sleipnir thundered through the night. His rider, Odin, spurred him on faster. The god had ridden for three days and nights—on a great mission of haste. For a week, his son, Balder, had suffered terrible nightmares— visions of death. Frigga, Balder's mother, was frightened for his safety. She had begged Odin to seek for answers—in a place where few were brave enough to venture.

The night was already black, but it somehow grew darker, and whatever warmth that was in the air, fled. The landscape had become nothing but ice and mist. Odin reined up his steed.

**ODIN:** We are very near the land of the dead.

**NARRATOR:** *(growling of a hound)* A pair of glowing eyes appeared in the gloom behind Odin, and the stench of blood filled his nose.

**ODIN:** Run swiftly, Sleipnir! Yah!

**NARRATOR:** The steed galloped forward again, with a monstrous beast in pursuit. It was Garm—the guard-dog of the dead.

**ODIN:** *(yelling)* Back, beast! Leave us in peace!

**NARRATOR:** Garm was no match for the swift legs of Sleipnir and soon gave up the chase. Odin slowed the steed to a trot.

**ODIN:** Now we have passed into Niflheim.

**NARRATOR:** A chilling fog covered the ground. Faint cries of pain lifted from it— the gasping breaths of the dead trapped beneath.

Odin dismounted, pulled his blue traveling cloak closer about him, and moved forward through the mist. Little ghostly wisps rose from it and clutched at him as he passed by. Ahead a mound of earth stood out like an island in the fog.

**ODIN:** This looks like a grave. Now for the runes.

**NARRATOR:** Odin raised his arms over the earth-mound and uttered the rune of awakening.

**ODIN:** Awaken, evil one. I summon you.

**NARRATOR:** The mound shuddered, and a hideous specter floated up from the grave. In life it had been a giantess.

**ANGERBODA:**    *(ghost-like voice)* Who awakens me from my sleep?

**ODIN:** I am Vegtam the Wanderer. I need answers, and you are the only one who can give them to me.

**ANGERBODA:** For centuries I studied the hidden arts of magic in Jotunheim. My knowledge allowed me to give birth to the three most fearsome creatures ever seen upon the earth. Many came seeking my knowledge. But even I could not escape death. And, now, even here among the frozen dead, I am not free from stupid questions.

**ODIN:** Your will is no longer your own. I will ask, and you will answer. You have no choice. Now listen! The world is changing. New evils are being born every day. Tell me why.

**ANGERBODA:** I speak only because you compel me to. *(pause)* Ragnarok is approaching, and the gods will finally meet their end. I have done my part to bring that about. But something that has never

happened before is about to happen, and it will change the rules of everything.

**ODIN:** What do you mean?

**ANGERBODA:** I am answering because you have compelled me. *(pause)* Look there into the distance—look into the hall of Hela.

**NARRATOR:** A ghostly hall appeared in the distance—its walls and roof were built from bones. Shreds of banners were hung from its rafters, and bony servants were laying a huge feasting table with cold, empty plates.

**ANGERBODA:** The dead prepare for a special guest.

**ODIN:** Who are they preparing this for?

**NARRATOR:** The spirit twisted—writhing against his command.

**ODIN:** Answer me!

**ANGERBODA:** I answer because you have compelled me. *(pause)* The son of Frigga! The son of Frigga will soon be joining us here.

**ODIN:** No!

**ANGERBODA:** Balder, the son of Odin, will soon die and be confined to Niflheim.

**NARRATOR:** These words seized Odin by the throat. Balder in Niflheim? It couldn't be.

**ODIN:** Impossible! No god should come here! Who shall send him here?

**NARRATOR:** The giantess' spirit grimaced and twisted.

ANGERBODA:  You ask too much! But I must answer! One of the gods themselves will send him here.

ODIN:  Loki is no longer among the gods!

ANGERBODA:  Loki will raise no hand against Balder. But I have already said too much.

ODIN:  You will say as much as a demand, giantess!

ANGERBODA:  Oh, that is where you are wrong, Odin—for now I see that is who you are. I will speak to you no more. Send me back into my grave and leave me in peace. Your son is doomed. You are doomed.

ODIN:  And I see that you are the spirit of that giantess-witch who gave birth to Fenrir. I gladly send you back to outer darkness. Go! Go back to your frigid grave forever.

NARRATOR:  Odin swiped his staff through the floating spirit, and it dissipated.

ANGERBODA:  (fading away) I will rise again, foolish god—when the Day of Doom comes. (low chuckling)

NARRATOR:  Odin quickly returned to Asgard, his heart even more troubled than before. He reported all he had heard from the giantess to Frigga.

FRIGGA:  (sobbing) I knew it! I knew it! You told me Balder's was just having bad dreams! I've always feared for his life—ever since he was born—and now I know why! But what creature on earth would ever want to harm Balder? Even the giants love and respect him!

ODIN:  The spirit said that it would be one of the gods.

FRIGGA:  One of the gods! Loki! I knew it!

ODIN:  No, she said Loki would not raise his hand against Balder.

FRIGGA:  Then who? Who? This will drive me insane with worry!

ODIN:  Then put it out of your mind. We received this message from a giantess-witch. We can hope that she was mistaken with her information.

FRIGGA:  But what if she wasn't? Oh, there are so many ways for him to die. By fire, by poison, by steel, by rock…

ODIN:  You would be better off to forget about this whole thing.

FRIGGA:  I'm through listening to you, Odin! You told me I was just overreacting! Well, now I know the truth. Someone is trying to murder my beloved son! But I will stop it—somehow!

ODIN:  (harshly) Your judgment is clouded by your fear! What will you do? Will you make every being in creation swear not to harm Balder?

NARRATOR:  Frigga's eyes opened wide.

FRIGGA:  That's it! Gods, men, dwarves, giants, and elves must all swear. And not just living beings—everything—every substance that could possibly harm him. Rock, iron, fire, water, pestilence! All will swear not to harm my darling Balder.

ODIN:  This is futile!

**NARRATOR:**    Frigga summoned her servant, Hermod, to expound her plan.

**FRIGGA:** *(crazy)* Hermod! Quickly! Round up the other servants. You must go to every single thing on the earth—animal, vegetable, mineral—and make it swear that it will never harm my Balder.

**HERMOD:**   Can plants and stone even speak?

**FRIGGA:**  Of course! Don't be stupid! I will show you the necessary runes. They will swear, or they will face the wrath of the gods! Now, go!  And be swift or you will be whipped!

**NARRATOR:**    The queen's servants departed from Asgard—going in all different directions, into all different worlds. Some went to the dwarves. Others went to the elves and giants.

The servants went to every type of rock and uttered the speaking rune over them.

**ROCK:** We rocks will not harm Balder.

**NARRATOR:**   They went to the deep waters of the world.

**WATER:**  We will not drag Balder under or steal his life-breath from him.

**NARRATOR:**   They went to every plant that sprang from the ground.

**PLANT:**   We will do nothing to poison Balder, the Beloved God.

**NARRATOR:**    As the servants reported back, Frigga greeted them eagerly.

**FRIGGA:** *(crazy)* What news?  What news?

**HERMOD:**  *(out of breath)* Everything is swearing an oath, my queen. We have gone into all the Nine Worlds.

**FRIGGA:**    Perfect! My plan is nearly complete. Now there is nothing under the sun that can harm my Balder. *(pause)* Wait a minute. Did you go to the sun and moon as well?

**HERMOD:**  I did. Their chariots are speedy, but I was able to catch them. They promised never to harm Balder and then laughed at such a foolish question.

**FRIGGA:**  *(laughing to herself)* It is a foolish question when you think about it, isn't it? Who would want to hurt Balder? Maybe this is all in my head.

**NARRATOR:**   Just then Balder himself entered the queen's chambers. Frigga smiled broadly and held her hand out to him.

**FRIGGA:**  Darling!  How I've missed you!

**BALDER:**   But, Mother, you saw me this morning.

**FRIGGA:** So I did.  So I did.

**BALDER:**  What is all this hubbub around Asgard? Something about an oath— connected to me? I hope I didn't cause trouble by mentioning my dreams to you and Nanna, my lovely wife.

**FRIGGA:**  Of course not. It was no trouble at all. I just sent my servants to every corner of the World Tree, asking all things to swear that they will never harm you—not even one of the glorious hairs on your handsome head. *(pause)* Wait a minute! Hermod! Did we ask hair? Balder could choke on hair.

HERMOD: *(sigh)* Yes, my lady. Hair. Toenails. Bellybutton lint. Everything.

BALDER: *(confused)* Am I in danger?

FRIGGA: *(shocked)* Of course not, sweetie. These are just some extra precautions. You can never be too careful, you know. But let me tell you the truly exciting part—as soon as this task is completed, I am planning to have a magnificent celebration for you!

BALDER: Like a birthday?

FRIGGA: Exactly. What a smart boy! I will send my servants out with an open invitation to everything under the sun.

HERMOD: *(groan)* Oh.

FRIGGA: Now, why don't you go back to your room, bolt the door, and get under the bed—just to be extra safe.

NARRATOR: Frigga shoved her confused son out the door and turned to Hermod once again.

FRIGGA: Now for our celebration.

HERMOD: I heard you. But you want invitations sent to *everything*? Even toe jam and pond scum?

FRIGGA: Of course! Of course! Everything is invited. Even giants! I have nothing to worry about now. That is—if you are positive that everything has taken the oath.

NARRATOR: Hermod hastily surveyed his scroll.

HERMOD: There is a small plant growing on the trees near the gates of Asgard that we did not ask. Something called mistletoe.

FRIGGA: *(relieved)* Is that it? Nevermind that plant. What harm could it do? *(pause)* Now! Prepare for the guests! There'll be dwarves and giants coming, so hide the good silverware.

HERMOD: Yes, my queen.

NARRATOR: Balder's face once again poked into Frigga's chamber.

FRIGGA: Darling! Shouldn't you be under your bed?

BALDER: I am sorry to disobey, Mother, but I thought since I am having a birthday, shouldn't we invite Hodur as well?

NARRATOR: Frigga's face fell.

HERMOD: Who is Hodur?

BALDER: He's my twin brother! Surely you've heard my mother mention Hodur.

HERMOD: No, actually—

FRIGGA: That's enough, Hermod. You have a banquet to prepare!

NARRATOR: Hermod scurried off to fulfill his queen's command.

BALDER: Don't you like my idea, Mother?

FRIGGA: Well, dear, I don't think Hodur likes to socialize. I haven't seen him in years. He could have died for all we know.

BALDER: But his birthday is my birthday, too.

FRIGGA: *(annoyed)* This isn't really a birthday party. I just said that because—*(pause)* Nevermind. Nevermind. Anything for my sweetie.  I will invite Hodur—if you insist.  Now you run along!  Shoo!

**NARRATOR:**  Frigga sighed. This was the last thing she needed. She stormed off in search of Hodur, her other son.

It was not that Hodur was a secret. He was just a fact that many chose to forget. Few now remembered that Balder had been born with a blind, sickly brother. As Hodur had grown, his attitude became even worse than his health. He was of a foul and sullen temperament.  To spare herself the embarrassment of his poor manners, Frigga had built him his own hall far away from the noble halls of the other gods.  Hodur had not been objectionable to this arrangement. He spent his days indoors, alone, and grew together with the darkness around him—deep and forgotten.

**FRIGGA:**  *(angrily)* Hodur!  Hodur!

**NARRATOR:**  The queen pushed her way into Hodur's darkened hall. Dust flew in all directions.

**FRIGGA:**  Hodur? Are you here? *(under her breath)* Of course, you are.  Where else would you be?

**NARRATOR:**  A voice spoke out of the darkness.

**HODUR:**  *(emotionlessly)* Mother dearest. How nice of you to visit. How long as it been? A year? Or longer? I lose track.

**FRIGGA:**  Show yourself, Hodur! Light a torch already!

**HODUR:**  A torch would do you no good. This is a little talent of mine. I call it my shield of darkness. I have become one with the dark and can hide myself from the light.

**FRIGGA:**  Hmmm. Fascinating. There used to be a window around here somewhere.

**HODUR:**  Believe it or not, I don't use it much. Why have a window anyway? So I could enjoy the view?

**FRIGGA:**  I see your attitude has not improved much!

**NARRATOR:**  Stumbling through the darkness, Frigga located a window and tore the covering from it. Light poured in to reveal the white, sickly shape of Hodur. His pallid features were like a mockery of Balder's.

**FRIGGA:**  There you are! I've come here to tell you that your brother wishes you to attend a celebration in his honor tomorrow.

**HODUR:**  *(sarcastically)* Brother Balder—darling brother Balder.  How is the favorite son?

**FRIGGA:**  He's fine, and he wants *you* there tomorrow at his birthday—I mean, celebration.

**HODUR:**  Yes, I know it's not his birthday—or mine either—not that anyone is interested.

**FRIGGA:**  *(angrily)* Try to show a little gratitude!  Your brother invited you to his party!  If it were up to me, I would have left you here.

**HODUR:**  Spoken like a true mother.

**NARRATOR:**  Hodur held out his pale hand.

**HODUR:**  Well, if I must attend, you'll have to lead me.

NARRATOR:  The day of Balder's celebration dawned. Creatures from throughout the World Tree came to shower praises and love upon the guest of honor. Even friendly giants and dwarves came for the festivities. Balder, dressed in his finest robes, sat proudly beside his newly-wed wife, the goddess Nanna. He had also insisted that Hodur have a special seat next to his. But his pale twin slumped in his seat, with a scowl on his face.

BALDER:  How I've missed you, brother! What have you been up to?

HODUR:  (hatefully) Breathing. Sitting alone in the darkness. Waiting for someone to visit me. By the way, it's been a while since you've bothered to visit me.

NARRATOR:  A look of pain crossed Balder's face.

BALDER:  (sadly) On my last visit you said that you never wanted to hear from me again. I was just respecting your wishes.

HODUR:  (hatefully) Yes, but here we are now. Pardon me if I'm not up for small talk. Point me toward the food, will you?

BALDER:  (lovingly) Hodur, do not let hatred and jealousy cloud your mind.

HODUR:  Jealousy? Ha! Jealous of what? Your privileged life?  Your pampering? Your life is a joke.  Your existence is a fantasy world.  Who could be jealous of that?

NARRATOR:  He sneered at his twin and hobbled into the crowd—grasping his way blindly and barking roughly at any who got in his way.

NANNA:  I cannot believe that creature is your brother.

BALDER:  (softly) He is hurt more deeply than we can ever know.  (pause) But I will not let him ruin this beautiful celebration that Mother has prepared for me. Oh! Here she comes now!

NARRATOR:  Frigga made her way up to the seats of honor and turned to address the great gathering of guests. A horn was sounded.  (sound of a horn) All the revelers turned their attention toward the platform where the queen now stood.

FRIGGA:  (grandly) Giants! Dwarves! Elves! Gods! Men! I have invited you all here today in peace to rejoice with us!

ALL:  Huzzah!

FRIGGA:  My son has been rendered safe from any harm in this world! Rise, Balder!

NARRATOR:  Balder was presented, and the crowd cheered. (cheering from the crowd)

FRIGGA:  To show the magical power of all your oaths, let me be the first to raise my hand against him.

NARRATOR:  Frigga held up a bow and a single arrow. (murmuring) Pacing back ten steps from her son, she tensed the string and nocked the arrow into its place. (louder murmuring)

FRIGGA:  (shouting) Behold!

NARRATOR:  The arrow twanged loose and shot straight to its target. (collective gasp) Balder flinched instinctively, but the arrow only shattered against his chest.

**BALDER:** *(laugh)* Ha! That tickled!

**ALL:** *(laughter)* Huzzah!  Huzzah!

**NARRATOR:**  The crowd erupted into cheers and beat upon the tables with their fists. *(pounding of tables)*

**FRIGGA:** Nothing can harm Balder!  Now, come!  Rejoice with us.  Join in our game of triumph.

**NARRATOR:**  Many of the guests came forth to try their hand at harming Balder.  An enormous ring was formed around the god, and the most-beloved laughed good-naturedly at the spectacle.

The giants came first with their iron clubs and stone swords.  They swung their weapons with all their might—but they, too, only shattered against the protected skin of Balder. *(shattering sounds)*

**BALDER:** *(laughing)* I am sorry, my friends. Iron and stone have sworn not to harm me either.

**NARRATOR:**  Then the giants beat at him with their bare fists.  They hammered their massive feet down upon him with all their might, but each time they rebounded off an invisible barrier, and the god remained unharmed.

**GIANT:** It is a good thing that Balder is a peaceful god—because now he is completely invincible!

**NARRATOR:**  Next the dwarves came forward, swinging axes forged with mighty spells.  They hacked at Balder's ankles, but their axe-heads broke away.

**FRIGGA:**  Not even magic can fortify a weapon enough to harm him!

**NARRATOR:**  Boulders, trees, and other projectiles were called for, and the merriment reached an all-time high.  With each failed attempt to harm her son, Frigga's eyes shone more and more.  She looked triumphantly to Odin, who was sitting gloomily at his feasting table.

**ODIN:** *(to himself)* Clever, Frigga.  But you cannot outwit Fate.

**NARRATOR:**  Of all the guests there that day, there was only one who had not been invited.  It was an old crone named Groa— or at least that is how she appeared.  On the inside Groa was Loki the dreaded trickster. After Loki had been expelled from Asgard, he had spent every moment plotting the best way to wound the Æsir the most deeply.  Here at this celebration he smelled a chance to do so.  In his disguise he made his way through the crowd until he stood at Frigga's side.

**LOKI:** *(old woman voice)* My stars! Look at what they're doing to that poor boy! I have never seen a stoning before!

**FRIGGA:** Oh, old woman.  You are mistaken!  This is a game we are playing. Nothing can harm my son, Balder.

**LOKI:** What a strange game!  What if he gets hurt?

**FRIGGA:** Didn't you hear me?  Everything in the world has promised not to harm him. *(suddenly worried)* Wait a minute.  Didn't *you* promise?

**LOKI:** Of course, of course.  A nice young man came to my hut and asked me to promise.  I didn't know why.  So I thought I would come here and see what all the fuss was about. *(pause)* But are you sure that *everything* has promised not to harm him? I mean, everything? In all the Nine Worlds?

**FRIGGA:** Yes! Now leave me alone.

**LOKI:** I mean, if I were you, I'd be worried I forgot something—missed something, you know.

**FRIGGA:** If you must know, there is one thing that did not promise—a patch of mistletoe growing on the trees by the gates. But that could not possibly harm him! So leave me be!

**LOKI:** Oh my. Who is that pale gentleman over there? He looks like he was raised in a cave.

**FRIGGA:** That is Hodur, my other son.

**LOKI:** Odor, you say? What a strange thing to name a child!

**FRIGGA:** *(loudly)* Hodur!

**LOKI:** Oh. Did *he* make your promise?

**FRIGGA:** You are really the most infuriating person I have ever met! Of course, he did not promise. He never comes out of his hall. He's only here because Balder invited him. Now, leave me alone!

**LOKI:** Fine. Fine.

**NARRATOR:** Loki could barely contain his excitement. All the ingredients for disaster were at his fingertips. He spied Hodur making his way out into the gloom of the evening.

**HODUR:** Who's there?

**LOKI:** Just an old woman. Why aren't you joining in all the fun?

**HODUR:** Old woman, I'm not joining in the "fun," because that is my brother they are celebrating in there. My twin brother, in fact.

**LOKI:** Twin? But he is so handsome—and you're—well…

**HODUR:** You don't have to say it. I know. *(pause)* I would certainly throw something at him if I thought it would hurt him. He deserves to be hurt! He has always been my mother's pet! His whole life he's had everything handed to him.

**LOKI:** Stay right here, sonny.

**NARRATOR:** Groa-Loki made his way to a nearby tree. Some mistletoe was growing there upon it. He plucked it loose and returned to Hodur.

**LOKI:** Look here. Here is some mistletoe.

**HODUR:** *(disgusted)* Look, old lady, I'm not in the mood for romance right now!

**LOKI:** *(suddenly angrily)* Listen, stupid. I am an enchantress. I will fashion a spear from this plant with my powers. Then you can join in on the fun.

**HODUR:** Fun? The spear will just bounce off him like everything else!

**LOKI:** Yes, but it will make you feel better! You can release some of that aggression—hatred that has been brewing inside of you these many years!

**HODUR:** Perhaps that would help. Make your spear, old woman.

**LOKI:**  I will enchant it so that it will always strike its target.  Your blindness will not hinder your aim.

**HODUR:**  Fine.  After I throw the spear, then I'm going back to my hall.  This has been enough fun for one day.

**NARRATOR:**  Loki began to mumble incantations, and the mistletoe twisted and formed itself into a long spike.  The tip of it was deadly-pointed.  He placed it into the blind grip of Hodur.  And in that moment, Loki's disguise faded away, and his voice regained its true nature.

**LOKI:**  *(normal voice)* Here is your spear.  Let your hatred guide you.  Find Balder and throw your weapon—and let the Æsir weep.

**HODUR:**  Huh? What was that?

**NARRATOR:**  But Loki had disappeared into the darkness.  Hodur made his way back into the festivities and pushed himself to the forefront of the ring around Balder.  Those gathered around cheered to see another participant. *(cheering)*

**FRIGGA:**  *(disgusted)* Hodur, what are *you* doing with that spear?

**BALDER:**  Brother, I'm so glad to see you've decided to join the fun!

**NARRATOR:**  Hodur took the mistletoe spear into his throwing hand and stepped forward.

**BALDER:**  All right! Let me have it!

**HODUR:**  Gladly!

**NARRATOR:**  The blind god hurled the spear. The spike cut through the air, and Balder flinched, anticipating a tickling sensation.  But when the spear hit, it did more than tickle—it penetrated. *(collective gasp)* They gasped in horror at the spear sticking from Balder's chest.

**BALDER:**  *(weakly)* I—I am struck.

**NARRATOR:**  With a confused look in his weepy eyes, Balder fell to the ground.

**FRIGGA:**  *(screaming)* Nooooo!

**NANNA:**  *(screaming)* Balder! Balder!

**HODUR:**  *(in shock)* What has happened? What's going on?

**NARRATOR:**  Odin rushed forward and knelt by Balder's side.

**ODIN:**  *(sadly)* He is dead! He is dead!

**NARRATOR:**  The hall erupted into chaos. Frigga fell upon the dead body of Balder—weeping uncontrollably.

**FRIGGA:**  *(weeping)* My baby! My son!

**NARRATOR:**  Thor grabbed Hodur and held him before the All-Father.

**THOR:**  Here! This pale lad is the one who threw the spear!

**ODIN:**  *(slowly)* Hodur, for this heinous act—the worst that has ever been committed here in Asgard—you are forever banished! All of the gods here have sworn not to harm one another, so we cannot punish you ourselves. But an avenger will come for you—someday. Now go and never come back!

**NARRATOR:** Hodur, his whole body trembling, stumbled through the crowd. All of the gods began to talk at once—lamenting, accusing, and wondering what the next course of action would be. Tyr knelt to examine the murder weapon.

**TYR:** This is a mistletoe spear, Father.

**FRIGGA:** *(crazy)* Mistletoe! Mistletoe did not promise! My son! My beloved son!

**ODIN:** Thor! Take Frigga to her chambers.

**TYR:** But how could Hodur have known about the mistletoe?

**ODIN:** I do not know, but I sense Loki in this somehow. He found the way to wound us the most deeply—and he used Hodur as his weapon. Even so, all this can still be undone. *(yelling)* Hermod! Hermod!

**NARRATOR:** The servant appeared before the All-Father.

**ODIN:** Take Sleipnir and go to Niflheim at once! Find the hall of Hela and tell her to release Balder back to us.

**HELA:** *(low laughing)* Ha! Ha!

**NARRATOR:** A ghoulish laughter filled the air, and the hall of the gods grew dark. A blue mist rose from the corpse of Balder—and in its light a grisly face appeared. One half of the face was a woman's. The other half belonged to a corpse—oozing with rotted flesh.

**ODIN:** *(angrily)* Hela! You witch! How dare you take one of the Asgard gods down into your realm!

**HELA:** Oh no, Odin. You *sent* him to me, and now he is mine forever. That's how it works, isn't it? I receive the dead and keep them down here in Niflheim.

**ODIN:** No god should ever reside in your kingdom, Hela. We are deathless.

**HELA:** Those were once the rules. But the rules have apparently changed, haven't they?

**ODIN:** *(quietly)* Then, Hela, we must ask you—humbly—to please release Balder to us.

**HELA:** *(evil laugh)* Ha! I love it. The Lord of Asgard begs! Father-Loki told me this day would come. *(pause)* Fine. I will release Balder on one condition.

**ODIN:** Speak.

**HELA:** If everything in creation will cry a tear for Balder, I shall release him. But, mind you, even if one thing does not comply, Balder is mine to keep forever. *(pause)* He's such wonderful company, and I would hate to lose him. *(laughter)* Ha!

**ODIN:** We agree to your terms. All things shall weep a tear for Balder!

**HELA:** We'll see. We'll see. Now, if you will excuse me, you are distracting me from my newly arrived guest. I must make him feel at home. He will be here for eternity after all. *(evil laugh)* Ha!

**NARRATOR:** Her foul cackle rose in the air, and the blue mist vanished as quickly as it had come.

**TYR:** Spoken like a true daughter of Loki.

**ODIN:** Æsir, you have heard her demands. Bottle up your grief.  We have a job to do. Go throughout every world.  All must cry a tear for Balder or face the consequences. When this is done, he shall be returned to us.

**NARRATOR:**     So the gods went throughout the Nine Worlds, beseeching all things to cry a tear for Balder.  The god was beloved of all creation, and all shed a tear when they heard of his death. Iron cried a tear. Fire wept. Even cold ice melted a bit around the edges.

After days of traveling, one-handed Tyr came to a broken-down hut, high in the mountains of Jotunheim.  He knocked rapidly on the door, and when there was no answer, he pushed himself inside. An old hag was rocking by the fire.  It was Groa the Enchantress—but deeper, it was Loki.

**LOKI:** *(old woman voice)* Barging in on an old woman, eh?

**TYR:** Old hag, Balder is dead.  He has been slain. All the world must cry a tear for him, and he will return to life. Will you shed a tear?

**NARRATOR:** Groa sucked thoughtfully upon her one tooth.

**LOKI:** And what if I do not?

**TYR:** *(angrily)* That would mean you have no heart. Balder loved everyone and did no wrong all the days of his life.

**LOKI:** Then I say he is a fool and deserves to die. I will cry no tears for him!

**TYR:** What? All the world weeps for him, and you will not! Why?

**LOKI:** I delight in his death!

**TYR:** How could you? He was beloved by everything upon the earth!

**LOKI:** Not everything, you fool!

**NARRATOR:** The old hag's body began to melt and shift and shrank down into the form of a crow.

**LOKI:** *(bird sounds)* Kaw! Kaw!

**TYR:** Loki! I should have known!

**NARRATOR:** Tyr slashed at the bird with his feeble left hand, but his blow missed, and the crow flew from the hut, crying as it went.

**LOKI:** *(bird-like)* Let Hela keep what she holds! Let Hela keep what she holds!

**NARRATOR:** In despair Tyr watched the bird's flight. Loki had succeeded in his plans. Brokenhearted, the god returned to Asgard to report what he had seen.

**TYR:** Father, all is lost. Balder must stay below—among the frozen dead.

**ODIN:** Why? What has happened?

**TYR:** I happened upon Loki, and he would not cry a tear.

**ODIN:** Then it *was* Loki who was behind all this. We have truly been defeated.  Begin the lament for my son.

**NARRATOR:** The same creatures who had gathered for Balder's celebration now remained for his funeral. They made their way down to the seashore to pay their last respects to the Most Beloved of the Gods.

The body of Balder was laid inside a magnificent ship—his possessions piled around him. But a group of unexpected visitors sent a murmur through the crowd. *(murmuring)*

**THOR:** *(angrily)* Look, Father!

**NARRATOR:** A group of fierce giants had arrived. They were led by a savage she-giant, who rode upon an enormous wolf. She used two twisted snakes for the wolf's reins.

**THOR:** How dare they interrupt this solemn occasion! *(yelling)* What are you doing here, giant-scum?

**NARRATOR:** The she-giant hissed, baring her fangs.

**HYRROKIN:** *(hissing)* Quiet, fool! Thor is our enemy—and always will be—but Balder was a friend to the frost giants. We come to mourn for him.

**ODIN:** Then you are welcome.

**NARRATOR:** The giants took their place among the mourners. One by one the gods placed mighty treasures within the burial ship. Frigga wept uncontrollably over her son, and Nanna, too. Finally, Odin leaned down and whispered his last words into the ear of Balder. No one knows what these words were, but they were the greatest words ever spoken. He removed the golden ring from his arm, the famous Draupnir, and laid it beside the body of his son.

**ODIN:** Now—he is ready to sail.

**NARRATOR:** The torches were brought forward, but before the ship could be kindled, Nanna cried out in one final burst of grief.

**NANNA:** *(cry of grief)* Ah!

**NARRATOR:** She collapsed, and when they raised her, she, too, was dead.

**FRIGGA:** Odin, can we bear much more? Her grief has killed her.

**ODIN:** Lay her beside her husband. It is only fitting.

**NARRATOR:** They laid them side by side within the craft. As the torches kindled the burial ship, even the giants wept.

**HYRROKIN:** *(sadly)* Balder the Beautiful is dead. Balder the Beautiful is dead.

**NARRATOR:** Odin approached the mighty giantess.

**ODIN:** I give you the honor. Please send my son on his way.

**NARRATOR:** The she-giant came forward and pushed the burning ship out onto the sea. All the spectators wept as flames consumed it. *(weeping)*

Thor, angrily wiping the tears from his eyes, turned to his thoughtful father.

**THOR:** *(angrily)* We can't let Loki get away with this!

**ODIN:** No. We cannot. He has taken from us what we loved most—just as he said he would. He must be punished.

**THOR:** I will smash his skull with my hammer! I will squeeze the life from him with these two hands!

**ODIN:** But we have sworn an oath, and so has he—never to slay the other.

**THOR:** Then he cannot be punished.

**ODIN:** No, there are punishments much worse than death, and these we will use.

**NARRATOR:** Using his magical sky-shoes, Loki had fled far indeed. He had found passage through the sky into Muspelheim, the Land of Fire, where Surt the fire giant and all of his brethren burn in outer darkness. Loki communed with them—telling them to await the day of Ragnarok, when they would split the sky wide open and have their revenge upon the gods. But after many months, he returned from that world to further his schemes.

Loki hid himself at the very edge of the world—in a hut with a door on each wall, so that he could easily escape. He knew the gods would be coming for him, and he knew no sleep.

Indeed Odin had spied Loki from his far-seeing throne, and the gods made their move. Loki sat in the midst of his hut, his eyes twitching from one door to another. He heard a twig snap outside in the darkness. *(twig snap)*

**LOKI:** *(angrily)* Fools! I hear you! I hear you!

**NARRATOR:** He darted forth from his hideout—running as swiftly as he could down the steep bank to the nearby river.

**LOKI:** Try catching me now!

**NARRATOR:** He leapt into the air, transforming into a salmon before he hit the water. There he lay in the shallows—waiting with ragged breaths.

**LOKI:** Heh heh. Lost them.

**NARRATOR:** A glowing light appeared above the water's surface. It was the light of Mjolnir.

**LOKI:** *(gurgling)* No! No!

**NARRATOR:** A net came down into the water—trapping Loki within it. The trickster was hoisted from the river.

**THOR:** Looks like Thor has made quite a catch! *(loud laugh)* Ha-ha!

**LOKI:** No! No!

**ODIN:** Ah, Loki. A cunning disguise—but one we anticipated. You should really try a little more variety. You played right into our hands.

**NARRATOR:** Loki returned to his true form and raged against the gods—shouting curses and threats. His captors carried him into a nearby cave.

**LOKI:** *(crazy)* I don't care what you do to me! It will never bring Balder back! I will never cry a tear for that fool!

**ODIN:** It is a pity that you cannot cry for Balder, for he is the only one among us who ever felt pity for you.

**NARRATOR:** Down, down, down, they took him—to the deepest bowels of the earth. There in the darkness, Tyr pulled forth a mighty chain—one as strong and everlasting as the chain that had been made to bind Fenrir.

**TYR:** The dwarves special-made this for you, Loki. It's just your size.

**NARRATOR:**  Tyr and Thor bound the writhing trickster to a rock with the magical chain. No matter how he transformed, he would never be able to escape its spell.

**ODIN:**  Now you will be chained here—for eternity.

**LOKI:**  *(hatefully)* That's where you're wrong! I will break loose! I'll be back, and when I'm free, you will pay! You will pay!

**TYR:**  Let us kill him! Forget our oaths.

**ODIN:**  If we kill him now, we will be no better than he is. We will do as Balder would do. We will show pity. Besides, I think that pity is the most painful thing to an evil creature such as Loki.

**LOKI:**  Grrrr. Release me! Release me!

**TYR:**  But his wolf-child took my hand, All-Father.  I will never fight as I did before. Can't his punishment be greater?

**ODIN:**  Very well.  Make it as gruesome as you wish, but you may not take his life.

**TYR:**  *(happily)* Thank you!

**ODIN:**  Thor and I will leave you to this. Farewell, Loki.

**LOKI:**  *(possessed)* I hate you!  I hate you all! Balder was just the first! Ragnarok will come, and death will claim you all! You all will die! Die!

**ODIN:**  Until that day, Loki.  Farewell.

**NARRATOR:**  Once Thor and Odin had departed, Tyr approached the chained Loki menacingly.

**TYR:**  So, we are finally alone.

**NARRATOR:**  Tyr uncovered the stump that had once been his sword-hand.

**TYR:**  Recognize this? Your wolf-son did this to me.

**LOKI:**  Do your worst! It won't change anything!

**TYR:**  Gladly.

**NARRATOR:**  Tyr found a viper in one of the crevices of the cavern.  A green, poisonous acid dripped from its sharp fangs.  The one-handed god chained this serpent to the top of the rock that held Loki.

**TYR:**  Now, I have my revenge.

**NARRATOR:**  As the snake hissed, the searing venom fell from its mouth and burned into the trickster's face like an acid. Loki howled and lurched against his bonds.

**LOKI:**  Ah! *(cries of pain)*

**NARRATOR:**  The entire cavern shook with his cries.

**TYR:**  Now, as its venom drips down, you shall feel the same pain that I have felt, day after day.

**LOKI:**  This is not the end! Do you hear me? This is not the end!

**NARRATOR:**  Loki was left to his fate. In pity, his wife, Siguna, searched for him— wandering until she finally heard his subterranean cries. Trying to ease his suffering, she held a bowl to catch the venom of the tormenting serpent. But she could never catch every drop, and when she turned away to empty her bowl, a bit would fall upon her husband's face, and he would spasm and curse—causing the whole earth to shake.

So was the punishment of Loki—chained in the depths of the earth until the day of Ragnarok, when he will be released. Then with the help of his foul children and giant brethren, he will bring final destruction upon the gods of Asgard.

As Odin and Thor journeyed back to Valhalla, the thunder god timidly addressed his father.

**THOR:** Father, I have one question.

**ODIN:** Yes, Thor?

**THOR:** What words did you whisper in Balder's ear?

**ODIN:** Ah. I cannot tell you, Thor. Those words were for Balder only.

**THOR:** Oh.

**ODIN:** But I can tell you this—they were words of hope.

**THOR:** Is Loki right? Will we all one day die? It seems so strange even to say it.

**ODIN:** Yes, I'm afraid we must.

**NARRATOR:** A faraway look came into the All-Father's eye.

**ODIN:** The World Tree will burn. All will be destroyed.

**THOR:** Then why should we fight? Why continue this struggle?

**ODIN:** For what good that can still be done. What Loki does not know is that a new world will be born from the ashes of the old. A man and a woman—miraculously preserved—will emerge, and mankind will continue. Balder will rise from Niflheim to rule over a new creation. It will be a better world—a brighter world.

**NARRATOR:** Thor furrowed his brow and then smiled.

**THOR:** (*thoughtfully*) Well, when you put it that way, it does not sound so bad.

**NARRATOR:** The All-Father smiled sadly.

**ODIN:** No. Not bad at all.

## DISCUSSION QUESTIONS

- Balder's death is considered the greatest tragedy in Norse mythology. Why is this so?
- Who is *most* to blame for Balder's death? Explain.
- In the original myth, as Balder's ship is pushed out to sea, a dwarf arrives late to the funeral and interrupts the solemn occasion. Enraged by the dwarf's rudeness, Thor punts him out onto the burning ship of Balder. How would this event spoil the moment of Balder's funeral?
- Do you feel sorry for Hodur? Explain. Why are the gods so cruel to him?
- Is Loki's punishment just? Does he deserve less or more? Explain.
- Should Siguna, Loki's wife, have taken pity on him? Explain. What can you tell about her character?
- Should the gods have broken their oaths with Loki and killed him? Explain.
- What is noble about the Norse gods? Explain.

# VALI, PRIVATE AVENGER
## TEACHER GUIDE

## BACKGROUND

Parody is one of the great art-forms, and Norse myths are not above a good ribbing. "The Death of Balder" leaves one loose end hanging—what will happen to Hodur, Balder's brother who was tricked into murdering him? Will he have to answer for his crime, or will he get away with it? The answer to that question is Vali.

In the original myth Odin is told through a prophecy that he must sire a son on a mortal princess. This son will grow to manhood in a single day and come to revenge the death of Balder. Vali is the name of this avenger, and Odin swears that Vali will neither comb his hair nor wash his hands until the death of Balder has been avenged. Vali is sired, grows to manhood in a single day, and fulfills the prophecy by tracking down Hodur and slaying him with his swift arrows.

Many modern readers will feel pity for Hodur since he "innocently" murdered his brother. But in the Norse code of honor, Balder must be revenged, no matter how accidentally he was killed.

In the 1940's and 1950's Hollywood produced a string of gritty detective movies. They usually featured a heavy-drinking private investigator lured into a web of crime by an attractive, but often duplicitous, female. Over the years this type of story has developed into a standard of sorts.

Until now no one has thought to combine these two genres—mythology and crime drama—and parody both of them at once. Here is the story of Vali the Avenger told as a hardboiled detective story.

## SUMMARY

Vali is born one day, and on the next he has grown to manhood. His adventure begins when a haughty valkyrie named Spear-Shaker comes into his mead hall and demands that he come to Asgard with her in order to speak to someone called "The All-Father." A recurring joke is that Vali is continually hitting on the valkyrie, who responds with physical violence.

Spear-shaker takes Vali to Asgard and introduces him to the All-Father. This is actually Odin, who reveals that he is Vali's father and has sired him for a specific reason—he must find Balder's murderer and kill him. In return for this, Vali will be one of the gods who survives Ragnarok.

Vali begins his investigation by questioning a group of suspicious-looking dwarves in the alley behind Valhalla. They tell him that Nanna, Balder's wife, is not a suspect because she died shortly after her husband. They tell him that Frigga invited all the creatures of earth to test out Balder's invulnerability. Vali decides to speak to Frigga.

Vali finds the Queen of Asgard in a seedy mead hall, drinking a strange drink. She tells him it is a mead of forgetfulness, but its effects are wearing off. She gives him more information about the murder, including the fact that mistletoe was the murder weapon. She is about ready to tell him the murderer's name, but she takes another drink of mead. Her memory is wiped clean.

Vali spots a thug-looking god standing along the walls of Asgard. He begins to question him, but the god does not respond. Munin the raven appears and tells Vali that this is Vidar, his long-lost mute brother whom Odin has sent to help him on his quest. The two brothers locate some mistletoe growing on a tree by the gates of Asgard. Vali questions the mistletoe, and it tells him that on the day of Balder's murder an old woman picked some of him loose and handed it to a blind man with her.

After questioning the mistletoe, Vali is confronted by Thor, who wants to know why he has been snooping around Asgard. The two gods are about to get into an altercation when Odin interrupts. He tells Vali that Hodur, the blind brother of Balder, is the murderer and commands him to go to the Norns and find out where Hodur has gone. Vali complies, and the Norns tell him that Hodur is hiding in the Forest of Darkness.

Vali and Vidar locate Hodur in the forest, and the blind god declares that he is a patsy in Loki's scheme. They try to bring Hodur back to Odin, but he makes a run for it. As he is fleeing, Vali shoots an arrow as a warning shot, but it accidentally kills the god. Their case is finished. The story ends with Odin vowing to punish Loki for his role in the death of Balder.

## ESSENTIAL QUESTIONS

- Should you always take revenge?
- What purpose does humor serve?

## ANTICIPATORY QUESTIONS

- What is a parody?
- Have you ever seen a story that featured a private investigator (or "private eye" as they're also called)?
- After Balder's death, what do you think happened to Hodur, his murderer?

## CONNECT

**Parody** Choose a story that you have read and write a parody of it. A parody contains many of the same elements as the story it is parodying but mocks these elements by adding plenty of exaggerated humor.

**Film Noir** Watch a film that fits into the film noir genre such as *Sunset Boulevard* (1950) or *The Maltese Falcon* (1941) in order to better understand the parody aspects of this play.

## TEACHABLE TERMS

- **Parody** This script-story is intended to be a parody of both Norse mythology and gritty detective dramas. What clues tell you that it is intended to be funny? What elements are broad exaggerations? What elements mock the story's source material?
- **Jargon** Terms like *dame, mug, suit, stool pigeon, etc.* in this play are all examples of jargon associated with crime dramas from the 40's and 50's.
- **Point of View** This script-story is told through one character's point of view. The audience knows this character's thoughts and feelings. This is an example of first-parson storytelling.
- **Running Gag** A joke repeated through the course of a story is often called a "running gag." Vali frequently references his one-day-old age, makes jokes about Odin's one eye, and messes up Spear-shaker's name. These are all examples of running gags.

## RECALL QUESTIONS

1. What is strange about the way Vali grew up?
2. What assignment does Odin give to Vali?
3. Who is Vidar?
4. Who tells Vali where to find Hodur, the murderer of Balder?
5. How does Hodur die?

# VALI, PRIVATE AVENGER:
## AN OLD NORSE DETECTIVE STORY

**CAST**

| | |
|---|---|
| **VOICEOVER** | *Narrating Voice of Vali* |
| **VALI** | *Avenger for Hire* |
| **VALKYRIE** | *Henchwoman of Odin* |
| **ODIN** | *The All-Father* |
| **FRIGGA** | *Odin's Number One Dame* |
| **THOR** | *One of Odin's Heavies* |
| **ANKLEBITER** | *Suspicious Dwarf* |
| **MUNIN** | *Bird of Odin* |
| **MISTLETOE** | *Parasitic Plant* |
| **HODUR** | *Blind God* |
| **NORN** | *Cosmic Know-It-All* |

**VOICEOVER:** It all started on a Tyr's-day. I was just a young sap—one day old to be exact. I mean, I was a full-grown man, but I had become that way in just one day's time. It's complicated.

Life for me had already been a whirl-wind, and it was just going to get worse. I was down in Midgard, trying to catch some z's in the old mead hall, when this dame walked in. For a second there, I thought I'd died and gone to Valhalla.

I could tell she was one of those militant gals. For starters, she was wearing some metallic-looking underwear as outerwear—plus she was carrying a mean-looking spear.

She had a body on her, too. It was thrown over her shoulder actually. It was Gunther the watchman—or at least it used to be. She threw the body down at my feet. Right then I fell for her. I was more of a goner than Gunther was. But I played it cool.

**VALI:** What can I do for you, doll-face?

**NARRATOR:** She had this I'd-rather-slay-you-than-talk-to-you look on her face. It was kinda cute.

**VALI:** What can I do for you, doll-face?

**VOICEOVER:** I guess she didn't like being called doll-face, because the next thing I knew, *my* face was slammed on the floor with 120 pounds of *doll* crushing the life out of me.

**VALKYRIE:** (*shouting*) Speak, mortal! Are you the one called Vali?

**VALI:** (*muffled*) You can call me anything you want, gorgeous.

**VOICEOVER:** She expertly dislodged one of my joints. (*cracking noise*)

**VALI:** (*cry of pain*) Ouch! Yep! They call me Vali.

**VOICEOVER:**  She jerked me up from the floor as easily as a sack of goat meat and glared at me like a rabid berserker.

**VALI:**  Easy on the robe, sugar. Anyone ever tell you that you're cute when you're violent?

**VALKYRIE:**  I am the valkyrie called Spear-shaker.

**VALI:**  Beautiful name. Is that Swedish?

**VALKYRIE:**  The All-Father wants to talk to you.

**VALI:**  The All-Father? I've heard of him. He lives uptown in Asgard, doesn't he? He's the kind of guy who has his hands in all kinds of dirty deeds, but somehow keeps them clean.

**VALKYRIE:**  I know nothing about his hands! But, come with me now, or I will break *your* neck!

**VALI:**  You say the sweetest things. But please—this is all happening so fast!

**VOICEOVER:**  It was true. Like I said, I'd just been born the day before.

I could tell that she was the kind of gal who didn't like to be refused. Plus, she was a definitely a valkyrie I'd like to know better. She grabbed ahold of my collar and took me for the ride of my life.

**VALI:**  Ahhh! (*cries of fright*)

**VOICEOVER:**  When I stopped screaming, I realized that we were somewhere new.

**VALI:**  We're not in Midgard anymore, are we, Skunk-stalker?

**VALKYRIE:**  Grrr! It's Spear-shaker! And we are in Asgard.

**VOICEOVER:**  The afterlife. The Big Sleep. Somehow I pictured it brighter. The place had a gloomy vibe—pale torchlight and long shadows. She led me into a mead-hall joint. Looked like the place was closed down for the night. Seated ominously at the end of a long table was a white-headed suit wearing a cape and a wingéd helmet.

**VALI:**  Is the circus in town or something?

**VALKYRIE:**  I have brought the man-creature, All-Father. The one called Vali Blankson.

**VOICEOVER:**  The icy dame shoved me into a seat and took her spot behind the All-Father's chair. I didn't like the vibe I was getting from this All-Father guy. One of his eyes had this shifty look in it. The other one had this less-is-more quality—a blank socket with a mean stare. It looked like he'd lost a poking match with a sharp stick.

**VALI:**  So what's the story here, All-Father? You send your lovely goon here to pick me up. Now what? What's your game?

**ODIN:**  Vali, I've had my eyes on you for a while now.

**VALI:**  Eyes? Check your math there. Looks like you're off one. (*pause*) What's the deal anyway? Are you saving up for a full pair?

**VOICEOVER:**  Spear-shaker came forward and ground my head into the tabletop. I could tell she was really starting to fall for me.

**ODIN:**  I've been impressed with your progress.

**VALI:** You should be. I was born yesterday, grew to manhood in a day, and here I am. A fine specimen, too, I might add.

**ODIN:** I have a proposition for you. First, I think you should know that I am Odin.

**VALI:** The Lord of Asgard. The Big Cheese. But the All-Father is just your cover, huh? I see. Crafty.

**ODIN:** I also thought you should know that…*I am your father.*

**VALI:** *(not surprised)* No kidding? You know, you got a nice place here. I bet you could host some killer parties.

**ODIN:** Did you not hear what I said? I am your father.

**VALI:** With a name like "All-Father," it sounds like you're everybody's father.

**ODIN:** No. I am literally your father.

**VALI:** *(not shocked)* Great. Now I can change my name from Blankson to Odinson.

**ODIN:** Aren't you shocked to find out that your father is one of the gods? How else would you be able to grow to manhood in a single day?

**VALI:** Well, I just thought I hit a growth spurt. Mom always told me you were my father, but I never believed her.

**ODIN:** Who wouldn't trust his own mother?

**VALI:** Eh. I haven't known her that long.

**ODIN:** Good point. I had to sire you because I have a quest for you. One of the gods has been killed.

**VALI:** One of the gods? Dead? Theocide, huh? Does that happen very often with you all?

**ODIN:** No. But still it has happened. I want you to track down the culprit and avenge the murder of my son—Balder.

**VALI:** Whoa, pops. I think you misspoke there. Don't you mean—your balder son?

**ODIN:** Balder is his name.

**VALI:** Yikes. What's your other son's name? Baldest? I'm glad you left *my* name up to Mom.

**ODIN:** *(dryly)* This is all very humorous, but I'm afraid we're short on time.

**VALI:** *You're* short on time? I was born yesterday. *(pause)* So you want me to track down the cheap hood who knocked off this Balder guy.

**ODIN:** Yes. Before you were born, I swore an oath that you would neither wash your hands nor comb your hair until you put Balder's murderer in his grave.

**VALI:** Sheesh. Can I at least brush my teeth? So what did this Balder fella look like? Was he a big, Nordic-looking guy?

**ODIN:** Yes. But we all are.

**VALI:** Good point. Hmmm. Was he bald all over, or just on top? Or is it one of those weird patchy things in the back?

**ODIN:** *(annoyed)* He had all of his hair. His *name* was Balder. He was killed right here in Asgard.

**VALI:** Any witnesses?

**ODIN:** Hundreds of them. Gods, dwarves, elves, even giants.

**VALI:** Sounds like tough crowd. Were you having a thug convention or something?

**ODIN:** It was supposed to be a celebration in his honor. We had no idea he would be murdered.

**VALI:** But in an ironic twist, his celebration turned into a funeral. It's the old it's-my-party-and-I'll-die-if-I-want-to case, huh? Everyone piles in for some mead and flax cake, and wham! Someone sends the guest of honor down to the old cooler, Niflheim. *(pause)* So why don't you gods avenge his murder?

**ODIN:** We're far too busy! Plus, we all pledged not to kill one another. There's also a strong possibility that Balder's murderer is...one of the gods! *(dramatic music)*

**VALI:** Stabbed in the back, huh?

**ODIN:** No. In the front actually. Right there in the atrium.

**VALI:** Ouch. That's a painful spot. Tell me this—where were *you* when all this went down?

**ODIN:** Me? What does that have to do with anything?

**VALI:** Defensive, huh? I'll make a note of that. *(pause)* Or I would if I knew how to write. Got any of those runes handy?

**ODIN:** Just get to it! I'm running short on time! Find Balder's murderer and kill him—or else!

**VALI:** I know you just said "or else," which was really intimidating—but I still have to ask, what is in this for me?

**VALKYRIE:** *(yelling)* How dare you speak to Odin that way!

**VALI:** Easy, Pot-licker.

**VALKYRIE:** Spear-shaker!

**VALI:** Sorry about that, babe, but I think the big guy can answer for himself.

**ODIN:** I don't think you understand—I'm making you one of those offers you can't refuse. But if you are looking for further compensation, the Norns have declared that Vali the Avenger will be one of the few gods to survive Ragnarok.

**VALI:** Hmmm. I'm a god, huh? Not too shabby! And nice to know. Mom must have missed that important piece of information. She probably tried to tell me yesterday—but I was going through my teenage years and wasn't listening to a word she said.

**ODIN:** Hmmmm. I see. Shall we continue?

**VALI:** Give me a break, pops! It's just a trip down memory lane. In my case, a short trip. So you said, after Ragnarok, I get to rule the world? *(pause)* But won't the world be just a huge pile of rubble by then?

**ODIN:** Yes, but you'll get to be the *king* of rubble.

**VALI:** *(sarcastically)* Hmm. Tempting.

**ODIN:** *(angrily)* Or I could reduce you to a smoking pile of ash!

**VALI:** I like your style. All right. You have a deal. Vali is on the job.

**ODIN:** Excellent. I have some wandering to do. Now I will take my leave.

**VALI:** Good. I never wanted it in the first place.

**VOICEOVER:** I could see that this first meeting between pops and me had not gone well. I made a mental note to check into family counseling later.

His valkyrie goon showed me out of Valhalla—rather roughly I might add. I saw through all her manhandling though. If she had a soft spot anywhere, it was for me.

After I located my kneecaps and reattached them, I started snooping around Asgard, asking questions.

**VALI:** The name's Vali, private avenger. What can you tell me about Baldy?

**VOICEOVER:** The reaction was always the same. When I mentioned the stiff's name, they got all weepy-eyed. Some of them turned on the water-works so bad, I couldn't get a word out of them. Come to find out the whole world was weeping for Balder.

On top of that, there wasn't a motive in sight. Balder was the most straight-laced guy who ever lived—handsome, kind, caring, faithful to his wife. Never did a bad deed in his life. But the question kept nagging at me, "If he doesn't have any enemies, who killed him?" I needed to get answers—and fast.

There's a narrow space between Valhalla and the next hall—kind of a dark alley—Valhalley, they call it. It's where the scum of Asgard go to hang out. I found a couple of dwarves lurking there. They were carving some graffiti about the goddess Freya into the wall.

I recognized one of them as a thug named Ankle-biter. I'd seen his ugly mug on a poster somewhere—wanted for lifting the golden horseshoes off Sleipnir.

**VALI:** I need some information from you low-lifes? *(pause)* Get it? *Low*-lifes?

**ANKLEBITER:** Hilarious.

**VALI:** I guess you're short on humor. Or maybe you're just short on everything. What can you tell me about Balder?

**ANKLEBITER:** I can tell you that I mind my own business, wiseguy!

**VALI:** Hey, buddy, when somebody bumps off a god, it's everybody's business. And I'm working for the All-Father.

**ANKLEBITER:** *(gasp)* The All-Father?

**VALI:** Yeah, so start spilling your guts! What do you know about Balder's wife?

**ANKLEBITER:** She was a dame named Nanna.

**VALI:** Was? What happened? Did she skip town after the murder?

**ANKLEBITER:** Nah. She died of grief, so she could be with her husband.

**VOICEOVER:** Two dead gods. The deities were really piling up.

**VALI:** Sounds fishy. Did anybody actually check if she was dead? She could have faked it.

**ANKLEBITER:** They burned her body.

**VALI:** Can't fake that. What are a couple of two-bit hoods like you doing here in Asgard, anyway?

**ANKLEBITER:** We was invited, pencil-neck. Queen Frigga invited all the creatures of the Nine Worlds. She said, "Come and throw an axe at my son. Nuttin's going to hurt him." And it was the weekend, and we had nuttin' better to do. Why not?

**VALI:** Frigga, huh? That's his mom. Talk about tough love. Maybe I need to be asking her some questions.

**ANKLEBITER:** Talk to whoever you want, pinhead. You ain't never going to crack this case!

**VOICEOVER:** I flipped them a coin.

**VALI:** Thanks for the info. Here's a gold piece to grow on, half-pint.

**VOICEOVER:** I found Queen Frigga in the last place I thought I'd find a royal dame like her—a mead-hall dive on the bad side of Asgard. The place was filled with smoke. Must have been goat-roast night. I recognized Frigga because she was wearing the same goofy winged cap that I'd seen on Odin. They must have got some two-for-one deal.

**VALI:** All right, queenie, what's your game?

**FRIGGA:** I'm shooting dice. Care to play?

**VALI:** No thanks. I don't play games—or at least ones that involve counting. But tell me, what's a classy lady like you doing in a mead hall like this?

**FRIGGA:** That's my business. Who are you, stranger?

**VALI:** My name is Vali, private avenger. I was sent here by Odin, my father.

**FRIGGA:** *(shocked)* Your father? Hmph. That two-timing cad! I should have known! Wait until I see him again!

**VALI:** Ah. Don't be too hard on him. He said he had to sire me.

**FRIGGA:** Ha! You think I'm going to believe that? I wasn't born yesterday!

**VALI:** *(offended)* I don't like what you're implying there, sister.

**FRIGGA:** Oh well. I always knew he had a wandering eye.

**VALI:** Yeah. Looks like it's taken a permanent vacation. Tell me, Frigga, you're acting pretty calm and collected for a mother who's just lost her darling son.

**FRIGGA:** It's this drink here. The witch who runs this place brews an ale of forgetfulness. It's pretty handy at times like this. I just need a quiet place to forget.

**VALI:** *(sarcastically)* Great. Then I doubt you'll be able to tell me any details about your son's death—like maybe why you invited a bunch of thugs to come attack him?

**FRIGGA:** Unfortunately, the ale's wearing off. Yes, I invited all the creatures of the world to come here and test out my spell of protection over Balder. How would I know that one thing—one tiny little plant—could hurt him? When has mistletoe ever hurt anyone?

VALI:  Depends on who you're standing under it with. So someone made a mistletoe missile and killed Balder? *(pause)* This doesn't add up.

FRIGGA:  You mean my story?

VALI:  No, these dice you just rolled. I can't do the math. But getting back to the case—you're saying that you *weren't* trying to get your own son killed?

FRIGGA:  No!

VALI:  No, you're not saying that you weren't—or yes, you are saying you weren't?

FRIGGA:  I didn't murder him, but I can tell you who did! That was the strangest thing about it! The person who threw the mistletoe spear was... *(coughing)* Hack! Hack!

VOICEOVER:  She took a swig of ale to clear her throat, but when she did, she wiped out her memory again. Try as I might, I couldn't get any more out of her. She couldn't even tell me her name or her day of the week. But at least I could check her off my list of suspects, and I had my murder weapon.

In a burg like Asgard you've got to know where to look for information. And I didn't. I scouted around and saw there was a big, shifty-looking thug leaning against the walls of Asgard like he was waiting for the next Bifrost outta town.

VALI:  Pssst. Buddy, who do I gotta ask around here about getting some... mistletoe?

VOICEOVER:  His eyes got wide, and he pointed on down the wall.

VALI:  Thanks, Mac.

VOICEOVER:  I headed on down the wall, but I noticed that the gorilla was tailing me. So I slowed down a bit, and when he got a little too close, I doubled around and grabbed him real tough-like. I held my dagger to his face.

VALI:  One more step, pal, and you'll have a new nostril.

VOICEOVER:  He just stared at me with this dumb look on his face and didn't say a word.

VALI:  All right, buddy! You asked for it!

MUNIN:  *(squawking)* Squawk! Stop! Stop!

VOICEOVER:  Some mouthy blackbird was perched on top of the wall.

VALI:  Get out of here, you lousy bird—before you make a mess all over the place!

MUNIN:  That's Vidar! The All-Father sent him to help you. He's your brother!

VALI:  *(confused)* My brother?

VOICEOVER:  I backed Vidar up, brushed him off, and looked him over.

VALI:  Yeah. He does have the family looks. Well, as long as he keeps out of the way and keeps his mouth shut.

MUNIN:  He's a mute.

VALI:  I like that in partner. Now, scram, birdy! And keep your beak shut about this! The last thing we need is some squawking stool pigeon.

**MUNIN:**  *(fading away)* I'm a raven, you dumb palooka.

**VOICEOVER:**  I shook hands with my long-lost brother.

**VALI:**  Put 'er there, Viddie. Sorry about that. This case is shaping up to be a real family reunion.

**VOICEOVER:**  He smiled a dopey smile and shrugged.

**VALI:**  So the question is, where did our murderer get his mistletoe? The stuff doesn't just grow on trees.

**VOICEOVER:**  Viddie pointed. Some mistletoe was growing on the nearby tree.

**VALI:**  Or maybe it does. Fetch me a torch, Viddie.

**VOICEOVER:**  I climbed up and nabbed the mistletoe.  Viddie came back with my torch, which I held up to the plant.   The mistletoe started feeling the heat real fast.

**VALI:**  All right, plant. Start talking or start sparking!

**MISTLETOE:**  What do you want? I don't know nothing!

**VALI:**  Double negatives, huh? Don't they teach you plants grammar? Where were you the day that Balder was killed?

**MISTLETOE:**  I was right here. Where else would I be? Plants can't move, you big maroon! I grow on this tree here.

**VALI:**  I despise parasites like you! But who picked you? Who put you up to this?

**MISTLETOE:**  I don't know. I didn't see her face.

**VALI:**  Her? So you're saying this was the work of a dame.

**MISTLETOE:**  Yeah. And she was ugly, too. Her chin and her nose were having a picnic. An old crone. She picked a piece of me and handed it to some guy she had with her. He was blind though.

**VALI:**  Blind? Blind to her intentions?

**MISTLETOE:**  No, he couldn't see.

**VALI:**  Oh. What did he look like?

**MISTLETOE:**   He was a Nordic-looking guy.

**VALI:**  Go figure. *(pause)* What a case! I've got a blind suspect, a mute sidekick, and a boss who's one eye short of a set.

**VOICEOVER:**  Suddenly, the moonlight was all but blotted out. The biggest goon I'd ever seen was towering over us. He was shaking a hammer that looked like it could put every nail in your coffin.

**VALI:**  Watch it, pal. I just got the dents pressed out of my helmet.

**THOR:**  Thor has heard that you have been asking questions around town.

**VALI:**  Who's Thor?

**THOR:**  I am Thor!

**VALI:**  I see. It's Speak-In-Third-Person Day again already? It always sneaks up on me.

THOR: What? Grrrr. You are causing trouble here in Asgard!

VALI: What's your deal? Are you the law around here or something?

THOR: You might say that. I bring the mighty thunderbolt!

VALI: Yeah, and I bring the potato salad, but who cares? I'm Vali, Private A., and this is my brother, Vidar. Don't try any of your double-talk with him though. He doesn't speak.

THOR: Why does he not speak?

VALI: I guess he has nothing to say. It's a condition that's contagious around here when it comes to this Balder person. Say, aren't you Balder's brother—from another mother?

THOR: Yes, Thor is Balder's brother.

VALI: Hmmm. Thor is, but *you're* not?

THOR: *(confused)* What?

VALI: Try to keep up. Is there any reason why you would want to hit your brother with a mistletoe spear and kill him?

THOR: No! Thor is honest and true.

VALI: Yes, Thor is. But we're talking about *you*!

THOR: What? I have a mind to—

VALI: That's good news. We were worried there for a minute. *(pause)* So you're not ruling yourself out as the murderer? That's what I'm getting here.

THOR: I will strike you with my mighty hammer, Mjolnir.

VALI: I'm surprised you can say that to me!

THOR: Ha! Why? Because you think you can stop me?

VALI: No. I'm just surprised you can say it. It's a big word.

THOR: Argh. Thor does not like you!

VALI: *(fake happiness)* Awww. Thor doesn't, but *you* do! How nice! *(pause)* I think I have enough information from you.

VOICEOVER: I turned to go, but a tall, shadowy character with a wide-brimmed hat was looming in my way.

VALI: *(screaming)* Ah! Who are you?

ODIN: It is I, Odin. I'm in a disguise.

VALI: It's a good one. I about had a heart attack here.

ODIN: Have you solved this case yet?

VALI: Give me a minute. My life just flashed before my eyes. It didn't take long.

VOICEOVER: Sure. I could see it now. Under all that get-up, it was Odin. He was eyeballing Viddie and me—or at least trying to.

VALI: I was just questioning Thor here. Or maybe I should say vice versa.

THOR: What did you call me?

**ODIN:** Thor is innocent. Do you actually think he would be smart enough to pull off a job like this? No offense, son.

**THOR:** None taken, Father.

**ODIN:** Hodur, the blind brother of Balder, is the one who killed him.

**VALI:** Killed by his brother, huh? I'm not sure I want to be a part of this family. You know, this would have been a handy piece of information *before* I wasted half my life on this investigation. For most people, that's just a figure of speech.

**ODIN:** *You're* the avenger. It's your job to figure it out.

**VALI:** Well, where do I find this Hodur crook?

**THOR:** Thor saw him flee Asgard!

**VALI:** Yes, and only if Thor was here to tell us which way he went.

**ODIN:** No one could know where he is. Hodur has a shield of darkness that hides him whenever he wishes not to be found.

**VALI:** Great. This has to be the worst day of my life. And it even rained yesterday.

**ODIN:** To find your man, I'm afraid you will have to consult the Norns. They live under a root of the World Tree. They are three weird, all-seeing sisters.

**VALI:** At least someone can see around here.

**ODIN:** Visit them and they will tell you what you want to know. Take Sleipnir. He will get you there quickly.

**THOR:** Thor wishes your quest well, avenger.

**VALI:** Well, when you see him again, say thanks.

**VOICEOVER:** Viddie and me climbed aboard Odin's built-for-speed steed. His eight legs took us to the Norn's root before we knew it. The three weird sisters—emphasis on weird—sat around a glowing fountain.

**VALI:** Shady little watering hole you have here, ladies.

**NORN:** We know why you've come, avenger! You seek Hodur the blind one. You want to kill him for the death of Balder.

**VALI:** Well, *want* isn't exactly the word I'd choose. Compelled to—against my will. That's more like it.

**NORN:** Hodur has lost himself in the Forest of Darkness.

**VALI:** Well, give him a break. He *is* blind. You'd get lost, too. But wait a minute. Let me get this straight. This Hodur guy's got a shield of darkness and is lost in the Forest of Darkness? So that's like double darkness?

**NORN:** Yes.

**VALI:** This is going to be fun. Any advice?

**NORN:** Take a light. *(pause)* Wait a minute. We're getting a vision! *(strangely)* Vali will be successful. Vali will slay Hodur.

**VALI:** I don't know if I'd call that successful. Knocking off a blind guy doesn't sound like a very honorable thing to do—even if he is a murderer.

**NORN:** There is more! Vidar the Silent One will one day slay the great wolf, Fenrir.

**VALI:** I like his future better. Do you think we could switch?

**NORN:** Farewell! Farewell!

**VOICEOVER:** It sounded like the Forest of Darkness would be a tough spot to find, especially about dusk, but Viddie had apparently paid attention in geography. We came to the forest somewhere between Jotunheim and Midgard. Three feet into it, you couldn't see your hand in front of your face. We kept bumping into trees.

**VALI:** This is pointless. Let's try another method. *(loudly)* All right, Hodur. We know you're in there! We have this forest surrounded. Come out with your hands up! No funny business.

**VOICEOVER:** Apparently, the bluff worked because Hodur appeared out of the gloom. He fit the description—a blind, Nordic-looking guy.

**VALI:** All right, Hodur. We know you took down Balder, so start singing!

**HODUR:** *(singing)* Have mercy! Have mercy!

**VALI:** Okay. Stop singing. It's a figure of speech. I can tell you're related to Thor.

**HODUR:** You've got me pegged all wrong!

**VALI:** Did you throw a mistletoe spear through your brother, Balder?

**HODUR:** Yes.

**VALI:** I think we have it about right then.

**HODUR:** But I didn't know it would kill him—honest! You gotta believe me. I was a patsy in someone else's scheme.

**VALI:** Then name names. Who set you up?

**HODUR:** I don't even know her name. It was some old lady who smelled like dead cats and onions. She saw I wasn't joining in on the fun, so she told me she'd make a mistletoe spear to hurl at Balder.

**VALI:** Ah, the dupe-the-new-guy-with-a-mistletoe-spear con. Why didn't you see through that?

**HODUR:** I know! How could I have been so blind?

**VALI:** Erm. Well, we're taking you back to Valhalla, and we'll let Odin sort all this out.

**HODUR:** *(realizing)* Wait a minute! I know who it was! It had to be him! Who else would want to do-in Balder but him?

**VALI:** Him? You said it was a her.

**HODUR:** It was.

**VOICEOVER:** I was beginning to think Hodur here had finally cracked.

**HODUR:** Loki put me up to it, and he took the form of an old lady.

**VALI:** He changed his gender. Man, this case has it all—fratricide, intrigue, and sex changes.

**HODUR:** It all makes sense now!

**VALI:** Well, that's great, but you still technically murdered your brother, and you're gonna have to answer for it. We've got to take you back to Odin's headquarters for questioning.

**HODUR:** But I just told you I was innocent. Can't you let me off with a warning?

**VALI:** No can-do. Book him, Viddie.

**VOICEOVER:** It was then that Hodur got the bright idea to run for it. You'd think that a chase scene where the chasé is blind would be a quick one, but old Hodur had chosen his hiding place well. In the Forest of Darkness we were just as blind as he was—in fact, blinder. I ran smack dab into about half a dozen trees before I finally saw a light at the end of the forest.

**VALI:** Don't do it, Hodur. There's no escape from the law!

**VOICEOVER:** The forest ended in a big dramatic cliff. But Hodur was running ahead full tilt. He didn't see it coming. Literally.

**VALI:** Stop, Hodur, stop!

**VOICEOVER:** I nocked an arrow into my bow. It was just a warning shot—just to let him know he was getting too close to the edge of the cliff.

*(twang of an arrow)*

**HODUR:** Argh! *(cry of pain)*

**VALI:** Whoops.

**VOICEOVER:** Hodur disappeared over the edge of the cliff. I turned and shrugged at Viddie.

**VALI:** So I'm not the best shot. I need a couple more days' practice, I guess. At least the case is closed.

**VOICEOVER:** So Balder was avenged. As we made our way back to Asgard, I realized I didn't feel good about this case. It had taken us on a wild goose chase, and now we were coming back goose-less. The real culprit was still out there. The sleaze-bag, Loki, was just gonna walk away a free man—or woman—or whatever he was.

When we reported our findings back to the All-Father, he didn't seem surprised.

**ODIN:** I had a hunch that Loki was behind this all along.

**VALI:** *(sarcastically)* Once again, thanks for sharing that hunch with the rest of us.

**ODIN:** Finding out information is what you get paid for.

**VALI:** *(surprised)* I'm getting paid for this?

**ODIN:** The rest of the gods and I will deal with Loki. You've done your part. Good job.

**VALI:** You know, pops, next time you need another avenger, find yourself someone else. I'm through with this racket.

**ODIN:** What will you do now?

**VALI:** For starters, I'm going to spruce up a bit—run a comb through my hair and wash this grime off my hands. It's been driving me crazy.

**VOICEOVER:** Quail-stomper the valkyrie was standing by the hall door, giving me the look.

**VALI:**  Now if you'll excuse me, I've got bigger herring to fry. *(to valkyrie)* Know any good mead joints around these parts, kitten?

**VOICEOVER:**  She must have liked being called kitten because she purred at me.

**VALKYRIE:**  Grrrrr.

**VOICEOVER:**  Actually, it was more of a growl.

**VALI:**  I know I might be a little young for you, doll. But I'll grow on you. Now where is that mistletoe?

**VOICEOVER:**  We walked out into the moonlight. It was the beginning of a brutal relationship.

## DISCUSSION QUESTIONS

- How can you tell this story is a parody?
- Two different genres of stories have been blended here. What are they?
- A running gag is a repeated joke. What was a running gag in this play?
- Word-play is a technique authors use to generate comedy. What are some examples of witty wordplay from this story?

# OTTER'S RANSOM
## TEACHER GUIDE

## BACKGROUND

Otter's ransom forms the earliest part of a long and complicated tale called the Saga of the Volsungs. This generations-long epic is often hailed as the *Iliad* of the Northern world. Its events focus on King Volsung, his descendants, and three magical treasures that they inherit—a cursed horde of red gold, a magical dwarf ring, and the legendary Sword of the Volsungs.

As you read this saga, you will notice many similarities to *The Lord of the Rings* and the other works of J.R.R. Tolkien. Norse and Anglo-Saxon mythology were a great inspiration for Middle-Earth, Tolkien's fantasy world. In fact, the Norse term for the world of men, Midgard, literally means "Middle-Earth."

The themes of the two sagas have connections, too. The red gold horde and magical ring first mentioned in this tale have a murderous curse placed upon them. All who see them desire them, and much like Tolkien's ring, they become a source of true evil and greed.

## SUMMARY

Odin and Loki are wandering through the world of men when they spy an otter sunning itself on a rock. Loki kills the otter with a rock and takes its dead carcass. The two gods seek shelter at a nearby dwelling and offer the otter's carcass as payment for a night's lodging. Unbeknownst to them the man who dwells there is a magician, and his son,

Otter, possesses the ability to transform himself into the shape of an otter. In actuality they are offering up the magician's dead son to him. The magician hides his shock and invites the two gods in for the evening, but secretly he begins to weaken them with magic. Finally, he and his two other sons bind the gods to their seats and are about to kill them when they decide to exchange their lives for a price. If the gods wish to live, they must completely fill and cover Otter's skin with gold. Since Loki was the instigator of the incident, Odin commands him to go out and find enough gold for this purpose.

The trickster does not have to go far before he sees Andvari the dwarf transforming himself into a fish. Since dwarves are notorious gold-hoarders, Loki catches the fish up in a net and threatens to kill the dwarf if he doesn't lead him to his horde. Andvari reluctantly agrees, and Loki steals all the dwarf's treasure—including a ring that is used in the making of more gold. The dwarf curses the gold horde and the ring.

Loki delivers the treasure back to the home of the magicians with plans of keeping the gold-making ring for himself. The treasure is stuffed into the pelt of Otter and mounded over his hide, but one whisker is left uncovered. In order to satisfy the magician's demands, Loki must give up the ring in order to cover the whisker.

The magician and his sons free the gods, who depart. Once they are gone, the family begins to argue over the treasure, and Fafnir, one of the sons, slays his father. He then threatens the other brother, Regin, with the same fate if he does not flee immediately. After Regin has fled, Fafnir takes the cursed horde into a mountain dwelling and transforms himself into a hideous dragon.

## ESSENTIAL QUESTIONS

- How can money be a curse instead of a blessing?
- Is greed ever good?
- What kinds of evil are committed in the pursuit of money?

## ANTICIPATORY QUESTIONS

- Would a million dollars solve all of your problems?
- Is wealth the most important thing in life?
- If you could transform yourself into an animal, what animal would you pick?
- Think about this quote:  "What would it profit a man to gain the whole world but lose his soul?" What does that mean?
- How do you know that someone is greedy?

## CONNECT

**The Works of J.R.R. Tolkien**  As a professor of Anglo-Saxon, Tolkien drew upon Anglo-Saxon and Norse mythology as the inspiration for many of his works, including *The Hobbit, The Lord of the Rings,* and *The Silmarillion.* The mythic connections in these works are too numerous to mention here. Read some of Tolkien's works (or watch the popular films based upon them) and try to spot some connections to Norse mythology.

## TEACHABLE TERMS

- **Figurative Language** On pg. 168 it says the magician's "eyes burned with fire." This is an example of figurative language.
- **Custom** In Norse society, if someone were accidentally murdered, it was customary to pay a *weregild* (or death fee) to the family. This custom is referenced on pg. 170.
- **Symbolism**  The gold horde and the magical ring in this story become a symbol for greed. They are cursed because they bring unhappiness and death to any who encounter them. How is this symbolic of greed?
- **Prologue** A prologue is an introductory section of story that sets up the later portions of the story. "Otter's Ransom" is a prologue to a longer story cycle involving the cursed gold horde. Before reading the rest of the cycle, predict what you think will happen in later events.

## RECALL QUESTIONS

1. How does Loki kill an otter?
2. How does this get Loki and Odin into trouble?
3. From whom does Loki steal a cursed gold horde?
4. What happens to the magician who inherits the gold horde?
5. Into what kind of creature does Fafnir transform himself?

# OTTER'S RANSOM

CAST

| | |
|---|---|
| **HREIDMAR** | *Ancient Magician* |
| **OTTER** | *Magician's Son* |
| **FAFNIR** | *Magician's Son* |
| **REGIN** | *Magician's Son* |
| **ANDVARI** | *Wealthy Dwarf* |
| **LOKI** | *Trickster God* |
| **ODIN** | *Lord of the Gods* |

**NARRATOR:** Long ago, the world was still filled with mystery, and there were magicians who possessed such great power that even the gods feared them. Deep in a wooded marsh, there dwelt Hreidmar the magician who had three sons—Fafnir, Regin, and Otter. Hreidmar taught his sons all that he knew of runes, troll lore, and other forgotten magic. The greatest spell of all was the spell of changing that allowed a man to change his shape at will. The magician's youngest and favorite son loved to swim in the cold pools near their home, but his natural body was too clumsy and constricting for such sport, so he would transform himself into the form of an otter for better swimming and sliding. For this reason they called him "Otter."

**HREIDMAR:** You should be careful, Otter. I have taught you my skill so well that some hunter may mistake you for the real creature and slay you!

**OTTER:** Don't worry, Father. I'll be careful.

**NARRATOR:** One day, two strangers came near Otter's pool while he was snacking on a salmon. Otter paid them no mind. After all, he could dodge the spear or arrow of any mortal man. But these were not mortal men. They were the gods Odin and Loki traveling through the marsh in disguise.

**LOKI:** Look at that otter over there! I hate otters! I bet I could knock it dead with this rock.

**ODIN:** Hmmm. I doubt it. You're not exactly a dead-eye.

**LOKI:** *(grumbling)* Look who's talking.

**ODIN:** Just leave the creature alone!

**NARRATOR:** But Loki skipped the rock across the waters with supernatural speed. *(zipping sound of a rock)* The rock struck Otter dead.

**OTTER:** *(cry of pain)* Ah!

**LOKI:** Got him!

**NARRATOR:** Loki retrieved the carcass of the otter, along with the salmon he had been devouring.

**LOKI:**  Ha! Two kills with one stone. Mmmm. Salmon.

**ODIN:** You are a strange one, Loki. Come on! We need lodging for the night.  I see smoke rising over the trees. Someone must live here in these miry woods.

**NARRATOR:** Of course, this was the home of Hreidmar the magician, and little did the traveling gods know that they had just murdered his son.

**ODIN:**  Greetings. We are travelers. We seek lodging for the night. We have no money to offer you in return, but we do have a nice salmon to give you as a gift.

**LOKI:** Er—actually…I already ate that.

**NARRATOR:** Odin glared angrily at Loki.

**LOKI:** But we do have this lovely otter!

**NARRATOR:** Loki held up the carcass.

**HREIDMAR:** *(gasp)*

**LOKI:**  Are you allergic to otter or something?

**NARRATOR:** The magician's eyes burned with fire.

**LOKI:** Well, you don't have to eat it. You could make a nice hat out of it—or maybe a lady's purse. I know they look like such mangy creatures, but they really do make nice accessories.

**NARRATOR:**  The magician ripped the otter out of Loki's grip.

**LOKI:** Touchy. Touchy. Must be an otter lover or something…

**HREIDMAR:** *(strangely)* Come inside. We will see that *you get what you deserve.*

**NARRATOR:** The magician turned and disappeared into his dwelling.

**LOKI:** *(sarcastically)* Well, that's not cryptic or anything.

**ODIN:**  *(whispering)* Loki! Do nothing to offend this man. He seems to have secret knowledge. There are many men in this world who have incredible powers.

**LOKI:** There are many men in this world who have an attitude problem!

**ODIN:** Loki!

**NARRATOR:** The gods entered the dwelling, and two boys seated them before a blazing fire. The magician himself was cradling the otter in his arms and seemed to be whispering to it.

**LOKI:** Uh, I wouldn't get that close if I were you. Otters are notorious flea-carriers. I'm just saying.

**NARRATOR:**  The magician snarled at Loki. Then tenderly stroking the dead otter's fur, he laid it upon a table. His two sons were staring at the dead animal with the same intensity as he did.

**LOKI:** *(to Odin)* Creeeeepy.

**HREIDMAR:**    *(strangely)* Now let me prepare you a dinner like you have never had before.

**ODIN:** We thank you for your hospitality.

**NARRATOR:** The magician skinned the otter, and as he did, great tears fell from his eyes.

**LOKI:** Otters make you cry, huh? Onions always do that for me.

**HREIDMAR:** Stranger, this otter was very special to me. But you will learn that—in time.

**NARRATOR:** He diced up the creature's meat and threw the pieces in a boiling pot upon the fire. He mumbled softly while the stew cooked. When he was finished, he placed two steaming bowls before the gods.

**LOKI:** *(hesitantly)* Hmmm. No thanks. I had otter stew for lunch.

**ODIN:** Just eat! It is rude to refuse your host's meal.

**NARRATOR:** The magician watched with a maniacal glee as they began to partake of the stew.

**HREIDMAR:** Yes, eat up. It would be a pity if you should lose your strength.

**LOKI:** *(between mouthfuls)* Mmmm. Not bad. Who knew? Otter tastes just like chicken.

**NARRATOR:** After the gods had greedily cleaned their bowls, they leaned back in their chairs and massaged their full bellies.

**LOKI:** *(weakly)* Odin, I feel strangely tired—almost weak.

**ODIN:** *(weakly)* I feel the same. My limbs are heavy, and my mind is dull. *(to the magician)* Friend, what was in that stew?

**NARRATOR:** The magician did not reply—but motioned to his sons who stood in the shadows.

**HREIDMAR:** Fafnir! Regin! Bring the chain!

**NARRATOR:** They came forward, bearing a length of chain between them.

**HREIDMAR:** Bind them!

**NARRATOR:** The magician did not give this order to his sons but to the chain itself. It sprang from the boys' hands and coiled itself around the gods, fettering them firmly to their seats.

**ODIN:** Ah! What is the meaning of this?

**HREIDMAR:** *(passionately)* You slew my son!

**LOKI:** We didn't kill anybody, you crazy old loon!

**HREIDMAR:** My son, Otter, is dead because of you!

**LOKI:** *(in disbelief)* You're kidding.

**HREIDMAR:** Would I joke about the death of my son?

**LOKI:** No, I mean you really named your kid Otter?

**ODIN:** There must be some mistake. We have murdered no one!

**HREIDMAR:** He was called Otter because that is the shape he loved to change himself into.

**LOKI:** Whoops. Okay, maybe we did.

**NARRATOR:** The gods' guilty eyes moved to the otter pelt still lying upon the table.

**LOKI:** *(weakly)* Er—sorry?

**ODIN:** Even if we did murder your son, it was an honest mistake. We had no idea. Do you plan to murder *us* then? That would be a worse crime!

**HREIDMAR:** Actually, it would be justice.

**ODIN:** Surely you must take *something* in return for the life of your son. Demand a weregild—a ransom for your lost son—and we will pay it!

**HREIDMAR:** No! I will take nothing from you—but your lives!

**NARRATOR:** The magician drew a knife and moved toward them.

**LOKI:** *(in fright)* No! I'm too clever to die!

**ODIN:** *(majestically)* Beware! We are not mortal men! We are gods!

**HREIDMAR:** Gods or men, it matters not. That potion I fed to you has rendered you helpless! Now, die!

**NARRATOR:** Fafnir caught his father's sleeve.

**FAFNIR:** Wait! Ask them to give us treasure for Otter's weregild. Then we will live like kings!

**HREIDMAR:** Stupid boy! That will not bring Otter back!

**FAFNIR:** Nothing can bring Otter back—not even their deaths. These men say they are gods. Surely, they can give us treasure, and that will ease our pain.

**NARRATOR:** Hreidmar paused thoughtfully and then re-sheathed his knife.

**HREIDMAR:** Very well.

**NARRATOR:** The magician picked up the otter skin and held it open sack-like before the bound gods.

**HREIDMAR:** One of you must go and find me enough red gold to fill my son's pelt. It must be enough treasure to cover every last hair of his body. Then—and only then—will we set you free.

**LOKI:** Seriously?

**ODIN:** Loki! You got us into this scrape! Now get us out of it!

**LOKI:** *(grumbling)* All right. All right. Same old story. Loki saves the day.

**ODIN:** But leave those magical flying shoes of yours behind, or you'll fly the coop and never return!

**LOKI:** You know me too well. Fine.

**NARRATOR:** The trickster god was freed. He handed his sky-shoes over to the magician and stormed out.

**LOKI:** Where am I going to find a treasure—and at this time of night? We're in the middle of a stinking marsh! I have half a mind to leave Odin there to rot.

**NARRATOR:** As Loki stalked through the marsh, the raspy singing of a dwarf filled the air.

**ANDVARI:** *(dwarvish singing)* La la la!

**LOKI:** *(sarcastically)* Oh great! Dwarves! That's just what I need. *(pause)* Wait a minute! Dwarves! That *is* just what I need! No one hoards treasure like those little boogers! They're bound to have a stash around here somewhere.

**NARRATOR:** Loki spied the dwarf ahead. His name was Andvari—a chubby, little fellow with an enormous red beard. He was skipping merrily toward one of the moonlit pools.

**ANDVARI:** *(more dwarvish singing)*

**LOKI:** *(kindly voice)* My, my! What wonderful singing!

**NARRATOR:** The dwarf whirled around.

**ANDVARI:** Who in the name of Durin are you? And what do you want here?

**LOKI:** Me? I'm just a kindly stranger. I was just admiring your singing talent there. I had always heard that dwarves were marvelous creatures, and now I see it's true.

**ANDVARI:** You look like a liar!

**LOKI:** A liar? No, no. Not me. Just an interested party. You know, I just met a magician who could turn himself into an otter. You dwarves can't do anything like that, can you?

**ANDVARI:** We dwarves are superior to humans in every way.

**LOKI:** Except in height, right? Heh. Heh. No offense.

**ANDVARI:** I could turn myself into a giant oak or a tiny acorn.

**LOKI:** Psssh. Trees? Not very impressive. Why not something challenging—like a fish?

**ANDVARI:** Very well. Then will you believe me?

**LOKI:** Of course.

**NARRATOR:** Loki watched as the dwarf transformed himself into a pike-fish and dove into the nearby pool.

**ANDVARI:** *(gurgling)* See? I'm a fish!

**LOKI:** Heh. Heh. Yes, you are.

**NARRATOR:** Loki jerked a drag-net from the satchel slung at his side.

**LOKI:** And this, my gullible friend, is a net. Never leave home without one.

**NARRATOR:** Loki caught the dwarf-fish up in his net and lifted him from the water.

**ANDVARI:** What are you doing? I can't breathe! I can't breathe!

**NARRATOR:** Andvari quickly transformed back into his dwarf form to find Loki's dagger poked in his face.

**LOKI:** Quit squirming and start talking, half-pint! Where is your treasure?

**ANDVARI:** You tricked me! How dare you trick me! What kind of person would do such a thing?

**LOKI:** Strangely, I am called Loki the trickster. Ever heard of me?

**NARRATOR:** The dwarf's eyes grew wide. Everyone had heard of Loki.

**LOKI:** Now, fish-face, tell me where to find your horde of gold, or I'll give you a permanent set of gills.

**ANDVARI:** *(gulp)*

**NARRATOR:** The only things dwarves prize more than their gold is their lives, so Andvari reluctantly guided Loki back to his cave. Within was his treasure—a heap of glittering, red gold.

**LOKI:** Perfect! I'll release you now, but don't try any funny business!

**NARRATOR:** As Loki greedily examined the hoard, Andvari snuck a ring from the pile and hid it behind his back.

**LOKI:** I saw that! Nice try, worm-breath. Hand it over!

**ANDVARI:** No! No! You can have all my gold, but I must keep this! Please! Please!

**LOKI:** *(annoyed)* You dwarves are so whiny! Give it to me!

**NARRATOR:** Loki wrenched the ring from the dwarf's grip and examined it. It looked so small and insignificant compared to the rest of the treasure. Loki smiled craftily.

**LOKI:** Fine. I'll let you keep the ring *if* you tell me why you want it so badly.

**ANDVARI:** All right. This ring is how I make more gold. Whoever wears this ring will always be rich.

**LOKI:** *(cruel laugh)* Wow. I can't believe it.

**ANDVARI:** It's true! That is how I made all this gold!

**LOKI:** No, I can't believe you actually told me that. What a sucker!

**NARRATOR:** Loki tucked the ring safely into his satchel.

**ANDVARI:** *(angrily)* Give me back my ring! You said you would give it back!

**LOKI:** Weren't you listening? Loki *the trickster*. They don't call me that for nothing! Some people just never catch on. Now beat it before I decide to end your meaningless, little life.

**NARRATOR:** The little dwarf grew red, tore at his beard, and spat upon the gold pile.

**ANDVARI:** Grrrrr. *(spitting sound)*

**LOKI:** If you think a little dwarf spit is going to keep me from enjoying this gold, you're mistaken.

**ANDVARI:** *(ranting)* A curse! I place a curse upon my ring and all my treasure! Whoever inherits it is doomed to despair and death! Death, I say! Death! *(maniacal laughing)*

**LOKI:** *(sarcastically)* Oooh. Not a dwarf curse! I'm shaking! *(cruel laugh)* Heh heh. Spare me your mumbo-jumbo.

**ANDVARI:** *(laughing)* Doomed! Doomed!

**LOKI:** Okay. Enough with the maniacal laughing. You're going to pop something.

**NARRATOR:** Loki bagged up the dwarf's treasure. As the trickster left the cave, the dwarf's crazed laughter was still ringing in his ears. When he reached the magician's dwelling again, Loki carefully slid the dwarf's ring upon his bony finger.

**LOKI:** A gold-making ring, huh? What will they think of next?

**NARRATOR:** The magician gruffly answered the door.

**LOKI:** Hello. I'm looking for Odin. Old, grouchy guy, big beard, empty eye-socket.

**NARRATOR:** The magician hoisted him inside.

**LOKI:** Oh, good. Odin, you're still here.

**ODIN:** It's kind of hard to leave—*when you're chained to a chair!* You better have found some treasure, Loki. Our *hosts* are getting impatient.

**LOKI:** Yes, yes. I have some gold. I have to fill up the pelt, right? Give it to me. I'll cram all this in, and we'll be off. *(grunting sounds)* Oh gross.

**NARRATOR:** When Loki had finished, the body of Otter had been stuffed with red gold and mounded over with priceless dwarf treasure.

**LOKI:** That was one of the most disgusting experiences of my life.

**NARRATOR:** The magician and his sons happily ran their hands through the coins.

**REGIN:** It's amazing!

**LOKI:** Okay, there's your treasure. *(under his breath)* I hope you choke on it. No big loss though. There's plenty more where that came from.

**NARRATOR:** He rubbed his red ring.

**ODIN:** Where did you get that ring, Loki?

**LOKI:** Oh, this old thing? You like it? It was a present from a new friend.

**HREIDMAR:** Wait a moment!

**NARRATOR:** The magician was pointing at the gold mound. A solitary otter whisker was sticking out from it, uncovered.

**LOKI:** You've got to be kidding me! It's just one stinking whisker!

**HREIDMAR:** Our pact will be null if even one hair of Otter remains uncovered.

**LOKI:** Is that in the fine print somewhere or something?

**ODIN:** Loki! Did you give them the *entire* treasure?

**LOKI:** Errr. I gave them *most* of it.

**NARRATOR:** Loki fidgeted with the ring.

**ODIN:** What about that ring?

LOKI:   My ring? You need more gold? Hang on a second. It's supposed to make more gold. Let me see here. Maybe there are some instructions on it. Oh great! They're in Dwarvish. Anyone have a Dwarvish-to-rune dictionary?

NARRATOR:  Odin's eye flashed angrily.

ODIN:  (angrily) Give them the ring, Loki!

LOKI:   Fine! Fine! (sadly) I didn't want obscene amounts of gold anyway… (whimpering)

NARRATOR:   The trickster slid the ring onto the exposed whisker of Otter. Immediately, the magical chain that bound Odin fell loose to the ground.

ODIN:   Now let's get out of here before anything else disastrous happens.

LOKI:  Just let me get one more look at that ring…

NARRATOR:   Odin grabbed Loki and dragged him out of the magician's dwelling. The trickster sulked as they continued their journey.

LOKI:   (grumbling) You could have let me keep the ring…

ODIN:  You could have not killed that otter.

LOKI:   At least there's a horrible curse on that treasure. (sarcastically) Oh no. Did I forget to mention that to them? Whoops. Silly me. Oh well. (snicker) Hee hee.

NARRATOR:   Back in the magician's dwelling, the curse had already begun to work. Hreidmar and his sons beheld the gold with a strange, red light in their eyes.

HREIDMAR:   At first I thought that nothing could make me forget my grief over Otter, but after I see this treasure…

REGIN:  We are richer than we have ever dreamed!

FAFNIR:  Father, let's divide the treasure three ways among us. That would only be fair.

HREIDMAR:   Fair? Who said anything about fair? I am the father. I am the keeper of the magic. Do either of you think you deserve this treasure more than I do?

REGIN:  No, Father. The treasure is yours.

NARRATOR:  Regin slunk back into the shadows, but Fafnir faced his father boldly.

FAFNIR:   I have some skill. I think I deserve at least some of the treasure!

HREIDMAR:  (laugh) You? Be silent, son, before I teach you a lesson about skill. You will have none of this gold as long as I live.

NARRATOR:  The magician turned back to his gold, but Fafnir was not done. There was a look on his face as he beheld that gold. It was the look a wolf gives his prey.

FAFNIR: So be it!

NARRATOR:  Fafnir drew a dagger. (shing)

FAFNIR:  Sorcery cannot protect you from steel!

NARRATOR:   Fafnir sprang toward his father.

REGIN:  Fafnir! No!

**FAFNIR:** The gold is mine! Mine!

**HREIDMAR:** *(cry of pain)* Ahh!

**NARRATOR:** The blood-stained corpse of Hreidmar lay upon the floor, and Fafnir smiled over it. He pointed the same bloodied knife toward his cowering brother.

**FAFNIR:** Now, Regin. You see what happens to those who stand between me and what I want. Run away—like the coward that you are—and never come back!

**NARRATOR:** Regin, his face white with fear, bolted from the house, and Fafnir was left alone with his treasure. He carefully picked up the red ring and placed it upon his finger.

**FAFNIR:** *(laughing)* It is mine! Mine!

**NARRATOR:** Soon after, Fafnir took his treasure and horded it in a deep cave. Then using his magic, he transformed himself into a great worm—an armored dragon. He multiplied his cursed horde of gold and gems with the help of Andvari's ring until it was mountains of wealth. He stretched his scaly body out over the mounds of gold and spent his days and nights guarding them.

Years passed. The poisonous fumes of Fafnir's breath caused the woods around him to wither into a wasteland. Many foolish warriors heard of the dragon's treasure and came to retrieve it, but they paid for such foolishness with their lives.

The red gold was indeed cursed, for Fafnir began to forget that he had ever been a man and eagerly feasted on those of his own kind. His greed lengthened his evil years, and he lived for centuries as the scourge of man.

## DISCUSSION QUESTIONS

- In Norse culture, a *weregild* was a price paid for the killing of another person. For instance, if you were responsible for someone's death (accidentally or otherwise), you would pay a certain price to the family. Is there anything like that in society today? Should there be?
- What lesson can be learned from the story of Hreidmar and his sons? What does wealth sometimes do to those who possess it?
- "Otter's Ransom" is the first part of a long story-cycle called *The Saga of the Volsungs*. What do you think will happen in later installments of this story?
- What do you think became of Regin, the other brother?
- Was Andvari right to put a curse on his treasure? Explain.
- How is Fafnir's dragon-form symbolic of his personality and emotions?

# THE SWORD OF THE VOLSUNGS
# TEACHER GUIDE

## BACKGROUND

Revenge for the Norse people was serious business—a bloody act that must be undertaken at all costs. Today revenge might mean humiliating someone in public, vandalizing their property, or sabotaging their career. For the Norse it meant the bloody annihilation of your enemies and their families. "An eye for an eye and a tooth for a tooth" also meant a death for a death. Codes of honor often demanded this, and the duty fell to the young men to avenge the murders of family members.   If they did not, their honor would be lost. Not surprisingly, this back-and-forth bloodshed led to a constant cycle of killing.   .

From Euripides' *Medea* to Shakespeare's *Hamlet* the question has been asked—how far should one go to achieve revenge? At what point do those seeking revenge lose their humanity? The next installment of the Saga of the Volsungs just might answer that question. Maybe even the Norse thought that there was such a thing as going too far.

## SUMMARY

Volsung, the powerful king of Hunaland, is the father of ten strong sons and one beautiful daughter, Signy. Volsung pledges Signy to King Siggeir, the ruler of the Goths from over the sea. During the wedding feast, a strange man appears. He is the god Odin in disguise, and he carries a powerful sword, which he drives into the live oak tree that grows in the midst of the king's hall. Then Odin declares whoever is able to draw forth the sword can keep it as a gift from the gods—until he comes to reclaim it.

Only Sigmund, the twin brother of Signy, is able to pull it forth. Siggeir tries to buy it from Sigmund, but he will not sell it. This angers Siggeir who secretly vows to murder Volsung and his sons and take the sword for himself. Signy journeys with her new husband to Gothland over the sea.

Soon after King Siggeir invites his in-laws for a visit but ambushes them with his army once they land on his shores. In the battle that follows Volsung is slain and his ten sons taken hostage.

Siggeir places the sons of Volsung in a set of wooden stocks within the forest. Each night a werewolf, who is actually Siggeir's mother, comes and devours one of the prisoners.   Meanwhile, Signy tries to develop a plan to save her brothers. By the time she does, only Sigmund is left alive. She instructs a servant to go to Sigmund and rub honey on his face. That night when the werewolf comes to devour Sigmund, the creature begins to lick the honey from his face. Sensing his chance, Sigmund bites onto the creature's tongue. In an effort to free its tongue, the werewolf breaks the stocks that hold Sigmund and then bleeds to death when Sigmund bites its tongue off completely. Sigmund flees into the woods.

Over the next ten years Signy develops a plan to have her revenge on her husband. She takes her youngest son, Sinfjotli (Sin), into the forest and seeks out Sigmund, who has been living as an outlaw in the forest. She tells Sigmund to take her son and raise him to be a great warrior, so together they can take their revenge on King Siggeir. Sigmund tests the boy's courage by mixing snakes into a bag of flour and then commanding the boy to knead it into dough. The boy calmly kills the snakes and bakes them into the bread. The boy grows up to be a fearless warrior.

After years of separation, Sigmund, Signy, and Sin reunite. The two warriors slay King Siggeir by burning down his hall. As the hall is in flames, Signy tells Sigmund that Sin is actually his son. Using magic, she had visited him in the forest in order to conceive a son who had full Volsung blood. Now that her revenge is complete, Signy regrets her actions and kills herself by throwing herself into the flaming hall.

Sigmund returns to Hunaland and reclaims his father's throne. Sin soon after is poisoned by one of his enemies. Sigmund grows old without an heir, until he marries a young princess who becomes pregnant with a son. Before his son is born, Sigmund is met in battle by Odin, who causes the Sword of the Volsungs to shatter. Sigmund is overcome by his enemies, but he commands his young wife to give the fragments of his sword to his son when he comes of age.

## ESSENTIAL QUESTIONS

- Should honor and duty be the most important things in life?
- When does the end cease to justify the means?
- Should a person ever take revenge?

## ANTICIPATORY QUESTIONS

- Would you seek revenge on someone who murdered your family?
- What is a werewolf?
- Should parents pick whom their children marry?
- Do twins have a special connection?

## CONNECT

*Le Morte D'Arthur* by Thomas Malory
Portions of the King Arthur legends are inspired by earlier Norse mythology. One example is that the pulling of the Sword of the Volsungs from the Branstock tree closely parallels Arthur pulling the sword from the stone.

## TEACHABLE TERMS

- **Figurative Language**  On pg. 180 when Signy describes the condition of Siggeir's heart as "shriveled and cruel," she is using figurative language to express her feelings toward him.
- **Dramatic Irony**  On pg. 182 the reader learns that King Siggeir is plotting to take revenge on Volsung's family, but the characters are oblivious to this. This is an example of dramatic irony, which increases suspense in the story.
- **Pyrrhic Victory**  This term applies to any victory that is won at too high a cost. Signy, in this story, wins a Pyrrhic Victory. Discuss the ways in which she sacrifices too much in the name of revenge.
- **Theme**  The theme of revenge and the effect it has on the avenger is apparent in this legend. Discuss what the story has to say on this subject.

## RECALL QUESTIONS

1. How does Sigmund receive his powerful sword?
2. What secret power does the mother of the evil King Siggeir possess?
3. How does Sigmund defeat Siggeir's mother?
4. How does Signy die?
5. What happens to the Sword of the Volsungs at the end of the story?

# THE SWORD OF THE VOLSUNGS

## CAST

**VOLSUNG** *King of Hunaland*
**SIGMUND** *Son of Volsung*
**SIGNY** *Daughter of Volsung*
**SIGGEIR** *Evil King of the Goths*
**ODIN** *Lord of the Gods*
**QUEEN** *Witch-Queen of the Goths*
**SERVANT** *Servant of Signy*
**SIN** *Son of Signy*

**NARRATOR:** King Volsung was larger-than-life. Physically, he was the largest man in his kingdom, standing head and shoulders above the other warriors, and he had a full, booming voice that sounded like thunder. According to some, Volsung was so large because his mother had carried him in her womb for six years before he was finally delivered.

Only a massive home would suit a giant-among-men like Volsung, so he constructed himself a hall whose roof was so lofty that a live oak tree grew in its midst. This was an ancient, sacred tree called the Branstock, and it had survived hundreds of winters.

Volsung's queen was rumored to be a valkyrie who had forsaken Valhalla on high to become his bride. She had made him the father of ten strong sons and one radiant daughter. The oldest two children were the apple of the king's eye—twins, a daughter, Signy, and a son, Sigmund. The luminous beauty of Signy was reflected in Sigmund's handsome features.

**VOLSUNG:** *(happy laugh)* Look at my ten strong sons and my beautiful daughter! All my conquests are nothing compared to the joy my children have brought to me!

**NARRATOR:** Indeed, every bit of Volsung's life seemed blessed by the gods—that is, until the princess, Signy, came of age. The maturing of such a beautiful girl did not go unnoticed by the other kings and warlords of neighboring realms.

A king named Siggeir traveled across the sea, from the land of the Goths, to see Signy for himself. Siggeir was known in his own kingdom as a cruel tyrant and was rumored to be the son of a shape-shifting witch. But here in Volsung's land, Siggeir was far away from his home—and the truth of his character.

**VOLSUNG:** Welcome, King of the Goths! I offer you the hospitality of my hall! Anything you require shall be given to you.

**SIGGEIR:** Anything, huh? *(crafty laugh)* Then it should be known that I come to ask for the hand of your daughter in marriage. Even across the sea we have heard of her beauty.

**VOLSUNG:** A perfect match, I say! Now our kingdoms will always be linked!

**NARRATOR:** Later that evening, Volsung broke the joyful news to his daughter, but she greeted it with a grim face.

**VOLSUNG:** Why do you look so sad, my dear? Do you oppose this union? Siggeir is a rich man with a large kingdom!

**SIGNY:** Father, you look only on the outward man. But I see his heart. It is shriveled and cruel.

**VOLSUNG:** The Goths are legendary warriors! He will make you a fine match.

**SIGNY:** You know that second sight is common in our family. I have seen the future! I see that much misery will come of this union if it is not dissolved immediately.

**NARRATOR:** Volsung frowned.

**VOLSUNG:** Such shameful words! And from my own daughter! We cannot break faith with this mighty king based on no reason at all.

**SIGNY:** My feelings are no reason at all?

**VOLSUNG:** Bah! The feelings of a silly girl! I will not break my agreement. It would be dishonorable!

**SIGNY:** *(quietly)* Then I guess my fate is sealed. I do not smile at it, but I cannot go against it. Very well. I will go and become the queen of the Goths.

**NARRATOR:** Volsung's hall was filled with feasting to celebrate the marriage. Tables had been spread around the Branstock tree, and lights hung in its high branches.

**SIGMUND:** Father, have you really given Signy away in marriage? What do we really know of this king from across the sea?

**VOLSUNG:** *(gruffly)* I know that he is fearsome and strong. And I know that we need allies.

**SIGMUND:** What does Signy say of this?

**VOLSUNG:** What does that matter? She is fulfilling her duty to her father. Now, let us say no more about it.

**NARRATOR:** Before the feasting had gone far, the lights flickered, and the hall went dark. *(collective gasp)*

**VOLSUNG:** What has happened?

**SIGGEIR:** What is the meaning of this, Volsung? Is this some kind of trick?

**NARRATOR:** The lights flickered back to life, but now a tall stranger was standing before the trunk of the Branstock. He leaned heavily on a walking staff, and a wide-brimmed hat shadowed his bearded face. *(murmuring from the guests)*

**VOLSUNG:** *(sternly)* Who are you? Explain yourself!

**NARRATOR:** The mysterious man revealed what he held in his free hand—a naked blade. The warriors there instantly drew their own swords. *(shinging of swords)*

**ODIN:** Hold!

**NARRATOR:** The mysterious visitor did not move to attack. Instead he turned and buried his sword—up to the hilt—into the ancient bark of the Branstock. *(shunk)*

**ODIN:**  Heed my words. Whoever draws forth this sword will have it as a gift from me, Odin. There is no better sword in all of Midgard! Use it wisely. He shall keep it until I return for it.

**NARRATOR:**  Then, as quickly as he had arrived, Odin vanished. *(murmuring from the guests)* A commotion ensued, following by a mad scramble for the enchanted sword. The shameless King Siggeir elbowed the other warriors to the side.

**SIGGEIR:**  Guests first! Out of my way! I'll be the first to try it.

**NARRATOR:**  Siggeir tugged violently at the sword.

**SIGGEIR:**  *(grunting)*  It's—sure—in—there—tightly. Argh!

**NARRATOR:**  After Siggeir finally tired, he cursed and spat upon the sword. Then the ten strapping sons of Volsung—one by one—tried to draw it forth. *(grunting of the sons)* Nine had tried and failed when Sigmund, the oldest and best among them, stepped forward. He locked eyes with the hateful King Siggeir.

**SIGMUND:**  Here. Let a real man try.

**NARRATOR:**  He jerked hard upon its handle, and the sword pulled free. *(cheering from the crowd)* He raised it high in triumph and called to Signy.

**SIGMUND:**  My sister, I give you the honor of this! I wish you happiness on your wedding day!

**NARRATOR:**  Signy only nodded grimly. Once the banquet resumed, King Siggeir drew near to Sigmund and spoke to him venomously.

**SIGGEIR:**  *(venomously)* That was quite a show, prince! But you never would have drawn that sword if I hadn't loosened it for you. I know in my heart that it should have been mine. Now, let me buy it from you.

**SIGMUND:**  Ha! Are you insane? Did you just see what happened? This sword was given to me by Odin himself!

**SIGGEIR:**  Fine! Enough games! I'll give you the sword's weight in gold.

**SIGMUND:**  You must think me a dishonorable fool. I cannot believe you are the man my father has picked to be my sister's husband.

**SIGGEIR:** Grrrr.

**SIGMUND:**  *(laughing)* Signy, come and control your husband. I think he has had too much ale.

**NARRATOR:**  The following morning, as Princess Signy bid her family farewell, she spoke to her twin brother in private.

**SIGNY:**  Sigmund, must I go with that villain? You can see as well as me what kind of man he is.

**SIGMUND:**  You have made an oath, and Father has sworn his word. All will be fine.

**SIGNY:**  I wish I had your confidence. I fear that I will never see my home again.

**SIGMUND:** We will see each other soon.

**NARRATOR:**  So Signy departed in her detested husband's ship to make her home in the land of the Goths. None of them knew how deeply Siggeir's treachery ran.

**SIGGEIR:**  That smug Sigmund thinks he's made a fool out of me, but I will have my revenge on the entire household of Volsung. Then I'll claim that sword for myself.

**NARRATOR:**  Three months lapsed, and then Siggeir sent Volsung an invitation for him and his sons to pay Signy a visit in the land of the Goths. Excited at the prospect of seeing his beloved daughter, Volsung set sail with his sons. As soon as they landed on those foreign shores, Signy herself met their ship—frantic with fright.

**SIGNY:**  *(shouting)* Father! Father!

**SIGMUND:**  *(in shock)* It's Signy!

**VOLSUNG:**  Daughter, why are you here? Why are you in such a state?

**NARRATOR:**  The poor girl was winded from running and could not reply.

**SIGMUND:**  Where is your husband?

**SIGNY:**  Oh, Father! Do you still trust that black-hearted beast? He has called you here to slay you—out of envy. Right now his armies lie over that rise, waiting to ambush you and my noble brothers. I came to warn you, so that you might flee back home.

**NARRATOR:**  Signy's brothers stared at one another in disbelief. *(angry murmuring)*

**SIGMUND:**  *(angrily)* Treachery! I knew that coward could not be trusted!

**NARRATOR:**  Volsung's brow darkened.

**SIGNY:**  Please, Father. Take me home. Take me away from this horrible place.

**VOLSUNG:**  No, daughter. You shall not flee—and neither shall we.

**SIGNY:**  Your enemies are too many. They will kill you!

**VOLSUNG:**  No one can escape dying—not even once. So for our part, we will act the bravest. We will face our enemy.

**SIGNY:**  *(weeping)* What will become of me if he should slay you?

**VOLSUNG:**  Go home, Signy. No matter what happens to us this day, you have made a vow, and you must return to your husband.

**SIGNY:**  *(in shock)* What? *(to Sigmund)* Sigmund? What do you say?

**NARRATOR:**  The girl turned to her brother, who looked away.

**SIGMUND:**  *(coldly)* Our father has spoken.

**SIGNY:**  *(coldly)* Then I have no choice but to obey. Farewell.

**NARRATOR:**  Signy departed that place, weeping—leaving her father and brothers as they prepared for battle.

Signy's life in Gothland had been even more horrible than she had imagined. The royal hall was ruled by Siggeir's mother, a cunning old sorceress, who kept her daughter-in-law a virtual prisoner. Signy had barely managed to escape in order to warn her family—but all for nothing.

When Signy returned to the royal hall, the witch-queen was waiting for her.

**QUEEN:** And where have you been? Out for a walk? It's a bit late in the season to be gathering flowers, don't you think?

**SIGNY:** My business is my own!

**NARRATOR:** The witch-queen had thin, glittering eyes like a wolf, and she caught Signy's wrist in her bony grip.

**QUEEN:** You little fool! You can do nothing to save your family! Siggeir will take the power of the Volsungs and make it his own. Your father will fall, and there is nothing you can do to stop it! Now get back to your room and don't let me catch you out of it again!

**NARRATOR:** Two days passed until Signy finally heard how the battle had fared. Her father and brothers had fought valiantly, charging their way through the Goth ranks eight times, but finally King Volsung had fallen, and her brothers had been taken captive. After hearing this news, Signy immediately went before Siggeir. Upon his throne her husband was grinning slyly.

**SIGNY:** My lord, I hear you have achieved victory.

**SIGGEIR:** I have—and look!

**NARRATOR:** He unsheathed a sword from his side. (*shing*)

**SIGGEIR:** Here it is at last—the sword that rightly belongs to me.

**SIGNY:** That is the Sword of the Volsungs!

**SIGGEIR:** But since there are no Volsungs left, it is now mine. Ha! (*evil laugh*)

**SIGNY:** I have heard that my father fell in battle but that my brothers still live.

**SIGGEIR:** For the moment. For the moment.

**SIGNY:** Please! If you feel any love for me at all, I beg of you to spare the lives of my brothers. Clap them in the stocks. Do whatever you want to humiliate them! But I beg you not to kill them!

**NARRATOR:** Siggeir raised his eyebrows.

**SIGGEIR:** Hmmm. I hadn't thought of that. What a wise wife I have! A slow, torturous death *would* be much more fitting than a quick, merciful one.

**SIGNY:** (*shocked*) What? No! That's not what I meant!

**SIGGEIR:** Starving to death in the stocks would be a much better fate for them.

**NARRATOR:** The witch-queen appeared out of the darkness behind her son and placed her bony hand upon his shoulder.

**SIGGEIR:** (*scream of fright*) Ah! Oh, it's you, Mother! Don't sneak up on me like that!

**QUEEN:** My son, you know my powers. You know that I can take on the skin of a wolf and kill as I wish.

**SIGGEIR:** Yes, it is one of your creepier traits.

**QUEEN:** Killing these Volsung princes is not enough. We must feed upon their power.

**SIGGEIR:** I don't follow you.

**QUEEN:** Let me go to them in my wolf-skin and devour them. Then their power will be ours.

**SIGGEIR:** Mother! Eating men alive! No wonder I never learned table manners!

**QUEEN:** Give them to me! I crave their young flesh!

**SIGGEIR:** Fine. Fine. But eat only one a night! Draw it out! And save that arrogant pretty-boy, Sigmund, until the last. I want him to suffer the most!

**QUEEN:** Fine! Tonight I feast on man-flesh!

**SIGNY:** *(weeping)* No. No. No.

**NARRATOR:** This news nearly drove Signy mad with grief, for it was she who had doomed her brothers to such a fate.

**SIGNY:** Oh no! This is even worse than I feared. I must find a way to free them.

**NARRATOR:** But the witch-queen had ordered that a guard be placed on Signy's chambers, and only her personal servants were allowed to enter or leave.

Meanwhile, the brothers were imprisoned in the midst of the dark woods to await their punishment. Siggeir ordered that a tree be felled and stocks built from it with enough clamps to bind the ten princes together in a line. The prisoners had no idea what a ghastly fate awaited them.

**SIGMUND:** At least we are still alive. There is still hope! I do not know what Siggeir has planned for us out here, but we will face it bravely.

**NARRATOR:** When evening fell, they heard a faraway howling. *(wolf howl)*

Through the dim light, they saw a humongous and frightening form rustling through the trees toward them. *(rustling)*

**SIGMUND:** Look! There!

**QUEEN:** *(roaring)* Roar!

**NARRATOR:** The wolf-creature pounced and fell upon one of the brothers. *(screaming of the victim)(shouting of the other brothers)*

**SIGMUND:** No!

**NARRATOR:** The other brothers struggled against their bonds—vainly trying to free themselves—as they listened to their brother's hideous screams. But, finally, the screaming stopped, and the creature disappeared back into the night.

This grisly ritual was repeated for nine consecutive nights. Each dusk the brothers bid one another a fond farewell—not knowing which one would meet his fate that night. Finally, it was only Sigmund who remained.

For nine nights Signy remained a prisoner in her chambers—helpless to aid her brothers. Siggeir came each morning to boast of his mother's actions the previous night.

**SIGGEIR:** Mother has been making quite a pig of herself. She's getting a nice little gut. But you know what they say about the Volsungs, "You can't eat just one!" *(cruel laugh)* Now, you're down to only one brother, my dear. And when your beloved Sigmund dies, it will be the last of your miserable line.

**NARRATOR:** Siggeir departed. Desperate to save the life of her twin brother, Signy wracked her brain.

**SIGNY:** There must be some way to free Sigmund!

**NARRATOR:** Just then her loyal servant arrived to deliver her daily meal.

**SERVANT:** I'm sorry, mistress. I hate to see you mistreated in such a way. There is only honey and bread for your evening meal.

**SIGNY:** Honey! That's it!

**NARRATOR:** She quickly explained her plan to the servant.

**SIGNY:** Go into the woods where my brother is being kept. Tell the guards that you have a message from me for Sigmund. Then when you are close, smear this honey all over my brother's face. He will know what to do from there.

**NARRATOR:** The servant nodded.

**SIGNY:** Hurry! It will be dark soon!

**NARRATOR:** The servant rushed away. When he reached the place where the prince was locked in the stocks, dark was already falling. He told the guards he had a message for the prisoner, and he drew close to Sigmund.

**SERVANT:** (*whispering*) Queen Signy has sent me to you! She said not to question what I do, but that you would know how this could bring you freedom.

**NARRATOR:** The servant smeared honey on Sigmund's face. After this was done, he disappeared back into the woods. Sigmund pondered what the meaning of the honey could be.

**SIGMUND:** Honey? What good will honey do me?

**NARRATOR:** As they did each evening, the guards abandoned their post and returned to the safety of the hall before nightfall.

**QUEEN:** (*wolf howl*) Ahhh-rooo!

**NARRATOR:** A pair of glowing eyes hovered in the darkness between the trees. The beast stepped forward to claim its final victim. For nine nights the moon had not been bright enough for anyone to see the beast that attacked them, but tonight the creature was bathed in moonglow. The wolf-creature stood upon its hind-legs, its cruel jaws hung open, and a serpentine tongue flicked between its teeth. True, it possessed the form of a beast, but its eyes were human.

**SIGMUND:** Nine times you have proved yourself a coward—attacking defenseless opponents. You have claimed the life of my brothers, and you may claim mine as well. But I have vowed to fear no man or beast.

**QUEEN:** (*hissing*) But I am both. Before the end, you will beg for mercy.

**NARRATOR:** The werewolf started to spring, but the sweet scent of honey made it pause. It drew close to Sigmund and sniffed. A bestial urge took over, and the werewolf's tongue shot out, licking the substance from Sigmund's face. It scoured every scrap of honey from his face, and Sigmund suddenly realized his sister's plan. It was his turn to attack.

Lunging out, Sigmund sank his teeth deep into the fleshy tongue of the wolf.

**QUEEN:** (*howl of pain*) Argh!

**NARRATOR:** The werewolf howled in pain and lashed out with all its might—but Sigmund only clamped down harder. *(crashing sounds)* As the beast flopped about, the powerful wolf-limbs thrashed at the stocks that held Sigmund, and the wood finally splintered underneath the assault. Sigmund sprang free from the remains of the stocks. He spat something from his mouth—the bloody end of the wolf's tongue. The beast fell upon the ground—its blood pooling about it.

**QUEEN:** *(whimpering)* No. No.

**NARRATOR:** The eyes of the werewolf clouded over, and then only the dead form of a shriveled woman lay there where a beast had once been. Sigmund fled into the woods.

When Siggeir's warriors dragged the bloody body of the witch-queen into his hall, he was beside himself with grief.

**SIGGEIR:** *(weeping)* Mother! Mother!

**SIGNY:** *(laughing)* Ha! Ha!

**SIGGEIR:** Silence! How dare you laugh!

**SIGNY:** The revenge of the Volsungs has begun.

**SIGGEIR:** This means nothing! Your brother is dead! Your line is dead! There will be no more Volsungs!

**SIGNY:** *(to herself)* We shall see. *(laugh)*

**NARRATOR:** Now Signy put a new plan into motion—a scheme she had been forming in her mind like a pearl—a way to return the Sword of the Volsungs to its rightful owner and make Siggeir pay for all that he had done to her family.

Ten years passed in the land of the Goths, and King Siggeir slowly lost his distrust of his Volsung queen. Signy dutifully bore him three sons, two who were the spitting image of their father, and one who shared the pale beauty of his mother. To them she never mentioned the atrocities Siggeir had committed against her family.

Siggeir believed Sigmund to be dead, but Signy sensed the truth. She knew that her brother had fled into the deep woods and built himself a hideout there. For the past decade he had lived as a woodland outlaw, killing those foolish enough to venture into his woods and stealing their goods. She knew that he, too, had been plotting a way to get his revenge on the evil king.

Signy bade her time and, at long last, made her move. She took her youngest son, the one who resembled herself, with her along the road that led through the deep woods. Before they had gone far, just as she expected, a tall, hooded man stepped into their path.

**SIGMUND:** *(roughly)* Halt! If you value your lives, hand over your money!

**NARRATOR:** Signy smiled. Her son beside her did not cry out or even blink at the sight of the armed man before them.

**SIGNY:** Tell me, outlaw, has it been so long that you have forgotten your own sister?

**NARRATOR:** The outlaw drew back his hood and stared at her in shock. It was Sigmund—older and heavily bearded.

**SIGMUND:** Sister? I can't believe it! What are you doing here in the woods?

**SIGNY:** I have come to show you how you might get your revenge—*our* revenge.

**NARRATOR:** She knelt down by her son.

**SIGNY:** This man and I must talk. Go into the woods and do not come back until I call for you.

**SIGMUND:** These woods are too dangerous for a child to be alone.

**SIGNY:** He will be fine. *(to the boy)* Go, Sin.

**NARRATOR:** The boy nodded and left them. Sigmund came forward and embraced his sister, but she coldly received him and shied away from his touch.

**SIGMUND:** All these years! I tried a thousand times to think of how I could reach you—to let you know I still lived.

**SIGNY:** I knew.

**SIGMUND:** If you knew, why are you only seeking me out now?

**SIGNY:** All the pieces had to be put into place. Only now do I have the weapon that you need to succeed.

**SIGMUND:** *(excitedly)* My sword? The Sword of the Volsungs? You have it?

**SIGNY:** No. My cowardly husband keeps it guarded at all times. *(pause)* I speak of the boy.

**SIGMUND:** Your son? A child is no weapon!

**SIGNY:** This one will be. He is my son, Sinfjotli. I have foreseen it. Once you were stronger, nobler, but you have been reduced to this cowardly practice. It has weakened you. Now you cannot defeat Siggeir alone. You will need another warrior to assist you—one of Volsung blood.

**SIGMUND:** That boy? Siggeir's own son will help me slay him? I think not.

**NARRATOR:** A strange look came over Signy's face—one of memory and pain.

**SIGNY:** He is not Siggeir's son. Two sons I bore to that evil man, and I hoped that each one would be strong enough to betray his father. I tested them to see if the blood of the Volsungs flowed strongly through them. I took my needle and sewed a piece of cloth to their tender hands. Of course, they cried out in pain. A pitiful display.

**SIGMUND:** That is a strange test for a mother to give.

**SIGNY:** Strange, yes. But a necessary one. I repeated the test with this boy, Sin. He did not cry out. I sewed the cloth to his hand and then even ripped it free! But he did not even bat an eye! I asked him if he did not feel pain. He replied that it would take much more pain for a Volsung to cry out.

**SIGMUND:** Ha! The boy has courage then! But who is his father, if not King Siggeir?

**NARRATOR:** Signy's face tensed.

**SIGNY:** It is no matter! You are his father now—as far as he is concerned. The boy is eight years of age. Train him up into a man. Show him the path to revenge, and he will not depart from it. Teach him to be ruthless.

**SIGMUND:** What will you tell your husband about the boy? Won't he notice his absence?

**SIGNY:** Siggeir has never cared for the boy. He favors the other two. They are more like him in spirit. When the boy is ready, send word to me, and together we will put my husband into his grave. The sword shall be returned to our family, and at last, I can know peace.

**NARRATOR:** Signy turned to go.

**SIGMUND:** Is this all? Will you not stay a while?

**SIGNY:** I must return home to my husband—lest he become suspicious.

**SIGMUND:** Will you bid the boy farewell?

**SIGNY:** He will be fine.

**SIGMUND:** Sister, much seems to have changed in you these past ten years.

**SIGNY:** Life changes us all, brother. Goodbye.

**NARRATOR:** Signy returned to her home and told her husband that the boy had been killed by bandits.

Meanwhile, Sigmund did as his sister commanded him and raised Sin to be a mighty warrior as he had been. He noticed that the boy was strangely aloof—almost above human emotion. He feared nothing.

One day Sigmund put the boy's fear to the test. He handed him a bag of flour.

**SIGMUND:** Boy, take this flour and knead it into some dough. Then bake some bread with it.

**NARRATOR:** Unbeknownst to the boy, Sigmund had placed live snakes into the flour sack. Sigmund returned to his room

and waited for the boy to cry out in shock, but later the boy came to him.

**SIN:** I have made the bread just as you requested. There were some vipers in the flour sack, but I strangled them and kneaded them into the dough. *(pause)* I would not eat that bread if I were you.

**SIGMUND:** *(laugh)* Ha! You *are* a Volsung!

**NARRATOR:** Years passed in this manner. When the boy had reached the age of sixteen, Sigmund sent secret word to Signy that the time had come for their revenge. Brother and sister met once again under the bare branches of the lonely wood.

**SIGMUND:** Years ago you gave me your son. Now I return him to you. He is trained to kill. He is ready to have his revenge, as we are.

**SIGNY:** Good. Then I shall give you this.

**NARRATOR:** Signy pulled a sword from beneath her robes. It was the Sword of the Volsungs.

**SIGNY:** Here is the blade that is rightfully yours. My husband has grown far too trusting of me. He thinks my memory is short. But it is long indeed.

**NARRATOR:** Sigmund timidly took the sword into his hands.

**SIGNY:** Tonight Siggeir and his men are feasting in the great hall. Go and avenge our family—once and for all.

**NARRATOR:** Sigmund took his sister's hand and kissed it.

**SIGMUND:** I will, sister.

NARRATOR: Later that evening King Siggeir sat in the midst of his men as they drunkenly feasted. Two warriors burst into the hall. *(murmuring)* Through the dim light the king could not see who they were.

SIGGEIR: Who goes there? What are your names, strangers?

SIGMUND: We are Volsungs!

SIGGEIR: *(laugh)* Impossible! All the Volsungs are dead. I carry the relic of their miserable line here at my side!

NARRATOR: The king moved to draw his sword but found his sheath empty. He looked up in fright.

SIGGEIR: It's gone! Stolen!

SIGMUND: Not stolen—but returned.

NARRATOR: Sigmund raised the sword, and Siggeir's face grew pale.

SIGMUND: Back in the hands of its rightful owner!

SIGGEIR: Sigmund! It can't be! Seize him!

NARRATOR: Siggeir's two dark sons rushed forward to protect him, but Sin sprang forward and cut them both down. *(dying cries of the sons)* A cold gleam was in the boy's eyes as he surveyed his handiwork. *(shouting of the men)* As the rest of the king's warriors drew their swords, Sin moved to engage them.

SIGMUND: Now, boy! Prove your worth! Avenge your ancestors!

NARRATOR: Sigmund reached King Siggeir and grabbed him by the front of his cloak.

SIGGEIR: Impossible! You are dead!

SIGMUND: No, cowardly king. The Volsungs are not all dead. One Volsung has come back for his revenge.

SIGGEIR: No! Impossible!

SIGMUND: Now, watch as your kingdom burns.

NARRATOR: A firepit blazed in the midst of the hall. Sigmund lifted the king and threw him into the fire. Siggeir's royal robes ignited immediately.

SIGGEIR: *(hideous screaming)* Argh!

NARRATOR: Sin singlehandedly battled the king's warriors. *(yelling of warriors)* Sigmund rushed to aid him. The Sword of the Volsungs sang as it cut through the air.

Outside the hall Signy sat in the gloom and listened to all that happened within— the cries of her two older sons as they perished, the wail of her husband as he burned alive, and the roar of the ensuing battle. Smoke began to pour from the opening in the hall's roof. She smiled to herself.

SIGNY: The hall must be alight. Fire. A fitting end to it all.

NARRATOR: Signy stood and threw open the hall doors. The heat of the fire washed over her like a blast. Through the smoke, Sigmund and Sin rushed out, their bodies bloody and bruised. They slammed the doors behind them and leaned heavily against them. Within the warriors battered vainly against the doors, as the flames continued to grow. Minutes passed, and the struggling on the opposite side of the door finally ceased. Sigmund sank wearily to the ground.

**SIGMUND:**  At last they have perished.

**NARRATOR:**  Signy turned to her son.

**SIGNY:**  Son, go look for survivors. No one in the kingdom must survive.

**SIGMUND:**  But, Signy, must our revenge reach so far?

**SIGNY:**  He tried to wipe out our people. I will wipe out his. Now, go, Sin!

**SIN:** Yes, Mother.

**NARRATOR:**  Sigmund stared at his sister in horror. She looked so strange to him—so much different from the girl he had once known.

**SIGNY:**  You look at me as if I am a monster, but there is something else I must tell you—before it is too late. *(pause)* You once asked me who the boy's father was, and I never gave you an answer. Many years ago, an enchantress came to my hall— a lady steeped in magic. I asked her to change forms with me. I took her likeness, and she took mine. Then in my beautiful disguise, I went into the deep woods and sought out the outlaw who lived there.

**NARRATOR:**  She looked into her brother's confused eyes.

**SIGNY:**  Perhaps you remember?

**NARRATOR:**  Sigmund's face turned pale.

**SIGMUND:**  No! No, it can't be!

**SIGNY:**  I knew only the full blood of the Volsungs could achieve our revenge. Sin has the blood of the Volsungs—from both mother and father.

**SIGMUND:**  How could you do such a thing?

**SIGNY:**  You would be surprised how far revenge can take a person. I do not regret my actions. But I do ask you to remember me the way I was—before all of this.

**NARRATOR:**  A tear fell from her eye, and she wiped it angrily away.

**SIGNY:**  The aim of my life became my enemy's death, and now I have it. I have poured all of myself into my revenge. All that is left is an empty vessel—unfit to live.

**NARRATOR:**  Sigmund held his head in wonder.

**SIGMUND:**  This is all too much! I cannot believe these things you say to me!

**SIGNY:**  Farewell, Sigmund. Long ago Father told me that my place was with my husband. He was right. I have achieved his death, but now I am no better than he is. I go to be with him now.

**SIGMUND:**  Signy!

**NARRATOR:**  Signy pulled open the hall doors. The fires were blazing even hotter than before, and the heat drove Sigmund backward. But Signy held out her arms—welcoming it—and walked boldly into her death.

Hours later, Sigmund and Sin stared at the smoking pile of rubble that had once been Siggeir's great hall. Sigmund told Sin, his son, of his mother's death. The boy showed no emotion. He had been trained well.

**SIGMUND:** Our revenge is complete. But I wonder who has lost more. All that is left to us now is to go back to the land of my father and see what has become of it.

**SIN:** The land of the Volsungs!

**NARRATOR:** Sigmund and Sin returned back across the sea to the land of Hunaland, back to the hall of King Volsung. The land had been overrun by lesser kings, but through many battles, Sigmund reclaimed it by the might of Odin's magical sword and the prowess of his strange son.

Sigmund moved back into his father's darkened hall. The Branstock tree still grew in the midst, and its lights were rekindled. In spite of Sigmund's homecoming, happiness did not return for him. He often thought back to his sister and all that had occurred in Gothland. Never did he tell Sin that he was truly his son. The hurt was too great.

Sigmund soon learned that it was not in Sin's nature to be at peace. The boy feared nothing. He went warring often, and made many enemies at home and abroad. It was no surprise when the young man collapsed during a feast in Sigmund's hall—dying from a poisoned cup. Sigmund knelt beside him to hear his last words.

**SIN:** *(slowly, painfully)* Uncle, I am glad you are here with me at the end. All my life I have never feared anything. Now that I face death, I know that I do not even fear it. But I do fear something. I fear life. I fear I have wasted mine.

**NARRATOR:** Sigmund had no words as the boy died. When he finally rose, he carried the young man in his arms.

**SIGMUND:** I go to bury him.

**NARRATOR:** Sigmund carried Sin's body into the woods. He did not know where he was bound. A wide stream soon blocked his progress. On the shore a ferry-boat was beached, and an old ferryman stood within. He wore a wide-brimmed hat.

**ODIN:** Who is that you carry in your arms?

**NARRATOR:** Sigmund spoke the words he had never spoken before.

**SIGMUND:** He is my son.

**ODIN:** Do you wish him to have passage upon my craft?

**SIGMUND:** I do.

**ODIN:** What kind of life did this young man lead?

**SIGMUND:** A short one. A sad one. But it was not of his own making.

**ODIN:** Then I will ferry him.

**NARRATOR:** Sigmund carried the body forward and laid it in the boat. The old man met Sigmund's gaze.

**ODIN:** The gods give many gifts—but they must be returned in the end. Death for life. Defeat for victory. Farewell, king—until our next meeting.

**NARRATOR:** Then the old man and his boat were no more.

In the elder years of his life, Sigmund

took a young queen, and soon she gave him the news that he would have a son. Sigmund did not tell her that it would not be his first. But before his new son could be born, Sigmund was called to war. His enemies had surrounded him, and the aging warrior battled valiantly against them. Even time could not cool the blood of the Volsungs.

In the thick of battle, an old man appeared—carrying a long staff. The frenzied Sigmund swung his sword against the old man's staff, and the unthinkable happened. The Sword of the Volsungs shattered. The old man evaporated and was seen no more. The gods had given, and now they had taken away.

Sigmund fell that day. Before he died, he was carried away from the battle. His young wife came to him.

**SIGMUND:**  Take the shards of my sword. When my son is born, give them to him. He will be a Volsung—the last of our line—and he will know how to use them well.

**NARRATOR:**  Then Sigmund started to slip from this world.

**SIGMUND:**  I will see my son in Valhalla.

**NARRATOR:**  Sigmund's wife cried and nodded her head—thinking that he spoke of their unborn son. But, in actuality, he spoke of another.

## DISCUSSION QUESTIONS

- How can you tell that honor was all-important to the Norse people?
- Does King Volsung deserve to die as he did? Explain.
- Some people believe that twins have a supernatural connection to one another. Do you think this is so? Do Sigmund and Signy have that kind of connection? Explain.
- Who is the stronger character, Signy or Sigmund? Explain.
- Was the sword of Odin actually a blessing or a curse for Sigmund? Explain.
- Who is a victim in this story? Explain.
- How can an unhealthy obsession change who people are? Explain.
- Through her actions, does Signy become just as evil as her detested husband? Explain.

# SIGURD THE DRAGONSLAYER
# TEACHER GUIDE

## BACKGROUND

Richard Wagner, pronounced "Vahg-ner," (1813—1883) is one of history's great composers. His masterwork is a cycle of four epic operas called *Der Ring des Nibelungen,* also known as simply "The Ring Cycle." For his sources he used the Norse Saga of the Volsungs and a Germanic interpretation of that saga, *The Nibelungenlied.* Wagner gave musical life to mythical characters such as Odin, Loki, Sigurd, and the valkyrie Brynhild. Since Wagner was German, he used the Germanic forms of these characters' names—Woden, Loge, Siegfried, and Brünnhilde. Wagner inserted his own themes into the story—making a magical ring, briefly mentioned in the original saga, into a weapon of power that could be used to rule the world.

With these operas Wagner sought to revive the Northern heritage and mythology that had been lost for so many years, and his work did lead to a revival of interest in the Norse and Viking world. Famous sections of his operas such as "The Ride of the Valkyries" are familiar to modern listeners, as well as the image of a female opera singer wearing a Viking helmet. Some have claimed that Wagner's operatic cycle, which runs over fourteen hours long, is the greatest work of art—ever.

## SUMMARY

Regin, a seemingly ageless blacksmith, has lived in the deep forest as long as anyone can remember. When the king of the land takes a new queen, she brings along a son—the child of King Sigmund, her former husband. Regin appears from the forest and asks to be the boy's guardian and train him at his woodland forge.

The boy Sigurd grows up as the apprentice of Regin the blacksmith. Regin is a harsh master and often taunts the boy about his lack of a father. Sigurd decides to prove to his master that his father was truly a great king by somehow locating the Sword of the Volsungs that once belonged to his line. Sigurd's mother tells him that the sword was broken, but she gives him the shards for him to re-forge. Sigurd is also granted the right to one of King Alf's horses from his royal herd. The boy goes to where the herd runs free. There he is greeted by an old traveler, who tells him to drive the horses into the river. Only the horse that makes it across the driving river is suitable for a hero. Grani the steed emerges from the river, and Sigurd takes this horse as his own.

Regin is overjoyed to see that Sigurd now has the shards of his father's sword. The smith has been waiting for hundreds of years in hopes of finding a sword that can kill his monstrous brother, Fafnir the dragon. Regin tells Sigurd he will re-forge his father's sword, but he must slay the dragon and win its treasure. Sigurd agrees.

The two ride to the nearby Gnita Heath where Fafnir the dragon lives. Regin tells Sigurd to dig a pit in Fafnir's path, and when the dragon passes over, Sigurd will stab him in the underbelly. Sigurd begins to dig his pit, but while his master is away the same old man appears again and warns him that such a plan will lead to his death. Sigurd decides to build two tunnels branching off from his pit. This way the burning blood of the dragon will not harm him. Sigurd waits in his pit, and Fafnir appears. When the dragon passes over his pit, Sigurd stabs him in the stomach and escapes the dragon's blood through the tunnels. Fafnir speaks to Sigurd as he is dying, telling him that he will be cursed by the treasure if he takes it. When Regin returns, he is shocked to see that Sigurd has survived and commands the boy to cut out the dragon's heart and cook it, so that Regin can eat it. Once Regin departs again, Sigurd complies, and as the heart is cooking, he accidentally gets a taste of it upon his fingers. Instantly, he can understand the language of the birds around him. They are speaking of Regin and how he plans to murder Sigurd. When Regin returns, Sigurd confronts him, and the smith tries to slay Sigurd, but the boy cuts off Regin's head. Sigurd intends to leave the treasure alone— thinking of the dragon's words—but he decides that he must see such a treasure for himself.

## ESSENTIAL QUESTIONS

- What happens when those whom we trust turn out to be deceitful?
- Can greed corrupt the human heart?
- Are family traditions important?

## ANTICIPATORY QUESTIONS

- How exactly does one slay a dragon? What obstacles must be overcome?
- What characters from the last story do you think will carry over into this one?
- What family traditions do you have?
- Do you have any items that have been passed from one generation to another? What are they? Why are they important?

## CONNECT

*Der Ring des Nibelungen* Richard Wagner's monumental opera-cycle retells events from the life of Siegfried (Sigurd) and a cosmic struggle over an enchanted ring. Watch or listen to some clips from these operas. You might not be able to understand their words. (They're in German.) But try to determine the character's emotions through the music. Clips from the operas can be found at *www.YouTube.com.*

## TEACHABLE TERMS

- **Motif: Orphaned Princes**  Many myths and legends feature orphaned (or at least partially orphaned) protagonists, who live a poor life only to discover they are the sons of kings. This is the case with Sigurd, as well as the famous King Arthur. Discuss other examples of this motif in literature, myth, or film.
- **Onomatopoeia**  Sound effects such as "shing" on pg. 201 and "Aaargh" on pg. 204 are examples of words constructed to imitate sounds.
- **Simile**  On pg. 199 Sigurd cradles his new sword "like a newborn child." This is an example of simile.
- **Slang**  The two ravens use slang— "chucklehead" on pg. 207 and "chump" on pg. 208—both meaning "idiot."

## RECALL QUESTIONS

1. Who raises Sigurd?
2. What does Sigurd's mother give to him?
3. How will Sigurd slay the dragon?
4. Who intends to murder Sigurd?
5. How does Sigurd find out about this plot?

# SIGURD THE DRAGONSLAYER

**CAST**

| | |
|---|---|
| **SIGURD** | *Young Apprentice* |
| **REGIN** | *Mysterious Blacksmith* |
| **ALF** | *King, Stepfather of Sigurd* |
| **HJORDIS** | *Queen, Mother of Sigurd* |
| **ODIN** | *Lord of the Gods* |
| **FAFNIR** | *Ancient Dragon* |
| **HUGIN** | *Raven of Odin* |
| **MUNIN** | *Raven of Odin* |

**NARRATOR:** As far back as anyone could remember, Regin the blacksmith had always lived in the deep forest. From his many years of toil in the fires of his forge, his body was stunted and grizzled like a dwarf. His weapon-making skills were unmatched, and when he spoke, his voice was filled with runes and ancient learning. Some even said that he must be a wizard or a dwarf or one of the eternal gods.

When King Alf, the ruler of that land, married a young queen from afar, she brought with her a young son named Sigurd. It was no surprise that the kindly King Alf agreed to adopt the boy.

Soon after Regin, the dwarf-like smith, emerged from the wood to appear before the king. He bowed respectfully with his grimy hat gripped in his blackened hands.

**REGIN:** For years and years I have served you, king, and I served your father before you. I have given you the greatest weapons and treasures ever seen. Now I ask you one favor.

**ALF:** Ask it, Regin! If it's in my power to give it, I will!

**NARRATOR:** Regin pointed to the boy, the son of the new queen.

**REGIN:** This child is not of your own. He will need to make his own way in the world. Let me take him to my forge and train him in my ancient arts.

**ALF:** A blacksmith? Ha! A forge is no place for the son of a king—even an adopted son.

**NARRATOR:** Regin scowled.

**REGIN:** I am more than a blacksmith. There is ancient craft in what I do. I know runes and secret teachings. Let me train the boy, and he will be great.

**NARRATOR:** The king could not argue that Regin was a wise master.

**ALF:** What do you think, my bride?

**NARRATOR:** The queen sat pensively for a moment.

**HJORDIS:**    If this man's craft and knowledge is as great as you say, then let Sigurd be trained by him.

**REGIN:**  Heh heh! Excellent! You will not be sorry.

**NARRATOR:**  So the boy was hoisted onto Regin's pony and led away to the smith's forge in the deep forest.

Ten years passed. There was no love or kindness in Regin's offer to become the boy's guardian. The smith was a hard master. But while the long hours in the forge had stunted Regin's body, they toughened Sigurd—making him tall and strong with powerful limbs.

Except for Sigurd's visits to the hall of his adopted father and his queenly mother, the boy was seldom heard from—and most of the kingdom forgot that he existed at all.

**REGIN:**  *(angrily)* Pump the bellows harder, you fool!

**SIGURD:**  I'm going as fast as I can!

**REGIN:**  Are you? Because this fire is about to die out! If we lose this sword, I'll take it out of your hide!

**NARRATOR:**  Regin rammed his tongs into the fire and drew forth the blade—still white-hot. He plunged it into the water barrel, and steam filled the forge. *(hissing)*

**SIGURD:**  How did it turn out?

**REGIN:**  Fine. No thanks to you! Maybe I could find a maiden to run the bellows for me! I bet even a girl could work faster than you!

**SIGURD:**  Maybe so. But will she work for nothing? Could she stand the sight of your ugly face day in and day out?

**REGIN:**  Bah! A boy should not speak that way to his master!

**SIGURD:**  A master should not make his student endure such conditions!

**REGIN:**  Let that sword cool down, and we will begin a shield.

**SIGURD:**  I can't today. I have to visit my mother at the king's hall.

**REGIN:**  What? You visited her two weeks ago! I swear, you have no work ethic, boy! Who's going to forge all this armor? It won't forge itself!

**SIGURD:**  I'll be back tomorrow.

**REGIN:**  And who will pump the bellows?

**SIGURD:**  Find one of those girls you were talking about. I hear there are some sturdy maidens in the village. Ask one of them!

**REGIN:**  Watch your tongue! I ought to whip you for such words!

**SIGURD:**  Now you're threatening to whip me? If my father, King Alf, knew about this, he'd—

**REGIN:**  *(cruel laugh)* Ha! Your father?

**SIGURD:**    Well, my adopted father, anyway. He treats me just like his real sons!

**REGIN:**  Is that a fact? Answer me this— where do his real sons live?

**SIGURD:**  At the king's hall, but—

**REGIN:** *(fake shock)* What? He doesn't send his real sons to live with a dirty blacksmith?

**SIGURD:** When I go to Alf's hall, they hail me as a prince!

**REGIN:** Maybe, but they also mock you behind your back. What kind of prince are you? What kind of prince wears smelly clothes and has a sooty face? You don't even have a horse to ride! Do other princes go about on foot? King Alf has a herd of wild stallions, yet why hasn't he offered to break one of them for you? Hmmm. Face it, boy! You're no prince. The life of a blacksmith is all that you have before you, so you might as well get used to it! The sooner you stop visiting the royal hall, the better! Get this nobility nonsense out of your mind!

**NARRATOR:** Sigurd was used to the smith's malicious words, but these cut deeply.

**SIGURD:** You're wrong! My *true* father was a king!

**REGIN:** Ha! Not this again! So who was this "true" father of yours? The King of the Elves? The Lord of Stardust? Where is his kingdom? Where is his mighty hall? Nowhere! That's where! Your mother has just told you a fancy tale to hide the truth from you. You are nothing but a fatherless urchin, and that is all you will ever be!

**NARRATOR:** Sigurd picked up the newly-forged sword and flung it into the forge-fire.

**REGIN:** *(cry of shock)* Ah! What are you doing? You'll ruin it!

**SIGURD:** Then go in after it.

**NARRATOR:** Sigurd turned his back on his railing master and marched out into the forest.

**REGIN:** *(shouting)* Curse you, boy! Curse you!

**NARRATOR:** The evening air greeted Sigurd coolly and gave his troubled mind time to think. One by one he recalled the stories his mother had told him about his real father.

**SIGURD:** My father is not some illusion! He was Sigmund, the son of Volsung! A mighty warrior! Regin is a fool!

**NARRATOR:** His favorite story that his mother told was of how his father had pulled a sword from a mighty tree called the Branstock. The sword had been driven into the tree by Odin himself and only the greatest of warriors could pull it free. It was the sword of the gods.

**SIGURD:** The Sword of the Volsungs! If only that sword still existed! Then everyone would see that I'm right.

**NARRATOR:** Sigurd reached a fork in the forest road. One path led to King Alf's hall. The other led to Gnita Heath, where no one dared to journey. The wasteland there was home to a giant worm, a dragon.

**SIGURD:** The sons of Alf allow a dragon to live on their very borders. They have cowardly hearts. If I were a true prince, I would slay that dragon.

**NARRATOR:** But all Regin's words came back to him. He had none of the princely trappings—a mighty steed, armor, a sword.

Sigurd continued on his journey. When

he reached the hall of his step-father, his mother greeted him warmly.

**HJORDIS:**  Sigurd! What a surprise! You came all the way from Regin's forge without even a cloak to keep you warm?

**SIGURD:**  It's warm, Mother. Spring is in the air.

**HJORDIS:**  Winter still has enough strength left to chill. Come to my chambers and sit by the fire.

**SIGURD:**  Mother, I've decided I'm not going back to Regin's forge. I want to stay here to live with you and King Alf!

**HJORDIS:**  Regin has given you an education.

**SIGURD:**  He's also a horrible grouch! He treats me like I'm nothing—but I'm the son of a king! *(pause)* Aren't I?

**HJORDIS:**  Of course, you are. I've told you many times about your father.

**SIGURD:**  Then I have a question, Mother. Where is his sword? Where is the Sword of the Volsungs? You said it was a weapon that was passed down through our line.

**NARRATOR:**  The queen's eyes became faraway and sad.

**HJORDIS:**  It was shattered.

**SIGURD:**  Shattered? But it was forged by the gods!

**HJORDIS:**  And it was shattered by the gods! Oh, I've never told you this because the heartbreak was so great for me. You see, your father died because of me. After he took me as his queen, another king challenged him for my hand. They fought a mighty battle. And no one could stand against your valiant father and his sword—but...

**SIGURD:**  But what?

**HJORDIS:**  Odin had decreed it was your father's time to fall. The god himself appeared on the battlefield. Your father did not recognize him amid the battle, and he swung his sword against Odin's staff. The sword shattered, and the god disappeared.

**SIGURD:**  Odin just left my father there weaponless—to die?

**HJORDIS:**  Death comes to us all—even the gods. And your father met it bravely. The white arms of the valkyries came to carry him to Valhalla, the hall of the valiant slain. So prove yourself worthy in this life, and one day you will meet him there in the golden-roofed hall.

**SIGURD:**  That's what I want to do! I want to be a great warrior like my father—not some nobody blacksmith!

**HJORDIS:**  *(proudly)* Then the time has come.

**NARRATOR:**  The queen opened an aged trunk and delicately drew forth a satin bundle. She unwrapped it before her son.

**HJORDIS:**  Here are the shards of your father's sword. When the battle had ended, I came to him. He had this last request— that the remains of his sword be passed onto you. For you see, Sigurd, you were growing in my womb at that time.

NARRATOR: The boy stared at his mother and took the bundle tenderly from her arms.

HJORDIS: Re-forge the sword. Continue our family's noble line.

SIGURD: I am speechless. It is almost like all my dreams are coming true at once.

HJORDIS: This was your destiny all along. Why do you think I ever agreed to apprentice my son to a blacksmith? I knew someday you would need Regin's skill. Only Regin can re-forge the sword of the gods.

SIGURD: Now I have a sword, but I also need a steed. Will King Alf give me one from among his stallions?

HJORDIS: I'm sure he would be happy to. I will speak to him. Now, go, and make me proud.

NARRATOR: Cradling the remnants of the sword like a newborn child, Sigurd received King Alf's blessing and struck out toward the meadow, where the royal horses ran free. As they gracefully swept the plain, Sigurd's breath was taken away.

SIGURD: *(to himself)* They are all so beautiful. Which one do I choose?

ODIN: Only one of them is truly worthy.

NARRATOR: The voice came from an old man, sitting underneath a nearby shade tree. His body was covered in a traveling cloak. A wide-brimmed hat shadowed his bearded face.

SIGURD: Who are you?

ODIN: A friend. If you wish to know which horse is best, drive them into the river. All of them will be carried downstream except for the mightiest. He will make it safely back to shore. I will help you.

SIGURD: Very well. Help me.

NARRATOR: The herd neared where they stood, and the old man rose and held his walking staff out before him. *(neighing of horses)* At the sight of this, the horses turned their course directly for the roaring river.

ODIN: Behold!

NARRATOR: The horses charged into the churning waters. As the old man had said, the current proved too strong for most of them, and they were swept downstream. Only one steed, flexing his great muscles, powered up onto the far bank.

ODIN: There he is. Grani—the steed sired by Sleipnir, the greatest of horses. Use him well.

SIGURD: Sleipnir? That's the horse of Odin himself!

ODIN: You're catching on.

SIGURD: But how did—?

NARRATOR: The deepening dusk consumed the old man, and he was gone.

When Sigurd returned to Regin's forge riding on a powerful stallion, the blacksmith could hardly believe it.

REGIN: Now you've stolen a horse?

SIGURD: It was gift from King Alf.

**REGIN:** A horse does not make a man. You're a fool for showing your face here again—after the stunt you pulled today!

**SIGURD:** That's not all. I also have a sword.

**REGIN:** A sword? I must be blind!

**NARRATOR:** Sigurd raised the bundle.

**SIGURD:** It is here in this bundle! My mother has given me the shards of my father's sword—Sigmund's sword!

**NARRATOR:** Regin's eyes grew wide.

**REGIN:** The sword of Odin! *(to himself)* After all these years! *(gruffly)* Come inside, boy. Now!

**NARRATOR:** The confused boy followed the blacksmith into his cottage, where Regin immediately barred the door and windows. The only light came from a small candle.

**SIGURD:** What's gotten into you, old man?

**REGIN:** Who else knows about this sword?

**SIGURD:** Just my mother. She is the one who gave it to me.

**REGIN:** But other than her? King Alf? The princes?

**SIGURD:** No. No one.

**REGIN:** Good! Good! Now show it to me!

**NARRATOR:** Sigurd opened the bundle, and the shining shards were revealed.

**REGIN:** *(laugh)* Heh heh! Finally! I have waited five hundred years to see a sword such as this!

**SIGURD:** *(laughing)* Five hundred years? What are you talking about, Regin?

**NARRATOR:** The blacksmith's face bore a strange expression.

**REGIN:** Do you know the wasteland at the edge of this forest? The one that is the home to Fafnir?

**SIGURD:** Fafnir the dragon?

**REGIN:** He is no dragon! He has taken the form of a dragon, but he's a man inside—just like me!

**SIGURD:** I don't know what's more shocking—finding out that Fafnir is really a man or that you are. *(laugh)*

**REGIN:** This is no laughing matter! He stole a treasure from me many years ago, and since that day, I have been watching and waiting for a way to defeat him! Now I have it!

**SIGURD:** This sword? The scales of a dragon can't be pierced with a sword!

**REGIN:** Oh, yes, they can. If the sword is tempered well. But I have never been able to forge one as mighty as this one. The sword of Odin—forged by the gods.

**SIGURD:** Yes, but it's in pieces.

**REGIN:** I can re-forge it. All these long years of waiting have paid off!

**SIGURD:** Waiting? What do you mean?

REGIN: Why do you think I took you in? You are a terrible blacksmith and practically a half-wit! I knew you were the son of Sigmund, and someday his sword might come to you.

SIGURD: So all these years, you've just been using me?

REGIN: Using you? No! Training you! For the greatest battle of your life!

NARRATOR: Regin held up a shield. Wrought into its surface was the image of a fire-red dragon.

REGIN: How else could you stand the creature's poisonous breath? Only if your skin had been seared by years of forge-fire. How could your arm drive the sword through the monster's scales? Only if it had been muscled and tightened by years of pumping the bellows.

SIGURD: I will slay the dragon?

NARRATOR: A demon-light had come into Regin's eyes.

REGIN: Yes, and you will slay him mightily and become the greatest warrior ever known to man! And if immortal glory is not enough for you, think of the treasure! We'll split it—you and I. Even then it will still make you richer than King Alf ten times over!

SIGURD: Gold is the goal of cowards. I want glory!

REGIN: You shall have it! What do you say?

NARRATOR: Sigurd thought of his father—of his great deeds. He thought of Valhalla, the hall of the brave.

SIGURD: I will need my sword re-forged.

REGIN: Of course. You shall have your sword, and *I* will have my revenge.

NARRATOR: Regin flew into the forge, bringing the fire to a vicious heat. He toiled upon the sword throughout the night, muttering strange runes over the shards, reshaping it with all the care of a master craftsman.

When the night was done, Sigurd held in his hands the Sword of the Volsungs complete once again.

REGIN: Behold! The sword is re-forged. It is Gram. Its craftsmanship is exquisite—its design, a work of elegance. All my years of training have come to this.

SIGURD: It's the greatest sight I have ever seen. But still it must be tested.

REGIN: Huh? What are you doing?

NARRATOR: Sigurd placed Regin's dragon-shield upon the anvil and raised his sword.

REGIN: Wait! No! Let it cool first!

NARRATOR: With all his might, Sigurd sliced downward.

SIGURD: *(battlecry)* Ah!

NARRATOR: The sword cleanly cut through the shield and the anvil it rested upon. *(shing)*

**SIGURD:**  Ha-ha! Now Fafnir has cause to fear.

**NARRATOR:**   A crooked grin spread across Regin's face.

**REGIN:**  Yes! That's my boy!

**SIGURD:**  All right, Regin. I will meet this worm—and I will slay him.

**REGIN:**  No. No. We have worked all night. You should rest, gather your strength. This is not some dumb beast. He is a wizard of old!

**SIGURD:**  Whatever he is, I know I will never have more strength than I have right now as I hold my father's sword. Today is the day that Fafnir will perish.

**REGIN:**  Then let us ride to Fafnir's lair!

**NARRATOR:**  Sigurd mounted Grani and lifted the smith up behind him. The steed reared, and his swift legs carried them forward into the dawn-light. Regin shouted over the thundering hooves.

**REGIN:**   You should know that Fafnir's breath is a poisonous fume! Many men have died from inhaling it.

**SIGURD:**  Is this supposed to encourage me?

**REGIN:**   It's better that you know what you are up against. The softest scales are on his underbelly.

**SIGURD:**  So I must be under him to defeat him? But then I will be crushed!

**REGIN:**  Don't worry! I have it all worked out. I've had many long years to plan for this day.

**NARRATOR:**  A sudden thought came to Sigurd's mind: Regin—this strange man who raised him—who was he really? Was he age-less like he claimed to be? And if so, what type of poisoned heart could harbor hatred for five hundred years?

**REGIN:**  You will dig a pit in the path that leads down from Fafnir's lair. He crawls down to the river everyday to drink from its waters. When he passes over the pit, you will stab upward through his underbelly.

**SIGURD:**  You've thought of everything.

**REGIN:**  Then all that gold will be mine! *(catching himself)* I mean—ours!

**SIGURD:**  You can have your gold—as long as I get the glory!

**NARRATOR:**   Soon they entered the devastated land where Fafnir dwelt. The very soil had been poisoned, and blackened trunks of trees stuck up sharply from the ground. Sigurd glimpsed a line of rocky hills, and a yawning cave-mouth in their midst.

**REGIN:**  There is Fafnir's lair. He sleeps during the day, so we will be free to dig. See the path here? This is the avenue he uses on his way to the river. Dig here.

**NARRATOR:**  The blacksmith produced a spade.

**SIGURD:**  Where are you going?

**REGIN:**  Nevermind! Dig! Dig!

**NARRATOR:** Regin disappeared and left Sigurd to his work. The hard earth did not easily yield, and Sigurd dug for many hours. The thought of his future great deeds spurred him on. But at last a strange voice caused him to stop.

**ODIN:** What are you doing? Digging your grave?

**NARRATOR:** From the bottom of his pit Sigurd looked up. There, staring down at him, was the old man in the wide-brimmed hat. One of his eyes seemed to be missing.

**SIGURD:** You again?

**ODIN:** This is a strange place for a grave—just outside a dragon's lair. Most men prefer to die inside of it.

**SIGURD:** I'm not digging a grave, old man! I'm going to slay Fafnir.

**ODIN:** Are you? From this pit?

**SIGURD:** Yes. Why not?

**ODIN:** Well, you look like a strong lad, but I'm worried about your wits. Don't you know that the blood of a dragon is like an acid? So when you stab Fafnir—from this pit—where will his blood will go?

**SIGURD:** Um…into the pit?

**ODIN:** Exactly. So I was right. You are digging your grave.

**SIGURD:** Wait a minute! Who are you?

**NARRATOR:** The brilliance of the sun swallowed the old man completely, and he was gone. With the words of the strange visitor ringing in his mind, Sigurd stopped to re-think the construction of the pit.

**SIGURD:** If I make a couple of narrow tunnels in the side here, I can shimmy through one of them and escape the dragon's blood. There! That is what I will do! *(pause)* Stupid Regin. His original design would have left me dead!

**NARRATOR:** It was nearly dusk when Regin reappeared at the top of Sigurd's pit.

**SIGURD:** I thought maybe you weren't coming back.

**REGIN:** *(whispering)* Have you finished yet?

**SIGURD:** Yes, but I had to reconfigure the—

**REGIN:** Shhhh! The dragon's time is nearly here. Smoke is coming from his lair. He awakens! I found a nice hideout not far away. I will wait there with Grani. Don't fail me, boy!

**NARRATOR:** As Regin disappeared, Sigurd raised his head above the rim of the pit. Green smoke was billowing out from the dragon's lair, and a scrabbling sound came from within it. It was the sound of claws passing over stone. *(scratching sound)* Sigurd gripped the hilt of his father's sword tightly.

**SIGURD:** I must remember the bravery of my father.

**NARRATOR:** At first, only blackness filled the cave-mouth, but then the scaly head of the dragon appeared there—his slitted eyes glowing like jewels in the dusky air. The dragon sniffed the wind and began to inch forward. Sigurd watched the creature's body emerge—his long, serpentine neck, his cruelly-spiked spine, his powerful legs tipped by scythe-like claws, and finally his barbed tail. Fafnir was the most wretched thing Sigurd had ever seen.

Sigurd fell back down into his pit—his hands shaking. As the dragon dragged his armored belly across the rocks, it grated loudly. The ground began to vibrate, and the scratching of the dragon's talons grew into a maddening din. Then it stopped.

**SIGURD:** (to himself) Patience! Patience!

**NARRATOR:** Sigurd slowly inched his eyes upward. The underside of Fafnir's head covered the opening above. The dragon had stopped above his pit, and he was sniffing. And then—to Sigurd's shock—the dragon spoke.

**FAFNIR:** (sniffing) A human. I have not smelled a human in this heath for a hundred years.

**NARRATOR:** The head swung downward, and the beast's yellow eyes locked onto Sigurd.

**FAFNIR:** Ah! There you are! Hiding in a hole, are you? Clever beast! (dragon snarl) Snarl!

**NARRATOR:** Fafnir struck downward, his snout gnashing at the pit. He hissed, and a spray of venom erupted from his glands. (hissing sound) Sigurd dove into one of the side-tunnels he had dug and crawled furiously. He emerged above ground yards away. He could now see the entire length of the dragon stretched out before him. The dragon was thrashing wildly at the pit, trying to fit his snout down inside it. Sigurd saw his chance.

**SIGURD:** Here, worm! Here I am! Here I am!

**NARRATOR:** The dragon looked up, hissed, and clawed his way toward Sigurd, spraying venom as he came.

**FAFNIR:** (raging) We shall see who is the worm! (dragon snarl) Snarl!

**NARRATOR:** With the dragon's jaws only feet from him, Sigurd dropped back into his tunnel and shimmied back toward the pit. When he reached it, the earth was smoking from the dragon's venom, and the body of the dragon covered the opening above. But this is what Sigurd had hoped for. Now the Fafnir's belly-scales were directly overhead.

**SIGURD:** Now, worm, you will taste the bite of Gram, the Sword of the Volsungs!

**NARRATOR:** With all his might, Sigurd drove his sword into the belly of the dragon up to the hilt.

**FAFNIR:** Aaaargh!

**NARRATOR:** As quickly as Sigurd's blow was struck, blood spewed in all directions from the wound. Sigurd dove into his second escape tunnel. Quickly crawling through the narrow passageway, he breathlessly emerged above ground.

The dragon was writhing madly—grasping with his claws at the wound in his stomach. Foul smoke was escaping the wound, which gushed venom and blood, and all the ground around smoked and cracked from toxic fumes.

Sigurd quickly examined his own body. Several spots had been burned from the splattering of the dragon's blood, but he was basically unharmed. He carefully wiped the sword on the ground to remove the dragon's blood. The blade itself was still flawless.

Fafnir had at last ceased his thrashing. His head rested upon the ground—his dull eyes watching Sigurd.

**FAFNIR:** *(weakly)* No blade could have struck me and survived.

**SIGURD:** This is no ordinary sword.

**FAFNIR:** Come closer. I wish to see it.

**SIGURD:** I am not a fool.

**FAFNIR:** *(laugh)* Heh heh. True. No mere fool could have beaten Fafnir. Who are you dragonslayer? Who is your father? Surely he was a great man.

**NARRATOR:** Sigurd wanted to boast of his noble line, but something told him this would not be wise.

**SIGURD:** I have neither father nor mother.

**FAFNIR:** Heh heh. Then it is a miracle that you were born. Please. I'm dying. As a last sign of respect, tell me the name of the man who killed me.

**NARRATOR:** Sigurd eyed the dragon suspiciously.

**SIGURD:** I owe you no respect. I will not tell you my name. Dragons can put a curse on those whom they can name.

**FAFNIR:** Someone wise has taught you. But I have no curse to give. I guess I shall have to go into the next world and tell them that No One the son of Nobody slew me.

**NARRATOR:** This was too much for Sigurd to bear.

**SIGURD:** Fine. I am Sigurd, son of Sigmund, son of Volsung.

**FAFNIR:** Ah! There is a name. Sigurd, the inheritor to my treasure, may it bring you all the happiness it has brought me. *(dry chuckle)*

**SIGURD:** I did not do this for treasure. I will claim none of it.

**FAFNIR:** Oh. It will claim you, dragon-slayer. And before the end, you will wish you had never seen it.

**SIGURD:** Enough! I will not be poisoned by your words!

**FAFNIR:** You have already been poisoned by the words of another. I am no fool. I can see the hand of Regin, my brother, behind all this. It only took him five hundred years, but now he has brought about my death—through you, his instrument.

**SIGURD:** Silence, worm!

**FAFNIR:** My only consolation is that he will bring about your death, as well! Greed and hatred know no bounds, no fidelity, no love. At least there is one lesson I have learned in my long life.

**SIGURD:** Then die and leave us all in peace.

**FAFNIR:** *(low chuckling)* Heh heh. Farewell, Fafnir's Bane.

**NARRATOR:** The light went out of the dragon's eyes, and all was silent.

The dank river from which the dragon watered flowed not too far away. Sigurd made for it and washed.

As Sigurd returned to where Fafnir had

fallen, he saw Regin there, practically dancing with glee. Regin taunted the dead dragon and did not notice Sigurd standing nearby.

**REGIN:** *(happily)* Who has the upper hand now, brother? You never thought I would be able to do it, did you? Ha! But it worked—and so neatly, too! Both of you are dead!

**NARRATOR:** Sigurd appeared at Regin's side.

**SIGURD:** Both of you?

**REGIN:** *(cry of fright)* Ahhh!

**NARRATOR:** The smith jumped at the sound of Sigurd's voice, and his face turned pale.

**REGIN:** *(in shock)* What? I mean—how?

**SIGURD:** How what?

**REGIN:** Oh, my boy! I thought you had perished in the pit! Thanks be to Odin! He has spared you for another day.

**NARRATOR:** Regin patted Sigurd furiously on the back.

**SIGURD:** You should never have doubted me!

**REGIN:** *(half-heartedly)* Well, isn't this great? That means we can *share* the treasure. I won't have to spend it all by myself. That's a relief.

**NARRATOR:** The smile of the blacksmith looked rather pained, but Sigurd failed to notice.

**SIGURD:** Yes, we should go into the dragon's lair and see what we can find in there.

**REGIN:** Hmmm. Good idea. But, first, let *me* go in and check it.

**SIGURD:** Check it for what?

**REGIN:** Oh, you know. Dragon traps and such.

**NARRATOR:** A hissing sound drew their attention. The body of the dragon began to decompose before their eyes. His flesh smoldered and flaked into fragments, which were caught up on the breeze.

**REGIN:** I'll go into the dragon's lair. You stay here and retrieve the dragon's heart for me.

**SIGURD:** His heart?

**REGIN:** *(angrily)* That's what I said, isn't it? *(calming)* I mean, I must eat his heart.

**SIGURD:** This creature was your brother?

**REGIN:** Yes, that's why I must eat the heart. Fafnir was actually a man. So you killed a man—not a monster. But all guilt for this deed will be removed from you and added to me if I eat of his heart.

**SIGURD:** Is that really necessary?

**REGIN:** Just do it! Use that oversized carving knife of yours, dig out his heart, build a fire, and roast it.

**SIGURD:** *(disgusted)* Very well.

**REGIN:** Now, let me go and check on this treasure. You will be a rich man—and a famous warrior, too, after everyone hears of this deed.

NARRATOR: The blacksmith bounded up the hill and disappeared into Fafnir's lair. Sigurd drew near to the dragon's cadaver. The meat of the creature had already been consumed by his rapid decomposition. Strips of skin hung from the massive ribs like tattered banners. The heart—the size of a human head—lay in the midst.

An hour passed, and Regin never returned. At last, Sigurd lit a fire and began to roast the dragon's heart upon a spit. The smell of it drew feathered scavengers—two ravens that perched on a nearby stump and watched his fire greedily.

SIGURD: I have always thought Regin was strange, but to eat a heart!

HUGIN: Squawk!

SIGURD: Shoo! None of this is for you!

NARRATOR: The skin and veins of the heart crackled over the fire. Sigurd reached out to see if the flesh was fully cooked and burned his fingers upon it.

SIGURD: Ouch! The fire must be burning hotter than I thought.

NARRATOR: He popped his burnt fingers into his mouth, and when he did, a tingling sensation spread throughout his entire body.

SIGURD: What is happening?

NARRATOR: He had tasted a bit of the heart of the dragon and absorbed a bit of Fafnir's knowledge. The birds were squawking again, but this time he could hear words within their calls.

HUGIN: Look at that chucklehead. He doesn't even know what's going to happen to him.

NARRATOR: Sigurd's head jerked toward the voice. Had he just heard a bird speak?

MUNIN: What an idiot! I have a brain the side of a seed, but even I could tell the creepy guy was up to no good.

HUGIN: Apparently, this fool doesn't know that eating the dragon's heart will give that other guy all the dragon's knowledge.

MUNIN: His mother must have dropped him on his head. Where does he think that guy has been all this time?

HUGIN: He must think that guy's still in the dragon's lair, but he actually double-backed into the woods.

MUNIN: I heard him muttering something about getting a spear.

HUGIN: Oooh. Then at least we will have some entertainment.

MUNIN: And some dead meat! Brawk!

NARRATOR: The pieces suddenly added up in Sigurd's mind. It had been Regin's plan all along to let him die in the pit—scorched by the dragon's blood. The birds' words told him that Regin must be planning an ambush. Sigurd carefully picked up his sword.

HUGIN: Here we go. There's the creepy one again. He's sneaking up behind the boy. He's got his spear all ready.

MUNIN: What? The chump's just going to sit there? He can slay a dragon, but he's going to be speared in the back by an old— Brawk!

NARRATOR: At that moment Sigurd spun around, his sword at the ready. Through the charred trunks of trees, Regin was coming toward him—a wicked-looking spear held in his grip.

SIGURD: Regin, what are you doing?

REGIN: What does it look like, you thankless brat? Why couldn't you just die like you were supposed to? That would be too easy! Well, now I'm going to fix the problem myself. You will have none of my treasure! (battlecry) Ah!

NARRATOR: Regin flung his expertly crafted weapon, and it cut swiftly through the air. (shoom) But Sigurd's arm was swifter, and he slashed at the spear— cleaving it in half. Its pieces flew harmlessly to either side.

REGIN: No! No!

NARRATOR: Sigurd ran forward and seized the cowering blacksmith in his powerful grip.

REGIN: Please! Please! You wouldn't harm your old master, would you? Think of all the years we spent together! All that I taught you! You are like the son I never had!

SIGURD: (angrily) You used me! You tried to kill me! All for a treasure!

REGIN: (crazy laughter) Heh heh. Oh, wait until you see it, boy. It is a treasure worth dying for—a treasure worth killing for. It

already has its grip on you, and you don't even know it.

SIGURD: This isn't about a treasure. It's about justice!

REGIN: Ha! Fafnir's curse is passed on! You will kill me now, and your heart will tell you it is for justice. But all that you do is for the gold—the treasure with the power to corrupt all men's hearts.

NARRATOR: Sigurd put his sword to Regin's throat.

REGIN: Ack! I knew I should have never re-forged that sword for you. It has shattered my spear and will soon shatter me. But not without a fight! Ah! (battlecry)

NARRATOR: Regin twisted loose from Sigurd's grip. He dove for the fallen shards of his spear, but Sigurd's sword split the air.

REGIN: Ah! (dying cries)

NARRATOR: The smith fell, and his head rolled free of his body.

SIGURD: So long, master.

NARRATOR: Sigurd dragged the body of Regin to lie beside the corpse of Fafnir. There he saw the dragon's skeleton had transformed into that of a man.

SIGURD: What power this treasure must have over men's hearts to make a brother betray a brother! It is truly cursed.

NARRATOR: Sigurd summoned Grani and started to ride away. But something made him turn back. His eyes fell upon Fafnir's lair. He knew deep in the darkness something glittered—a treasure like none other. And his heart desired it.

**SIGURD:**  The treasure is cursed. But you know, Grani, curses are for lesser men. I am a Volsung. *(pause)* I will just have a little look and see what treasures this worm has kept.

**NARRATOR:** Sigurd, Fafnir's Bane, made his way toward the dragon's lair.

## DISCUSSION QUESTIONS

- Is Sigurd a hero? Explain.
- What makes Regin an evil character?
- Does wealth have the power to corrupt? Explain.
- What do you think will happen in the next part of Sigurd's story?
- Why does Sigurd decide to go ahead and see the dragon's treasure—even when he has said that his quest is not about treasure?
- Why does Sigurd believe he will be able to avoid the curse of the treasure?

# THE FALLEN VALKYRIE
## TEACHER GUIDE

### BACKGROUND

Women enjoyed almost equal rights in Norse society. Marriages were arranged, but divorce was easy. Women could publicly state their reasons for divorce, and the marriage was dissolved. (One woman divorced her husband for wearing a shirt that was too fancy for a man.) Women could also inherit property under Norse law. Women lived by the same code of honor as men, spurring their husbands on to be as brave a warrior as they could be. Even the sagas celebrate valiant shield-maidens who fight alongside the men.

Another symbol of equality in life was equality in death. Ceremonial burial ships have been unearthed, wherein male and females are buried alongside their prized possessions. One burial ship contained a rich woman, her wagon, cooking objects, and the body of her female servant. This was the ship designed to bear her through death to Valhalla.

### SUMMARY

Sigurd makes his way into the dragon's lair, where the cursed gold horde lies. The two ravens of Odin warn him that he should not touch the gold, but the hero does not listen, and he takes the treasure and a cursed ring as his own. The birds tell him of a kingdom over the mountain and a mysterious maiden trapped in an enchanted hall on the heights of the mountain. They direct Sigurd to a magical helmet within the horde that allows its wearer to change shape. Taking the dragon's gold, Sigurd sets out for the mountaintop hall. Once there, Sigurd bravely spurs his horse through the wall of flames that surrounds the hall. On the other side he discovers a sleeping maiden, whom he awakens by pulling a thorn from her neck.

The maiden is Brynhild, a valkyrie cursed to a mortal life for disobeying Odin. The man who is brave enough to make it through the wall of flame is to be her husband. Sigurd pledges himself to Brynhild by giving her the cursed ring he took from the dragon's horde. Then he rides off to become a lord in the kingdom of Burgundy.

Once in Burgundy, Queen Grimhild decides that Sigurd should be wed to her daughter—in order to keep his treasure in their kingdom. Sigurd is not interested in the princess though. He tells the queen about his valkyrie maiden atop the mountain. The queen, who is secretly a witch, feeds Sigurd a potion to make him forget his love. Once all memory of Brynhild has been erased, Sigurd marries the princess.

The queen encourages her son, Gunnar, to ride to the mountain and claim the valkyrie maiden as his own wife. She tells him to use Sigurd toward this end. Gunnar cannot make it through the flaming walls because his fear is too great. He asks Sigurd to use his magical helmet to change his shape into that of Gunnar and ride through the flames to claim the maiden in his name. Sigurd does so. Brynhild is shocked to see someone other than Sigurd accomplish this feat. She does not realize it is really Sigurd in disguise, and he does not remember having met her before. Disguised as Gunnar, Sigurd seizes her and takes her back to Burgundy disguised as Gunnar.

Brynhild is forced to marry Gunnar, and she is shocked when she sees Sigurd married to the princess. What is even more shocking is that Sigurd does not seem to remember her. Soon after, the princess tells Brynhild the truth—Sigurd had taken on Gunnar's form in order to retrieve her. Brynhild feels betrayed and decides to take revenge.

Giving Gunnar a potion of rage, Brynhild tricks him into murdering Sigurd in his bed, but Gunnar is also killed in the process. Brynhild orders the son of Sigurd and the princess to be killed as well. The body of Sigurd is laid out in a funeral boat, and the ship is lit. With her revenge complete, Brynhild lies down upon the flaming boat with her love, and they go to Valhalla together.

## ESSENTIAL QUESTIONS

- Should young people listen to the warnings of others?
- Should you always defend your pride?

## ANTICIPATORY QUESTIONS

- What is a valkyrie?
- Can you overcome a curse?
- If you make a promise (but you are tricked into breaking it), should you still be punished?
- Is revenge ever justified?

## CONNECT

*Die Nibelungen (1924)* This pair of epic films is often called *The Lord of the Rings* of the silent era. The director used intricate sets and then-unheard-of special effects to re-tell Sigurd's story. While these films may not inspire the awe today that they did upon release, they are still a fun way to see the story brought to life. Clips from the film can be found at *www.YouTube.com*.

**"What's Opera, Doc?"** This classic Looney Tunes short parodies many aspects of the Volsung saga and Wagner's operas—placing Elmer Fudd in Sigurd's magic helmet and Bugs Bunny in the role of Brynhild.

## TEACHABLE TERMS

- **Myth Motif** This myth bears a striking resemblance to the fairy tale "Sleeping Beauty." A maiden under a spell is a common motif in European mythology and folklore. Discuss other examples of this motif.
- **Idiom** On pg. 214 the raven says, "My beak is sealed." This is wordplay on the common idiom "My lips are sealed" meaning "I will not tell."
- **Plot** The last four script-stories form a cycle known as the Volsung Saga. Discuss how the plot has progressed from the very beginning. The saga covers multiple generations of a single family. How are their stories interrelated?
- **Protagonist** Sigurd enters this script-story as the main character. Discuss whether he is still the protagonist by the end of the story. Has Brynhild assumed that role in his place?
- **Culture** Discuss the ritual of Norse burial ships and funeral pyres. Why were ships used? Why were possessions piled aboard with the deceased?

## RECALL QUESTIONS

1. What does Sigurd's helmet do?
2. Why has Brynhild been put to sleep?
3. How does Sigurd awaken Brynhild from sleep?
4. What makes Sigurd break his promise to Brynhild?
5. Why does Brynhild take her revenge?

# THE FALLEN VALKYRIE

## CAST

| | |
|---|---|
| **SIGURD** | *Hero, Dragonslayer* |
| **HUGIN** | *Raven of Odin* |
| **MUNIN** | *Raven of Odin* |
| **BRYNHILD** | *Fallen Valkyrie* |
| **QUEEN** | *Queen of Burgundy* |
| **GUNNAR** | *Prince of Burgundy* |
| **GUDRUN** | *Princess of Burgundy* |

**NARRATOR:** Sigurd the Dragonslayer stood bathed in gold-glow. Deep within the lair of Fafnir the dragon, mounds of gold cast an eerie, red light over the young warrior. Once this treasure had been Fafnir's, but now it rightfully belonged to Sigurd. Yet, as he had been warned, it came with an ancient curse. He had planned only to view it—to glimpse what horde the dragon held—but now that he saw it, he desired it, like nothing he had ever desired before.

**SIGURD:** *(to himself)* I am a dragonslayer and a Volsung. Curses are for lesser men. This gold will be mine.

*(cawing of crows)*

**NARRATOR:** As Sigurd bent down to examine the treasure more closely, two ravens flew in through the cave-mouth and perched upon a rock.

**HUGIN:** Kaw! Oh boy! Look at that fool!

**NARRATOR:** By eating of the dragon's heart, Sigurd had learned the speech of animals.

**SIGURD:** Be careful, bird. I am wise enough to understand your words.

**HUGIN:** Is that so? If you're so wise, why do you even consider touching that cursed gold?

**MUNIN:** That treasure has been cursed for hundreds of years.

**SIGURD:** It may have cursed Fafnir, but it won't curse me. I am the dragonslayer!

**HUGIN:** *(to Munin)* Kind of conceited, isn't he?

**NARRATOR:** Sigurd pointed to a stunning ring within the horde. It glowed with the same strange, red light as the rest of the treasure.

**SIGURD:** See that ring? A lesser man would quake in fear just to touch it—but not I.

**NARRATOR:** Sigurd picked up the ring and slipped it onto his finger.

**HUGIN:** Oh pinfeathers! He's really asking for it now!

**MUNIN:** Boy, that ring is the most cursed item here! The dragon himself wore it for many years, and it corrupted his heart.

**SIGURD:** He was a beast. I am a man.

**HUGIN:** Fafnir was once a man, too—long ago.

**SIGURD:** All this talk is foolishness. What do a couple of filthy birds know about curses anyway?

**HUGIN:** Plenty.  We are the birds of Odin.

**SIGURD:** Really?

**MUNIN:** How else would we have so much wisdom? We are Thought and Memory.

**SIGURD:** Hmmm. If you are Odin's birds, you can answer me this question—how do I become a mighty lord of Midgard? A single sack full of this treasure will make me richer than any other man in the world. But it is all meaningless without a title—without a kingdom.

**HUGIN:** What will a kingdom prove?

**SIGURD:** It will prove that I am great. *(pause)* But if you cannot answer my question, you must not truly be the birds of Odin…

**MUNIN:** *(sarcastically)* Reverse psychology. How tricky. We can tell you how to become a lord. There is a kingdom over the mountains called Burgundy. There men are made lords because of their bravery and deeds in battle.

**SIGURD:** Burgundy sounds like my kind of place. How do I reach it?

**MUNIN:** You must travel over the high mountain of Hindfell.

**HUGIN:** *(whispering)* Pssst. Don't send him that way! It will take him too close to *you know who*…

**MUNIN:** Oh yeah.  I'd forgotten about her.

**SIGURD:** Who is that?

**HUGIN:** Oh, no one. No one. Just a maiden trapped in a mysterious hall. Nothing you'd be interested in, dragon-boy.

**SIGURD:** Of course, I'm interested.  Tell me more about it.

**HUGIN:** Oh, it's just your typical enchanted hall—surrounded by a wall of flame. But other than that, nothing special. My beak is sealed.

**NARRATOR:** Sigurd stroked his chin shrewdly.

**SIGURD:** Hmmm. What other secret knowledge do you know?

**MUNIN:** See that helmet there? It is priceless.

**SIGURD:** This thing? Don't you mean *worthless.* It's just a beat-up, old helm. There aren't even any jewels on it.

**HUGIN:** Ha! And they say we birds have small brains! That's a *magical* helmet! The

Helm of Awe! With that helmet on your head, you can take any shape you wish.

**SIGURD:** *(in wonder)* Amazing!

**HUGIN:** But we have already said too much. Our master will be displeased with us.

**MUNIN:** Now, we will leave you, dragon-slayer. Fare thee well. Kaw! Kaw!

**NARRATOR:** The two ravens flew from the dragon's lair. Sigurd thoughtfully examined the beat-up helmet.

**SIGURD:** We'll see if these birds know what they're squawking about.

**NARRATOR:** Sigurd placed the helmet upon his head and concentrated on the image of a raven. In an instant he felt his body shrink down into a small, feathered form.

**SIGURD:** I am a bird! *(squawking)* Amazing! Amazing!

**NARRATOR:** He transformed back into his human form.

**SIGURD:** This helmet and this treasure will make me the most famous warrior who ever lived! Now, I must find this mysterious hall and maiden the birds spoke of.

**NARRATOR:** Sigurd packed as much of the treasure as he could onto the back of Grani, his steed. He kept expecting the load to be too much for Grani, but the horse bore much more than he thought possible.

**SIGURD:** You are truly a son of Sleipnir to bear such a heavy burden.

**NARRATOR:** Sigurd pulled at the reins to lead Grani from the cave, but the horse did not move.

**SIGURD:** What is the matter? Is the load too heavy after all?

**NARRATOR:** The steed lowered his head and rubbed his muzzle against his master's arm.

**SIGURD:** Are you sure? Ha! You are the greatest steed in the world!

**NARRATOR:** Sigurd mounted Grani. *(horse neigh)* Grani whinnied and galloped from the cave. *(hoofbeats)* From the scorched realm of Fafnir, Sigurd turned his course toward the towering mountain, Hindfell.

**SIGURD:** We must head up that mountain there, Grani. My destiny awaits me there! I can feel it!

**NARRATOR:** The winter winds blew cruelly against the horse and rider, but they climbed higher and higher up the mountain. Sigurd saw something ahead flickering against the dark sky. He spurred Grani on. At the summit, a towering wall of fire appeared. *(whoosh of flame)*

**SIGURD:** There is the wall of flame. The enchanted hall must lie on the other side. Come, Grani, summon your courage. Run fast and hard! Yah! Yah!

**NARRATOR:** Grani charged forward. No fear stirred in Sigurd's heart, and, sensing this, Grani did not falter. The horse leapt toward the wall of flame and passed cleanly through. *(fiery whoosh)*

**SIGURD:** Good boy! We have made it! Look! There is the hall!

NARRATOR:    Sigurd dismounted and drew his sword. *(shing)*

SIGURD:  Wait here while I investigate.

NARRATOR:  The hall was dark and silent. Sigurd advanced and passed inside. A single candle burned within, and only one thing adorned the strange hall—a carved block of stone and upon it lay a body. Sigurd drew closer.

SIGURD:  Hello?

NARRATOR:  A hanging veil surrounded the body, and Sigurd pulled it back. The form appeared to be a corpse—bedecked in the armor of a warrior.

SIGURD:  Is this a hall or a tomb? Where is the maiden the birds spoke of? And who is this warrior?

NARRATOR:  Sigurd sheathed his sword and leaned down to examine the body. The man's face and features were very delicate, and his chain mail seemed to be so old that it had grafted onto his skin.

SIGURD:    Perhaps there is some clue beneath his armor.

NARRATOR:  Sigurd took the brittle chain mail into his grip and easily ripped it asunder. *(ripping sound)*

SIGURD:  *(shocked)* What is this?

NARRATOR:  Beneath the armor were rich garments—the clothing of a maiden.

SIGURD:  This is most strange!

NARRATOR: Then Sigurd removed the warrior's helmet, and a cascade of golden hair fell loose from it.

SIGURD:  *(shocked)* A maiden!

NARRATOR:  Before Sigurd lay the most beautiful woman he had ever seen.

SIGURD:  She must be under some kind of enchantment! I must wake her—at any cost.

NARRATOR:    He leaned forward and planted a tender kiss upon her lips.

SIGURD:  *(amorously)* Awake, my beauty.

NARRATOR:  The maiden remained still.

SIGURD:    Hmmm. I thought that would work.

NARRATOR:    Sigurd ran his fingers through the maiden's hair, and as he did, the action revealed a thorn stuck into the flesh of her white neck. He plucked it loose. Her beautiful eyes flew open.

BRYNHILD:  Ah! *(battlecry)*

NARRATOR:  The maiden sprang up with full force, and Sigurd was thrown backward to the ground. She stood upon her stone bed—hair flowing and eyes flashing.

BRYNHILD:    *(roaring)* Who awakens Brynhild, the mightiest of the valkyries?

NARRATOR:  Sigurd stared up at her in wonder, as he struggled to regain his voice.

SIGURD:    I—I do! Sigurd the dragon-slayer.

NARRATOR: The maiden arched a delicate eyebrow.

BRYNHILD: Dragonslayer, you say? Stand up and face me!

NARRATOR: She reached down and jerked the young hero to his feet.

BRYNHILD: Stand up straight! Hmmm. Your stature is not as intimidating as I hoped, but you will do.

SIGURD: Do for what?

BRYNHILD: My husband.

SIGURD: Husband?

BRYNHILD: Since you have passed through the fire and awoken me, you are to be my husband.

SIGURD: Who are you?

BRYNHILD: I am no one now. But once I was a mighty battlemaiden. The daughter of Odin All-Father! I was the leader of the valkyries—immortal and invincible!

SIGURD: I have always heard stories of the valkyries.

BRYNHILD: They are more than stories! They are truth! My shieldmaidens and I rode the clouds, dropping the gods' judgment upon the warring lords of the earth. Kings died bitter deaths when *I* turned the tides against them. And when I placed my shield over them, they lived to fight again. When noble warriors fell in battle, we valkyries carried them to Valhalla with our white arms.

SIGURD: But you are beautiful. I had always heard that the valkyries were skeletal hags with vicious nails and eyes that dripped blood.

BRYNHILD: To the defeated, yes. But to the victorious we look like this.

SIGURD: This is much more pleasing! So what are you doing in this place?

BRYNHILD: My pride became too much for me. I was given orders by Odin, but I chose to disobey them. I caused a battle to turn against his will. And for that, I was punished. He declared that I should lose my immortality and marry a mortal man.

SIGURD: I pulled this thorn from your skin.

BRYNHILD: Yes. That is the Thorn of Sleep that he stuck into my flesh. Before he condemned me though, I begged him to give me only the bravest of men as my husband. My father had enough love left for me to grant me that! Imagine *me* wed to a man who was not my equal in bravery and deeds. Ha! So he put me here, in a magical hall surrounded by fire, so only the bravest man alive would ever find me.

SIGURD: That is I!

BRYNHILD: Yes. Apparently. Tell me more of your deeds, and I shall do the same.

NARRATOR: Neither of them knew how long they spoke together in the enchanted hall. Brynhild shared much of her secret knowledge with Sigurd, who in turn told Brynhild of his ancestors the Volsungs, the forging of his sword, Gram, and his adventure with the dragon.

**BRYNHILD:** I see that you are a great warrior, but I assume you are also some kind of king or prince.

**SIGURD:** I am neither. *(pause)* Like I said before, I used to be a blacksmith. *(pause)* Well, a blacksmith's apprentice actually…

**NARRATOR:** The maiden wrinkled her nose disdainfully.

**BRYNHILD:** Hmmm. This is not good.

**SIGURD:** I have no title, but I do possess great wealth—all the treasure I took from the dragon.

**BRYNHILD:** *(not impressed)* Wealth is nothing without a title.

**SIGURD:** I have plans to be great though. I'm journeying to the land of Burgundy. I hope to win fame among its people and claim a title there.

**BRYNHILD:** Very well. I will wait here.

**SIGURD:** Wait for what?

**BRYNHILD:** For you to gain a title. Then you can return and claim me as your bride.

**SIGURD:** You mean, you won't come with me?

**BRYNHILD:** Most certainly not! I'm not leaving here to become the wife of some commoner! *(pause)* But, not to worry, I am yours when you return to claim me.

**NARRATOR:** Brynhild extended her hand to Sigurd, and he kissed it.

**SIGURD:** I do desire to have you as my wife. What man wouldn't?

**BRYNHILD:**    Naturally! Now pledge yourself to me!

**SIGURD:** Brynhild, I give you my pledge to return and make you my wife.

**BRYNHILD:** I think it is customary to give a token of affection to your lady.

**SIGURD:** I have nothing to give you.

**BRYNHILD:** What about that ring?

**NARRATOR:** The cursed ring glowed upon Sigurd's finger.

**SIGURD:** Oh, yes. Take the dragon's ring and wear it. It is a symbol of my pledge to you.

**NARRATOR:** He slipped the ring onto her finger.

**BRYNHILD:** Hmmm. The sight of this ring pleases me. Very well. I will consent to be your wife. But let me warn you—I am not one who is lightly dishonored. Do not forget your promise.

**NARRATOR:** Sigurd drew near and kissed the maiden.

**BRYNHILD:** You have proven yourself worthy to be my husband. And I admit—I smile at the thought of our marriage. Do not lose your way back to this place.

**SIGURD:** Never!

**BRYNHILD:** Now, go!

**NARRATOR:** So Sigurd left his newfound love there in her enchanted hall—the cursed ring of the dragon glistening upon her finger.

As Sigurd traveled on, the thought of the beautiful sky-maiden made his heart light. He traveled down the far side of the mountain into the land of Burgundy. A great hall stood in the valley, and Sigurd spurred Grani toward it.

Heralds signaled his approach, and when Sigurd entered the great hall, he was taken before Grimhild, the queen of that land.

**QUEEN:** Welcome, stranger. What brings you to Burgundy?

**SIGURD:** I have heard tales of your kingdom and your great respect for warriors. Do you rule here?

**QUEEN:** My son, the prince, rules our kingdom. But he is away hunting. What is your name, stranger?

**SIGURD:** I am Sigurd, the slayer of Fafnir.

**QUEEN:** Fafnir? Ha! What a wild story! If you slayed Fafnir, you would have a mighty treasure at your disposal.

**SIGURD:** I do.

**NARRATOR:** Sigurd displayed a sack of treasure before the queen. Its red glow filled the hall.

**QUEEN:** *(breathlessly)* My boy!

**SIGURD:** There is more where that came from, too.

**QUEEN:** You must stay here with us! I have told you of my son, but I also have a beautiful daughter. It would be a great honor for us if you would take her as a wife.

**NARRATOR:** Sigurd bowed humbly.

**SIGURD:** I am sorry, my queen. My heart is already pledged to another and cannot be swayed.

**QUEEN:** *(annoyed)* But you have not even seen the princess yet. I assure you that you will find her most pleasing.

**SIGURD:** No woman on earth can rival the lady I love. She is not of this earth.

**QUEEN:** *(intrigued)* Really? Tell me more.

**NARRATOR:** Sigurd told the queen about the mysterious hall high in the mountains and how he had bravely woken the maiden within. He held no detail back, and as he told his story, the features of the queen grew colder and colder.

**QUEEN:** Hmmm. An amazing tale. Well, if you are pledged, then you are pledged. But, please, stay and feast with us! My son will return tomorrow.

**NARRATOR:** What Sigurd did not realize was that Queen Grimhild was no ordinary woman. She was a witch studied in the dark arts.

That very evening, in the secrecy of her chambers, she brewed a special potion—one that clouded the memory of love. Then at the feast that evening, the witch-queen served the potion up to the warrior.

**QUEEN:** We welcome a mighty hero to our hall—the mighty dragonslayer. Drink, Sigurd! Drink to your new home and your new friends here in Burgundy.

**NARRATOR:** Sigurd drank deeply, and the potion caused him to forget. He forgot the mysterious hall upon the mountain. He forgot the magical wall of fire. He forgot his love, who waited in the midst of the flames.

Sigurd dwelt in Burgundy for years. He fought many battles with the young prince, Gunnar, and made the name of the Burgundians great. The queen's magic held firm. Never once did the memory of Brynhild enter into Sigurd's mind.

As the queen had planned, Sigurd married the princess Gudrun and became a lord of Burgundy. He had gained the title he sought—but he had forgotten the reason he had first sought it.

Because of Sigurd's prowess as a warrior, his popularity among the people grew. But the queen and the prince began to view him with a jealous and suspicious eye.

**QUEEN:** Sigurd grows more beloved every day! If the people had a choice, they would pick him as their ruler instead of you.

**GUNNAR:** If only…

**QUEEN:** Watch your tongue! Ever since your father died, I have worked tirelessly to make you a mighty ruler. Now you're going to throw it away and let him steal your throne? I had your sister marry him because of his gold, but he must never inherit the crown. Burgundy will not be ruled by a nobody!

**GUNNAR:** He's not a nobody. *(mockingly)* He's a dragonslayer.

**QUEEN:** Ha! Any fool can slay a dragon. The people are too easily swayed. They love those foolish stories and tales. If only you had done some great feat instead of Sigurd. *(pause)* Wait a minute. *(thinking)* Yes, it just might work! *(to Gunnar)* Son, I think it is time that you took a wife.

**GUNNAR:** Mother, I'm enjoying my freedom. The last thing I need is a wife.

**QUEEN:** *(angrily)* I command you!

**GUNNAR:** Try your mind-control spells on someone else.

**QUEEN:** Sigurd may have slain a dragon, but you will have your own adventure to tell. You will marry the very daughter of Odin himself—a beautiful valkyrie maiden who lies trapped in an enchanted hall atop the mountain.

**GUNNAR:** You don't really believe that old story do you?

**QUEEN:** I do! Sigurd has been there. He saw her himself! He told me about it when he came here!

**GUNNAR:** That's funny. He's never mentioned it to me. And he thinks we are the best of friends.

**QUEEN:** That's because he's forgotten.

**GUNNAR:** How could he forget such a thing?

**QUEEN:** Ha! You underestimate your mother. I *made* him forget with one of my potions.

**GUNNAR:** Clever Mother.

**QUEEN:** Now you must go to this hall and claim the maiden for yourself. The people will eat it up! A mysterious maiden rescued from an enchanted hall. Why, they'll forget all about the dragonslayer!

**GUNNAR:** Then I guess I'll leave at once.

**QUEEN:** Take Sigurd with you.

**GUNNAR:** Why? I don't need *him.*

QUEEN:   Use him to your advantage, however you can. But remember, you have sworn a blood-brother oath with him! So do not harm him.

GUNNAR:  Fine.

NARRATOR:  Gunnar told Sigurd of his new quest, and they readied themselves for the ride to the peak of Hindfell.

SIGURD:  (strangely) A mysterious hall, you say? All surrounded by fire?

GUNNAR:  (shrewdly) Yes. Are you sure you've never heard of it?

SIGURD:  (pause) No. I have not.

GUNNAR:  Interesting…

NARRATOR:  They rode to the mountain summit, and there the flaming walls came into view. At the sight of them, Gunnar's courage started to fail.

GUNNAR:  (nervously) Hmmm. Those walls are higher than I expected. And that fire looks pretty hot. Maybe this isn't such a good idea.

NARRATOR:  Sigurd was staring at the fires strangely.

SIGURD:  I feel as if I have seen these walls before—as if in a dream.

GUNNAR:  (angrily) Then dream me to the other side of them!

SIGURD:  You have nothing to worry about. Just ride hard and fast.

GUNNAR:  That's easy for you to say! All right. I'll give it a try. Yah! Yah!

NARRATOR:  Gunnar charged close to the flame, but the heat caused his steed to rear. (nervous neighing)

GUNNAR:  Argh! The horse is spooked. I can go no further. This will never work!

SIGURD:  Here. You can ride Grani. As long as you feel no fear, he will not.

NARRATOR:  Sigurd dismounted and offered Gunnar his steed.

GUNNAR:  Very well.

NARRATOR:  But neither would Grani approach the flames. The horse could sense the fear in the Gunnar's heart.

GUNNAR:  It's no use! You must go for me.

SIGURD:  Me?

GUNNAR:  My mother told me that old helmet you wear has magical powers. It allows you to change your shape, right? You must change forms to look like me. Then ride through these flames and claim the maiden who sleeps on the far side.

SIGURD:  It is your place to win her.

GUNNAR:  Do it, Sigurd! As your prince, I command you to do this for me!

SIGURD:  What should I tell the maiden?

GUNNAR:  Tell her nothing. She will think I was the one who saved her. By our oath of blood-brotherhood, I command you to do this.

SIGURD:  Fine. I do not like it, but since you press me, I will.

**NARRATOR:**  Sigurd placed his helmet upon his head, closed his eyes, and in a flash, he took on the likeness of Gunnar.

**SIGURD:**  *(different voice)* I am Gunnar!

**GUNNAR:**  Ha! Perfect! My own mother would not be able to tell us apart!

**NARRATOR:**  Sigurd mounted Grani, who nimbly leapt through the walls of flame. Sigurd thought this act had a strangely familiar feeling to it, but the magic of Grimhild still clouded his mind. The valkyrie's hall now stood before him—a single candle burning in its window.

   The years of Sigurd's absence had been long for Brynhild. She thought often of the handsome warrior who would be her husband. He was off in the world winning glory, which was fitting. Only the greatest of men would be worthy of a valkyrie.

   Within her hall, Brynhild heard the sound of an approaching horse.

**BRYNHILD:**  My husband has returned! At last!

**NARRATOR:**  She ran to the doorway but stopped short. A stranger was approaching.

**BRYNHILD:**  *(in shock)* It can't be! That is the same horse but a different rider. *(loudly)* Halt! Who are you? What do you want here?

**SIGURD:**  Maiden, I have passed through the flames. I now claim you as my wife.

**BRYNHILD:**  Only one man is brave enough to reach this place—and you are not he.

**SIGURD:**  I am Gunnar of Burgundy. I have passed the test. You must come with me!

**BRYNHILD:**  Never!

**NARRATOR:**  Sigurd-Gunnar swung from his horse and approached the maiden.

**SIGURD:**  Come with me or face the consequences!

**BRYNHILD:**  No!

**NARRATOR:**  Sigurd seized the woman's wrists, but she struggled violently against him.

**SIGURD:**  There is no need to resist. You are to be my wife.

**BRYNHILD:**  I won't! I won't!

**NARRATOR:**  Brynhild suddenly realized she was helpless. She was a slave to Odin's curse. This man had passed the flames, and she must go with him.

   The man eyed the ring glowing upon her finger.

**SIGURD:**  This ring…

**BRYNHILD:**  See! My *true* husband gave me this ring.

**SIGURD:**  I *am* your true husband now.

**NARRATOR:**  He forced the ring from her finger.

**BRYNHILD:**  *(to herself)* My husband! Where are you? Why is this happening?

**NARRATOR:** Sigurd hoisted the maiden onto Grani, and at his spurring, the steed leapt back through the flames.

**GUNNAR:** I can't believe it! You actually did it! What has happened to her?

**SIGURD:** The flames must have caused her to faint. Here. Take her. Quickly!

**NARRATOR:** Gunnar laid the limp maiden upon the ground as Sigurd removed his helmet—returning to his true form.

**GUNNAR:** Now, remember, Sigurd. Don't breathe a word of this! As far as anyone is concerned, *I* saved this maiden.

**SIGURD:** I have done what you asked, but I will not lie to my wife.

**GUNNAR:** Fine. Tell her if you must. But no one else shall know.

**NARRATOR:** So Brynhild, the mysterious maiden of the flaming hall, became the bride of Gunnar, prince of Burgundy.

Brynhild's shock was great when she beheld Sigurd in the royal hall—married to the princess Gudrun. The unfaithful cad even pretended that he did not recognize his former love. Brynhild wanted to go to him, speak to him, ask him why he had forsaken her, but her pride prevented it.

**BRYNHILD:** He has thrown me over for a princess. So be it.

**NARRATOR:** Gunnar used the tale of Brynhild's rescue to bolster his popularity among his own people.

**GUNNAR:** Sure, Sigurd slew a dragon, but did he brave ten-foot-high walls of flame?

Only the bravest man in the world could have done so. *(to Brynhild)* Isn't that right, dear?

**BRYNHILD:** *(coldly)* It is as you say.

**NARRATOR:** Brynhild could not understand how a foolish coward like Gunnar had passed the fires of her hall. She resolved herself to a lifeless existence. The sight of Sigurd, his wife, and young son caused Brynhild daily pain, and she nursed a bitter hatred toward them all.

Brynhild treated Sigurd's wife with an icy indifference, and the princess came to resent Brynhild in return. One day, when the women of the royal household went down to the Rhine River to swim and bathe, the princess confronted Brynhild.

**GUDRUN:** Why do you always stare at me with such contempt? Is it because you are jealous of my husband?

**BRYNHILD:** Jealous of Sigurd? Ha. Your husband is a faithless fool.

**GUDRUN:** How dare you say such things! He slayed a mighty dragon!

**BRYNHILD:** A coward like him could never have done that. The dragon must have died from old age—or was suicidal. *(snotty laugh)*

**GUDRUN:** And what has *your* husband ever done?

**BRYNHILD:** Well, let's see. He charged through flaming walls to rescue me.

**GUDRUN:** Did he?

**BRYNHILD:** Are you calling me a liar?

**GUDRUN:** Oh, foolish Brynhild. Do you really think my weak-livered brother could ride through supernatural flames? Only a *real* man could do that.

**BRYNHILD:** What do you mean? Explain yourself.

**GUDRUN:** Gunnar didn't rescue you. Sigurd did.

**BRYNHILD:** Ha! I knew you were ugly, but now I see you are stupid as well!

**GUDRUN:** (*yelling*) It's true! Sigurd has a magical helmet, and he made himself look like Gunnar. But it was Sigurd who saved you! He told me himself!

**BRYNHILD:** A liar can say anything.

**GUDRUN:** Where do you think I got this ring? Sigurd said he took it from your very finger.

**NARRATOR:** Brynhild stopped short. There was the red ring upon the princess's finger. Why hadn't she ever noticed it before? Everything suddenly made sense to her. Only Sigurd could have claimed her as his bride—and only Sigurd did.

**BRYNHILD:** I—I—

**NARRATOR:** Brynhild blushed—humiliation rushing upon her. Sigurd had tricked her, made her the wife of a fool. Things were far worse than she ever could have imagined. She ran from the river, back to the royal hall, and locked herself in her room.

For three days and nights, she would admit no one to her room. At last she heard a voice entreating her through the wooden door. It was Sigurd.

**SIGURD:** Brynhild? Open the door.

**BRYNHILD:** (*to herself*) Fine. I will see what the snake has to say for himself.

**NARRATOR:** Brynhild allowed Sigurd to enter.

**BRYNHILD:** You have a lot of nerve to come here!

**SIGURD:** Your husband asked me to speak to you. He does not know what my wife has said to you, but he knows you are upset.

**NARRATOR:** All the emotions that Brynhild had felt for so long broke free.

**BRYNHILD:** (*passionately*) Sigurd, how could you do this to me?

**SIGURD:** What do you mean?

**BRYNHILD:** On the mountain, you promised me—you promised to marry me. Why did you dishonor your promise?

**SIGURD:** What? What do you mean? (*pause*) Wait.

**NARRATOR:** Brynhild's words caused memory to flood back into his mind. The witch-queen's magic had grown too weak to hold back the tide.

**SIGURD:** (*gasping*) No! No! I have been tricked, Brynhild! I remember it all now. Something made me forget!

**BRYNHILD:** A likely excuse! Admit it! You promised yourself to me, but when you saw this pretty princess, you had to have her—even if it meant dishonoring me.

SIGURD: No! That's not it! I don't know what happened, but as soon as I came here, I forgot all about you—

BRYNHILD: Ha! I didn't expect you to admit it so freely.

SIGURD: No, that's not what I meant! But I remember my love for you now! I love you, Brynhild! I do!

NARRATOR: Sigurd covered his face with his hands.

SIGURD: What can we do? What can we do?

BRYNHILD: Nothing. You have your wife. I have my husband. What a wonderful existence you have made for us here.

SIGURD: Please. What if I leave her? What if we run away from this place?

BRYNHILD: (enraged) Do not dishonor me! I fell for your lies once! I'll never believe them again!

SIGURD: Brynhild! Please!

BRYNHILD: Get out of my sight. You disgust me.

NARRATOR: Brynhild would not listen to any of Sigurd's pleas for forgiveness. Finally he went away—brokenhearted and helpless.

BRYNHILD: That, wolf! He must think I'm a complete fool! I will punish him for this! No one dishonors Brynhild.

NARRATOR: Brynhild went at once to find her husband. She flew at him and struck him roughly across the face. (smack)

GUNNAR: Ah! (cry of pain)

BRYNHILD: You sniveling coward!

GUNNAR: What is the meaning of this?

BRYNHILD: You deceived me! I should have known that no spineless worm like you could have braved the walls of flame!

GUNNAR: Lower your voice! Do you want someone to hear you?

BRYNHILD: I know that it was Sigurd who claimed me! I thought it was you all these years. You fooled the whole world into believing you were a hero—even me!

GUNNAR: You won't tell anyone about this, will you?

BRYNHILD: Is that all your worried about? Your reputation? Ha! Well, fine. I promise I won't tell a soul—if you end Sigurd's life.

GUNNAR: Well, that seems a little hasty—

BRYNHILD: Do it! Or the whole kingdom will know your secret!

GUNNAR: I can't! Sigurd is a mighty warrior. He slayed a dragon!

BRYNHILD: Weakling!

GUNNAR: I'd like to see him dead as much as you! I'd love to be rid of him! He's always lording his precious dragon-treasure over us! But it's not worth risking my neck over. The answer is no!

BRYNHILD: Coward!

**NARRATOR:** The old valkyrie fire had come into Brynhild's eyes.

**BRYNHILD:** I will not rest until I see him dead before me!

**NARRATOR:** Brynhild stormed off to the chambers of the old queen. Grimhild, who had become hunched and emaciated with age, huddled in a chair by the fire.

**QUEEN:** *(old voice)* What do you want from me, sky-maiden?

**BRYNHILD:** Give me the last bit of your rune-knowledge.

**QUEEN:** *(dry chuckle)* Why should I give it to you?

**BRYNHILD:** Because I'm going to use it to kill Sigurd.

**NARRATOR:** The eyes of the old witch glittered.

**QUEEN:** Ah! Then the red gold will be finally ours. It will be with our house forever.

**BRYNHILD:** You can keep the gold. I want revenge! Now teach me to make a potion that will drive a man wild with murderous rage.

**QUEEN:** Gladly.

**NARRATOR:** The old queen spoke the words, and as soon as they were whispered, the last breath of life left her. She slumped forward in her chair.

**BRYNHILD:** So long, foolish witch. You have spoken the words that will doom your house forever. *(cruel laugh)*

**NARRATOR:** Brynhild went to work mixing a concoction of serpent venom and wolf's flesh. She dipped it out into a goblet and carried it to her husband.

**GUNNAR:** What is this?

**BRYNHILD:** A toast to the death of Sigurd.

**GUNNAR:** I'll drink to that.

**NARRATOR:** Gunnar drank deeply. The goblet clattered to the floor, and Gunnar grasped his stomach.

**GUNNAR:** *(cry of pain)* Ughn. What is happening? What have you put inside of me?

**BRYNHILD:** It is my rage, Gunnar. My wrath! My courage! You will now become the instrument of my revenge.

**GUNNAR:** *(painful cry)* I—I—I must do whatever you command me to do.

**BRYNHILD:** Spoken like a true husband. All the household is now asleep. Go to Sigurd's chambers and drive a sword into his unfaithful heart.

**GUNNAR:** But—I have sworn an oath of brotherhood—

**BRYNHILD:** Do it!

**NARRATOR:** Gunnar writhed in pain.

**GUNNAR:** *(cry of pain)* I must! I must!

**NARRATOR:** The potion took hold of him. His eyes became red with a supernatural rage, and he seethed like a berserker.

**GUNNAR:** *(raging)* Arrrrrrrgh!

BRYNHILD: *Strike!*

NARRATOR: Gunnar seized up his sword and disappeared into the darkness.

Brynhild smiled a satisfied smile. She seated herself, smoothed out her robes, and waited. In the quiet corridors, a sudden succession of cries rang out. *(screaming and wailing)* Men-at-arms were rushing through the hallways—confused shouting coming from all directions.

BRYNHILD: Now. Gunnar has done his deed. Let us see his handiwork.

NARRATOR: Passing through the hallways, her robes billowing about her, Brynhild recalled her former valkyrie glory.

BRYNHILD: Once I rode the black clouds over the battlefields of Midgard—doling out death. Tonight I do the same.

NARRATOR: She neared the chambers of Sigurd. Blood ran red on the floor. Servants were running this way and that, crying out. Two of them held the weeping form of the princess between them.

GUDRUN: *(weeping)* No! No!

NARRATOR: Brynhild sneered and stepped past the princess and into Sigurd's chamber. Upon the blood-stained bed was a body. It was Sigurd—run through with Gunnar's sword.

BRYNHILD: *(softly)* I'm sorry, my love. This was the only way I could have you.

NARRATION: Another mangled body lay upon the floor. It belonged to Gunnar. Gram—Sigurd's sword—stuck up from his back.

BRYNHILD: Well, husband, I guess the dragonslayer still had enough strength to kill. This has all worked out so neatly. Now I am rid of you as well.

NARRATOR: The servants were amassing in the doorway. They were looking to Brynhild with terrified glances. What did this all mean?

BRYNHILD: *(sternly)* Sigurd is dead. He was a traitor. Prince Gunnar was punishing him for his treachery, but he was slain in the process.

NARRATOR: The frantic princess appeared from the hallway.

GUDRUN: *(screaming)* She's killed my husband! She's killed my husband!

BRYNHILD: The princess is mad with grief. Take her to her chambers and lock her there.

GUDRUN: You can't do this! No!

BRYNHILD: For Sigurd's treachery, the son of Sigurd must die as well.

GUDRUN: No! He's just a boy! You can't!

BRYNHILD: I am the ruler of Burgundy now! I do what I will. Prepare Sigurd's body for the death ship. I will see him burn.

GUDRUN: No! No!

BRYNHILD: Oh. I almost forgot.

NARRATOR: Brynhild caught the shaking hand of the princess and pried the gleaming ring from her finger.

**BRYNHILD:**  I claim this ring which is rightfully mine.

**NARRATOR:**  So much sadness was dealt that night. Sigurd, a hero whom ten men could not have slain in battle, lay murdered by the hand of his blood-brother. Sigurd's young son, too, had been put to the sword. The fury of the valkyrie had descended upon Burgundy.

The morning broke, but the shamed sun hid behind a layer of gloom. The body of Sigurd—dressed in grave-clothes—lay in a ship upon the waters of the river Rhine. Gram had been cleaned and fixed into his grip. Upon his pale brow was the Helm of Awe. The dead form of his son and Grani, his freshly-slain steed, lay beside him. Dry twigs and sticks had been packed in all around them.

Brynhild stood near the death-ship's prow and watched all this with a stony gaze.

**BRYNHILD:**  *(loudly)* So passes Sigurd, Fafnir's Bane. Let this be a lesson to all. Even the mighty can fall.

**NARRATOR:**  Servants came forward and applied torches to the kindling of the ship. Flames sprang up to engulf everything within. *(crackling of a fire)* The fire reflected in Brynhild's eyes.

**BRYNHILD:**  *(quietly)* You have died bravely, my mortal love. Do not worry. I will bear you to Valhalla.

**NARRATOR:**  Of its own accord, the ship began to drift out to sea. Brynhild turned and faced the onlookers.

**BRYNHILD:**  Sigurd travels to the next world! But he will not go alone.

**NARRATOR:**  Brynhild threw herself onto the flames of the boat. Amid the blaze, she laid her body down by the side of her love—and died.

Some who were gathered there swore that they saw a strange sight that day. It was Brynhild, as a shining valkyrie once again, riding the billowing smoke of the pyre up to the heights of Valhalla. And thrown across her steed was the fallen form of Sigurd, her beloved.

## DISCUSSION QUESTIONS

- Why is this story a tragedy?
- What is Sigurd's tragic flaw?
- What is Brynhild's tragic flaw?
- What part does Sigurd's treasure play in his downfall?
- Was Brynhild right to take her revenge as she did? Explain.
- Since Sigurd and Brynhild will be together in Valhalla, does this story actually have a happy ending? Explain.

# SO YOU WANT TO BE A VIKING

There are plenty of legends about Vikings: They were menacing warriors with names like Eric Bloodaxe and Thorfinn Skullsplitter, who wore horned helmets and drank mead from the skulls of their enemies. But what is the reality behind this race of ferocious fighting men?

As most people know, the Vikings were raiders from Scandinavia (modern Norway, Sweden, and Denmark). They sailed their well-engineered long-ships across the seas to ransack the other kingdoms of Europe. With their swift shifts they could attack in lightning swoops with no advance warning. Most of their long-ships were powered by sixty oarsmen, who (once the ship was beached) drew their swords to become sixty fearsome warriors. Europe lived in fear of these types of raids for three centuries.

But in spite of all these fearsome details, Vikings may be one of the most misunderstood groups of people in history. Sure, they did do most of the things the history books say they did—plenty of murdering and pillaging—but, in their defense, they didn't know any better! The Europeans who wrote about the Vikings classified themselves as "highly civilized" and, along with all other Christian kingdoms, shared a code of rules that all people should live by. The trouble was that the Vikings didn't know the rules of "civilization." They weren't civilized and didn't care to be.

The first recorded Viking act of terror happened at Lindisfarne, an island off the coast of England that was home to a wealthy Christian monastery—full of gold and other valuable trinkets used in the service of the Church. Everyone in civilization knew that it was bad manners to attack a monastery. After all, the monks who lived there were in peaceful service to God. But here came the Vikings, who had no idea what a monastery was. They weren't Christians. They had their own gods, who told them the strongest person is always the best. So what did they do? They sailed right up to the monastery and began looting it. It had no defenses because who would ever attack a monastery? After butchering most of the monks and enslaving the rest, the Vikings sailed back home—patting each other on the back for doing such a good day's work.

When the civilized kingdoms of Europe heard about this, they were in shock! Who were these long-haired demons from across the sea—these monsters that would dare murder holy men in cold-blood? They feared the Vikings for the same reason they hated them—they had no rules.

The word *Viking* most likely comes from the Norse word for "bay" and is a verb that means "raider" or "pirate." But the truth is that many Vikings were first farmers. And while this may diminish their bloodthirsty image, they were farmers who were willing to cross the sea and ruthlessly kill in order to obtain new land. In fact, while some Vikings raided other lands and returned home, others came, conquered, and stayed. The other lands of Europe offered them more of a life than their old home.

There are many different theories about what made the Vikings leave their home. The most likely is that Scandinavia became overpopulated, forcing many young men to sail out and look for land elsewhere. Good farmland was in short supply. Plus, laws said all property should pass from a father to his oldest son. If he had five sons, that left four sons with no land—no way of supporting themselves. What could they do? A-Viking they will go!

Vikings weren't the upper-class of Norse society—not kings and dukes and such. Those types of people had plenty of land. Vikings were the outcasts—social misfits, criminals, or sons who couldn't get any land from their fathers. (Eric the Red was an outlaw in Iceland before he left for Greenland.) They were men who were left with no choice but to journey afar and look for their living.

The Vikings were amazing colonizers. Around 860 A.D. Viking settlers moved to Iceland and colonized it. Then about a hundred years later, Eric the Red discovered Greenland, and by its name, tricked settlers there. Around 992 A.D. Eric's son, Leif Ericson, became the first European to discover North America. The Vikings even tried several times to settle there, but the Native Americans drove them away.

The Vikings were not polite about what they took. This was a thousand years before real estate agents. If a home looked good to them, they'd take it. Imagine a boat-load of single men arriving on the shores. After land, the next thing they needed was a wife. Once again, Vikings took what they wanted. Where did the Vikings get their horrible manners and their low regard for human life?

Living in Scandinavia was no picnic. For many weeks during the year the temperature was below zero, and there was little daylight. Getting crops to grow there was always a struggle. Starvation was always a very real possibility. This grim environment caused the Norse people to be tough. If the crops failed, then the old and sick would not be fed. If a baby was delivered during lean times, it would be left outside to die. The code of life was survival. Strength was prized, and weakness was spurned. Long-lasting blood feuds, which pitted family against family, caused murder and arson to be frequent in the Norse world. A Viking could just as easily be killed at home as on a raid.

Eventually, the Viking raids did settle down. The kings of Scandinavia adopted the religion of the rest of Europe, Christianity, and converted their people to the same. Once the Vikings shared a religion with their victims, it seemed a bit rude to be pillaging their lands. Plus, there was that puzzling Christian commandment, "love your enemies." When it ended, the Viking age had lasted from 790-1100 A.D.

## DISCUSSION QUESTIONS

- What piece of information about the Vikings do you find most surprising? Explain.
- Devise a Viking nickname for yourself. Frequently, these nicknames were given for some personal characteristic or habit (for example, "Eric the Red" and "Thorfinn Skullsplitter.")
- Listen to the song "Immigrant Song" by Led Zeppelin. What is the connection between the song and the Vikings? Explain.

# RAGNAROK

*Also known as "the Twilight of the Gods," Ragnarok, the Norse Doomsday, is the ultimate battle between good and evil—an event similar to the apocalypse of the Bible. According to the Norse myths, Ragnarok will contain a number of specific events, which are related here. But is it the end of the world—or just the beginning of a new one?*

What tidings are to be told of Ragnarok? First, there will come a winter called the Fimbul-winter, where snow will drive from all quarters, the frost will be so severe, and the winds so keen and piercing that there will be no joy to be found—not even in the sun. There will be three such winters in succession without any intervening summer. Great wars will rage over all the world. Brothers will slay each other for the sake of gain, and no one will spare his father or mother in that carnage.

Then a great supernatural tragedy will happen: The two wolves of darkness that have pursued the sun and moon since the beginning of time will finally catch their prey. One wolf will devour the sun, and the second wolf will devour the moon. The stars shall be hurled from heaven. Then it shall come to pass that the earth and the mountains will shake so violently that trees will be torn up by the roots, the mountains will topple down, and all bonds and fetters will be broken and snapped. Loki and the Fenrir-wolf will be loosed. The sea will rush over the earth, for the Midgard Serpent will writhe in rage and seek to gain the land.

Three immortal roosters will crow to signal that Ragnarok has begun. The Fenrir-wolf will rampage with wide-open mouth—fire flashing from his eyes and nostrils. His jaws will be so wide that even though his bottom jaw rests on earth, his top jaw will reach to heaven. The wolf would open his jaws even wider on that day if he could. The Midgard Serpent will vomit forth venom, defiling all the air and the sea.

In the midst of this clash and din the heavens will be torn in half, and the fire giants of Muspelheim, the realm of fire, will come riding through the opening. Surt the fire giant will ride first—an army of fierce flame coming before and behind him. He has a terrible, fiery sword which shines brighter than the sun. As these fire beings ride over Bifrost, it will break to pieces. The fire giants will direct their course to Vigard—a plain one hundred miles on each side. Meeting them there will be the Fenrir-wolf and the Midgard Serpent. To this place will come

Loki and with him all the frost giants of Jotunheim. In Loki's army will be all the ignoble dead of Hela.

While these things are happening, Heimdall will stand up and blow with all his might on his horn to awaken all the gods, who will then hold counsel. Odin will ride to Mimir's well to ask advice of Mimir. Then the World Tree, Yggdrasil, will tremble, and all things in heaven and earth along with it. The gods will speedily arm themselves and rush forth to the battlefield. First will be Odin riding out with his golden helmet and his spear Gungnir—advancing against Fenrir. Thor will stand by his side but can give him no assistance, for he will have his hands full in his own struggle with the Midgard Serpent. Frey, the godly brother of Freya, will encounter Surt and heavy blows will be exchanged before Frey falls. Things might have been different if he had not lost that famous sword which he gave up to the giants.*

On that last day even the dog Garm, the watchdog of Hela, will break loose. He will rage against Tyr, and they will kill each other. Thor will slay the Midgard Serpent, but retreat only nine paces before falling to the earth dead, poisoned by the serpent's venom. Fenrir will swallow Odin and thus cause his death. But then, Vidar (one of Odin's noble sons) will immediately turn and rush at the wolf, pinning the beast's lower jaw to the ground with his foot. With his hand Vidar will seize the upper jaw and rip the beast's mouth apart—killing him for good. Loki will battle against Heimdall, and the two will kill each other. Thereafter, Surt will fling fire over the earth, burning all the world. The World Tree will be consumed in flames— and so a world that has always been, will end.

But what will happen *after* heaven and earth are consumed in flames? When all the gods and all men are dead? Something new. The earth will rise again from the sea—green and fair. The fields will produce their harvests—even without being sown. Vidar and Vali, two of Odin's sons, will survive Surt's fires, and they will dwell on the plains where Asgard stood before. The two sons of Thor will come forth, too, and with them, Mjolnir, the mighty hammer. Then Balder and Hodur will come up from Niflheim—hand in hand, for Balder will have forgiven his brother. They will all sit together and talk about the things that happened aforetime. They will find lying in the grass those golden game pieces which the gods once had.

In another secret place there will be concealed two mortals—surviving Surt's fire—called Lif and Lifthrasir. They will feed upon the morning dew. From these will come so numerous a race that they fill the whole world with people. But that is not the greatest wonder. Sol the sun will have somehow hidden away a daughter—just as fair as she was—and she will rise and ride across the sky in the same heavenly course as her mother once did. And the world will be whole once again.

\*   **In one of the Norse myths, the god Frey has to give up his magic sword when he courts and marries a giantess.**

## DISCUSSION QUESTIONS

- How does Ragnarok compare to other descriptions of the end of the world?
- What do you think of the death of the most famous gods? Do they meet a noble end? Explain.
- Do you think each god is equally matched against his opponent?
- What do you like about the idea of a new world reborn from the ashes of the old? Explain.

## AN INTERACTIVE END·OF·THE·WORLD BATTLE GAME

**INTRODUCTION:** The two wolves of darkness swallow the sun and moon. Fire giants break free from Muspelheim and fling ravaging flames over the world. The Rainbow Bridge shatters, as do the chains that bind Fenrir and Loki. The enemies of good overpower the gods and their allies, and the world is lost. Or at least—that's how it's supposed to happen. Now is your chance to rewrite mythology. In this game you can play as one of two sides—the Æsir gods and their allies or Loki and the jotuns (giants). (A third team of dwarves is available for advanced play.)

**PREMISE:** This roleplaying game is played using game-sheets and dice. Every player fills out a game-sheet (see pgs. 240-243) and assumes the identity of a character from Norse mythology. Each player chooses a set of troops to command in battle. Using dice, players "battle" characters from the opposing team. Players roll a die to determine who wins a particular battle-round. When all the troops under a player's control have been killed through successive battle-rounds, the player "dies," and a point is awarded to the other team. There are two different options for determining which side "wins the war" (see "Winning the Game"). Also there is a dwarf army component that can be added for advanced play (see "Dwarf Addition").

**NUMBER OF PLAYERS:**     10-40 (over 40 can play, but you will need more character names than are listed in these rules)

## ITEMS NEEDED

3 six-sided dice
1 marker for every player
3 pairs of desks facing each other, labeled as "battle stations"
1 piece of scratch paper

## SETTING UP AND GETTING STARTED

- *Note: In these instructions, the teacher or activity organizer is referred to as "The Gamemaster."*
1. There are four sheets included with this game. The first is the rules sheet pg. 240. The second is the god game-sheet pg. 241. The third is the giant game-sheet pg. 242. The fourth is the dwarf game-sheet pg. 243. (This fourth sheet will only be used if the dwarf addition is incorporated into the game.)
2. For a two-team game, you will need to photocopy two sets of game-sheets. One set will have the rules sheet on one side and the god game-sheet on the other. The second set

will have the rules sheet on one side and the giant game-sheet on the other. Make an equal number of both sets.

3.  Equally divide your class into two sides:  gods and giants. (These numbers do not have to be perfectly equal but should be as close as possible.) **Note:**  *The giants are technically "the bad guys," so make sure students placed on this side are comfortable with roleplaying.*

4.  Have the god players sit on the opposite side of the room from the giants.

5.  Assign god or giant character names to players according to their side, or you can let players pick their own character name. (See the chart below for a list of character names. Balder and Hodur are not included on this list, as they were deceased at the time of Ragnarok.)

| GODS | GIANTS | DWARVES |
|---|---|---|
| Bragi | Angerboda | Andvari |
| Brynhild | Fafnir | Bifur |
| Frey | Fenrir | Bofur |
| Freya | Garm | Bombur |
| Frigga | Hela | Brokk |
| Heimdall | Hreidmar | Dori |
| Iduna | Hugi | Dvalin |
| Mani | Logi | Fili |
| Mimir | Loki | Frag |
| Odin | Midgard Serpent | Frosti |
| Sif | Regin | Gandalf |
| Sigmund | Siggeir | Gloin |
| Sigurd | Skrymir | Kili |
| Sol | Surt | Nori |
| Thor | Svadilfare | Ori |
| Tyr | Thiazi | Sindri |
| Vali | Thrym | Thorin |
| Vidar | Utgard-King | Vig |

6.  Make a list of every character name that is assigned. This will be important later.

7.  Pass out a god or giant *Ragnarok Now* game-sheet to every player

8.  Distribute a brightly colored marker to each player.

9.  Have each player choose 20 units to command. Each type of troop costs a different number of units. The top troopers cost 4 units and are very powerful, while the lowest only cost 2 units but can be very easily killed. Players should indicate which troops they choose by circling them with a bright marker. Players should carefully double-check their totals, and players whose troops do not add up to 20 units should be removed from the game.

10.  Have players choose a special skill from the front side of the game-sheet. Have them write this skill in the indicated space on the back side of the game-sheet.

11. Designate at least 3 battle stations. A battle station is two desks facing one another in the middle of the room. This is where the students will "do battle." **Note:** *You can create as many battle stations as you desire, but 3-4 is a good number for a typical group.*

12. Place one die at each battle station.

## SPECIAL ABILITIES FOR THE GODS

- *Note: When players choose their special abilities, they must choose from the list that corresponds with their side. For example, characters from the side of the gods cannot use abilities associated with the giants. (For dwarves, see "Dwarf Addition.")*

- <u>Thunderstrike (Offensive)</u> **If a 2 is rolled, it is automatically converted to a 6.**
  - o **Example:** Odin rolls a 2 against Loki's top warrior. A 2 cannot harm Loki's warrior, but the number is converted to a 6 and, therefore, kills the warrior. *(If Loki's special ability is protection from 6's, this conversion will not harm him.)*

- <u>Hammer Throw (Offensive)</u> **If a 3 is rolled and does *not* result in a kill, the player has the option to roll again for a higher number. If the 3 results in a kill, the player may not roll again.**
  - o **Example:** Odin rolls a 3 against Loki's top warrior, but a 3 cannot beat him. This gives Odin a second chance to attack before Loki's turn. *(The maximum number a player may roll is twice, no matter how many 3's are rolled in a row.)*

- <u>Bifrost Covering (Defensive)</u> **If a 5 is rolled against the player, the player cannot be harmed by it.**
  - o **Example:** Loki is attacking one of Odin's bottom warriors, and he rolls a 5, which should kill the warrior. But since Odin is protected from 5's, it does nothing.

- <u>Apples of Iduna (Defensive)</u> **If a 1 is rolled, the player may roll again (but not for an attack). If the player rolls another 1, a bottom warrior may be added to the player's game-sheet.**
  - o **Example:** Odin is attacking Loki's bottom warrior and rolls a 1, which does not result in a kill. Before Loki takes his turn, Odin rolls again. The point of this roll is not an attack but to see if Odin can roll another 1. If Odin does, he can add another bottom warrior to his sheet. If he does not, the game continues.

## SPECIAL ABILITIES FOR THE GIANTS

- <u>Wolfbite (Offensive)</u> **If a 1 is rolled, it is automatically converted to a 5.**
  - o **Example:** Loki rolls a 1 against Odin's top warrior. Loki's roll is converted to a 5, which will kill Odin's top warrior. *(If Odin has a special ability that protects him from 5's, this conversion will not harm his top warrior.)*

- **Thievery (Offensive)** If a 3 is rolled, the challenger "steals" the opponent's turn. The challenger attacks twice, and the opponent does not attack at all. This ability only works when the player is the challenger.
  - **Example:** Loki is the challenger in a battle-round, and he rolls a 3 against Odin. Whether or not the 3 kills any of Odin's warriors or not, Loki steals Odin's turn. Now Loki is able to attack again, and Odin gets no turn during this battle-round.

- **Shield of Darkness (Defensive)** If a 6 is rolled against the player, the player cannot be harmed by it.
  - **Example:** Odin rolls a 6 against Loki's top warrior, which should result in a kill. But Loki is protected from 6's, so nothing happens.

- **Rise from Niflheim (Defensive)** When a player's last troop is killed, one troop type of the player's choice may be brought back to life and play can continue. (This can be used only once during the entire game.)
  - **Example:** Odin kills Loki's last troop (one of his bottom warriors). Normally, this would mean that Loki's character must die. But since his special ability is Rise from Niflheim, Loki gets to bring one of his troops back from the dead. This could be a top, middle, or bottom warrior. Loki gets to use this ability only once per game. As soon as his final warrior is killed again, Loki's character will die.

## PLAYING THE GAME

1. Each battle-round is made up of:
   - The challenger's attack
   - The opponent's attack
2. Using a list of character names, the Gamemaster will call out the first character name on the list. (*Tip for Gamemaster: Place a tally mark by each name every time you call it. This way you can make sure everyone receives the same number of turns.*)
3. The character whose name was called is now the challenger.
4. The challenger makes his or her way to a battle station and chooses an opponent from the opposite side.
   - **Example:** The Gamemaster calls the character name "Odin." The player designated as Odin goes forward to the battle station and says, "I challenge Loki!" The player designated as Loki must come forward to the battle station.
5. Once both players are at the battle station, the challenger examines the opponent's sheet. The challenger chooses which type of unit on the opponent's sheet to attack.
6. The challenger indicates which type of troop he or she is going to attack on the opponent's sheet.
   - **Example:** Odin says, "I'm going to attack your top warrior, a fire giant."
7. The challenger and opponent re-examine the numbers needed for a kill. (This same chart is listed on each player's rule sheet.)

| | |
|---|---|
| **Top Warrior** | **Challenger must roll a 4 or higher to kill** |
| **Middle Warrior** | **Challenger must roll a 3 or higher to kill** |
| **Bottom Warrior** | **Challenger must roll a 2 or higher to kill** |

8. The opponent must reveal his or her special ability. Some special abilities are offensive, and some are defensive.
9. The challenger rolls the die.
10. If the challenger rolls the required number for a kill (and it is not affected by the opponent's special skill), the challenger can mark out the attacked troop on the opponent's paper.
    - **Example:** Odin is attacking one of Loki's top warriors (a fire giant). He knows he must roll a 4 or higher, but Loki reveals that his special ability is "Shield of Darkness," which means a 6 cannot hurt him. This means Odin must roll a 4 or 5. Odin rolls and gets a 5. He reaches over and X's out one of Odin's top warriors.
11. If the challenger does *not* roll the required number for a kill, it is deemed a "miss." It is now the opponent's turn to attack.
12. After the challenger attacks, the opponent has a chance to attack (following the same procedure).
13. Once both players have had a chance to attack, they should leave the battle station and go back to their respective sides.
14. The Gamemaster will repeat the process of calling out characters' names, keeping track of how many times each character has gone, and making sure all the battle stations are filled.
15. When all of a player's troops have been killed, the player should take his or her game-sheet to the Gamemaster. This means the player is out of the game, and the opposing side gets a point for "killing" that player.
    - **Example:** If Loki kills Odin's last troop, Odin is removed from the game, and the giants get 1 point. Also remember to remove the player's character name from the list since he or she will no longer be called to battle.

## WINNING THE GAME

There are two ways of winning the game. The Gamemaster should select which option will work best for time and the group involved.

- **Option #1: The game can be played until every player on one side has been defeated.**
  o **Example:** All the gods die, so the giants are declared the winners. (Or if the Dwarf Addition is being used, two of the other armies would have to die.)
- **Option #2: A certain time limit can be declared before the game begins.**
  o **Example:** The game will be played for two class periods, and the side with the most points at the end of the second class period will be declared the winner. (Depending on the time available to you, this game can be played over several class periods. **Note:** Due to set-up time, the game is probably too complicated to play in a single class period.)

## DWARF ADDITION (ADVANCED)

The dwarves are skilled craftsmen and weapon-makers, who stay to themselves and only interact with the other creatures of the world when it appeals to their greed. According to mythology, the dwarves play no part in the final battle of Ragnarok. But what if they did? On whose side would they fight? Or would they fight only for themselves—thinking only of the riches such a war would bring them?

**There are two different ways to incorporate the Dwarf Addition into this game.**

- **Option #1:  Battle of Three Armies** When dividing the class into teams, create three equal teams—the gods, the giants, and the dwarves. (Since the dwarves have their own game-sheet, you will need to copy three sets of game-sheets—a different type of game-sheet for each of the three teams.) In this scenario, all three teams will battle each other, and the winner will be the team who scores the most kills against the others.
- **Option #2:  Dwarf-Warriors for Hire** When dividing the class into the god and giant teams, leave a small group of players (3-5) to be designated as dwarves. They will fill out a separate game-sheet. All players will fill out their game-sheets as normal (receiving 20 units per player). But after this, the few dwarf warriors will be available "for hire" by the two other teams. Holding with the greedy nature of the dwarves, the gods and giants must try to buy their allegiance. This can be done by the gods and giants offering the dwarves units from their own game-sheets.
  - **Example:** Brokk the dwarf shouts, "Who wants me on their side?" Loki offers to give him a top warrior in return for his allegiance. Odin offers two top warriors, so Brokk decides to join the gods' side. Odin crosses two of his top warriors off his own game-sheet and circles two top warriors on Brokk's sheet.
    - *Note: Two members of a team can offer an incentive together. For example, both Odin and Thor can offer to give Brokk two of their top warriors. This would mean Brokk would receive a total of four top warriors.*
    - Dwarves cannot accept more warriors than they have spaces for on their game-sheet. For example, no dwarf can have more than five top warriors, four middle warriors, etc.
  - If no one bribes the dwarves onto their side, it is up to the dwarf players to pick which side they would like to join.

**NOTE:**  Since the dwarves are not associated with either the gods or the giants, their special abilities can be drawn from either the god or giant ability list.

## GAMEMASTERS: TIPS AND FUN ADDITIONS

- **Tip:** It is best to do several "sample" battles before actually beginning the game.
- **Tip:** It will take about 10 minutes before the players completely understand the rules, but once they do, they will enjoy it immensely!
- **Addition:** At the beginning of a game ask several questions about Norse mythology. Those players who answer correctly can be given extra units to add onto their game-sheet.
- **Addition:** Take on the role of a god and choose to enter the battle at any point with your own game-sheet.
- **Addition:** Give a fun prize to the side that wins the war.
- **Addition:** Divide the room into their respective teams (gods, giants, etc.) several days before you actually play the *Ragnarok Now* game. Have the sides face their desks toward one another. Have each group make a banner for their team and hang it on the wall.
- **Addition:** Assign characters a few days before you actually play the game. Have the players research their characters, finding out what role they played in Ragnarok or Norse mythology as a whole.
- **Addition:** Make a spying rule. When characters "die," it frees their spirit from the rules of the mortal world. They can cross over to the opposite side and scout out opponents' sheets, looking for characters who are near death and reporting this back to their teammates.

# RAGNAROK NOW

## AN INTERACTIVE END·OF·THE·WORLD BATTLE GAME

The two wolves of darkness swallow the sun and moon. Fire giants break free from Muspelheim and fling ravaging flames over the world. The Rainbow Bridge shatters, as do the chains that bind Fenrir and Loki. The enemies of good overpower the gods and their allies, and the world is lost. Or at least—that's how it's supposed to happen. Now is your chance to rewrite mythology!

**PICK YOUR TROOPS:** Every player (that's you) gets 20 units to command. Different types of warriors count as more or fewer units. For example, a top warrior costs 4 units, while a bottom warrior only costs 2 units. Keep in mind though that a top warrior is much harder to kill in battle. To indicate how you would like to disperse your 20 units, circle the troops you choose on your game-sheet. (Make sure your troops add up to 20 units, or you'll be removed from the game.) **Remember:** Choose wisely. When all of your troops are killed, your character "dies," and the opposing team gets a point!

| TYPE OF TROOP | COST | ADVANTAGE |
|---|---|---|
| Top Warrior | 4 units | Challenger must roll a 4 or higher to kill |
| Middle Warrior | 3 units | Challenger must roll a 3 or higher to kill |
| Bottom Warrior | 2 units | Challenger must roll a 2 or higher to kill |

**PREPARE FOR BATTLE:** Using the opposite side of this sheet, choose your troops. **Remember:** Your units must add up to 20. Then choose **one** special ability (either offensive or defensive) and write its effect in the provided blank.

| GODS AND ALLIES | GIANTS AND ALLIES |
|---|---|
| **THUNDERSTRIKE (OFFENSIVE)** If a "2" is rolled, it is automatically converted to a "6." | **WOLFBITE (OFFENSIVE)** If a "1" is rolled, it is automatically converted to a "5." |
| **HAMMER THROW (OFFENSIVE)** If a "3" is rolled and does not result in a kill, the player has the option to roll again. | **THIEVERY (OFFENSIVE)** If the challenger rolls a "3," it "steals" the opponent's turn. The challenger attacks twice. |
| **BIFROST COVERING (DEFENSIVE)** If a "5" is rolled against the player, the player cannot be harmed by it. | **SHIELD OF DARKNESS (DEFENSIVE)** If a "6" is rolled against the player, the player cannot be harmed by it. |
| **APPLES OF IDUNA (DEFENSIVE)** If a "1" is rolled, the player may roll again (but not for an attack). If a bottom warrior may be added to the game-sheet. | **RISE FROM NIFLHEIM (DEFENSIVE)** When a player's last warrior is killed, one warrior type of the player's choice may be brought back to life and play can continue. (This can be used only once per game.) |

# THE GODS AND THEIR ALLIES

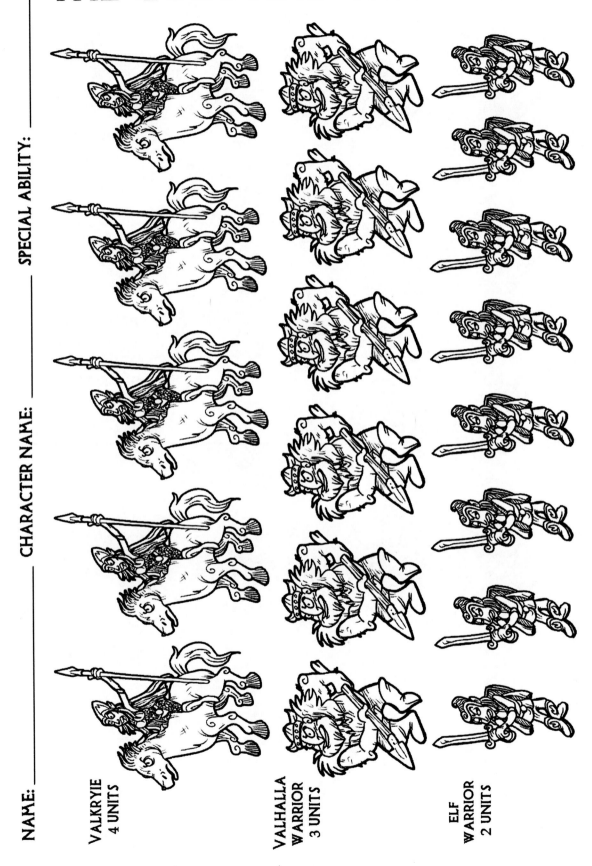

NAME: _____

CHARACTER NAME: _____

SPECIAL ABILITY: _____

**VALKRYIE**
**4 UNITS**

**VALHALLA WARRIOR**
**3 UNITS**

**ELF WARRIOR**
**2 UNITS**

# THE GIANTS AND THEIR ALLIES

SPECIAL ABILITY: _____

CHARACTER NAME: _____

NAME: _____

**FIRE GIANT**
**4 UNITS**

**JOTUN WARRIOR**
**3 UNITS**

**NIFLHEIM WARRIOR**
**2 UNITS**

# THE DWARVES

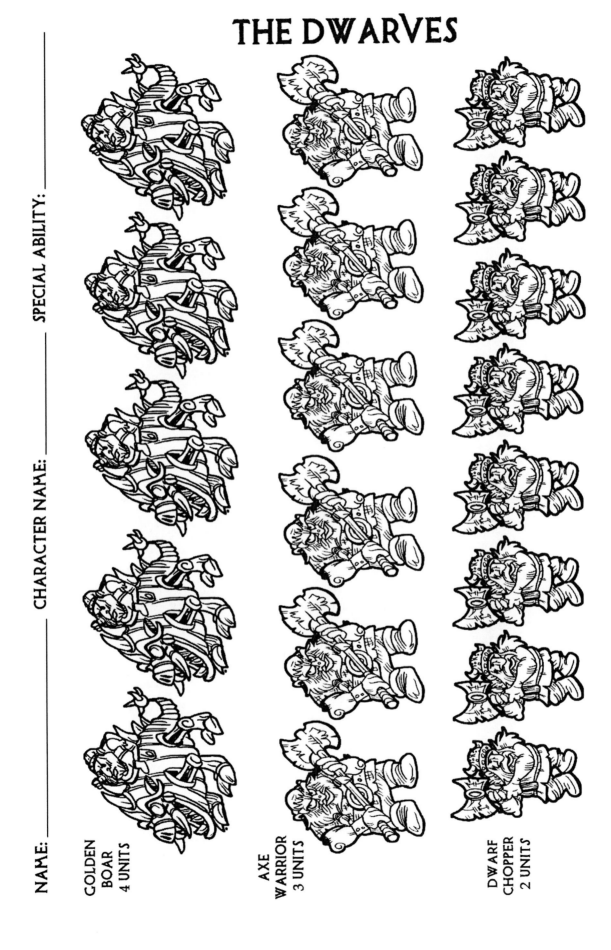

SPECIAL ABILITY: _____

CHARACTER NAME: _____

NAME: _____

GOLDEN
BOAR
4 UNITS

AXE
WARRIOR
3 UNITS

DWARF
CHOPPER
2 UNITS

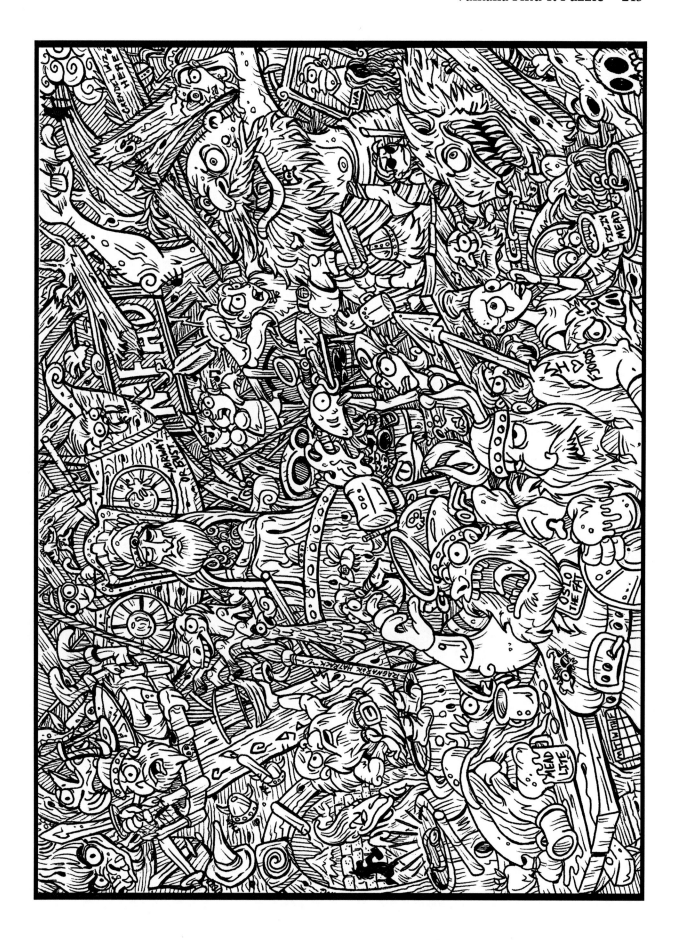

# VALHALLA FIND·IT PUZZLE

## CAN YOU FIND ALL OF THESE ITEMS HIDDEN IN THE PICTURE?

- Apples of Iduna (4)
- Axes (3)
- Bat
- Bones (3)
- Brisingamen
- Calendar
- Catapult
- Eye of Odin
- Fafnir the Dragon
- Fenrir the Wolf
- Frost Giant
- Great Cow
- Hair of Sif
- Hand of Tyr
- Heimdall
- Hela
- Hodur
- Horned Helmets (11)
- Hugin and Munin
- Jormungand
- Loki
- Love Potion
- Miniature Viking Ship
- Mjolnir

- Mouse
- Newt
- Odin
- Otter
- Portrait of Richard Wagner
- Runes
- Salmon
- Scissors
- Scroll
- Shields (5)
- Sif
- Skulls (5)
- Sleipnir
- Small Snake
- Spears (5)
- Spider
- Stinging Fly
- Svadilfare the Horse
- Thor
- Tyr
- Valkyrie
- Wide-Brimmed Hat
- Word: "Ragnarok"

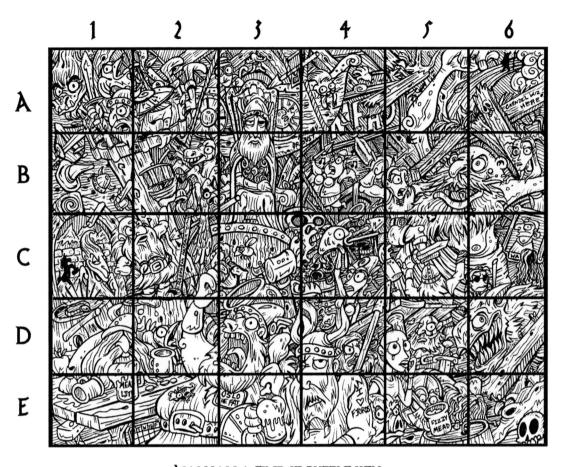

## VALHALLA FIND·IT PUZZLE KEY

Apples of Iduna (4) **B3, C5, D1, E6**

Axes (3) **C3, D1, E5**

Bat **A3**

Bones (3) **C5, D6, E3**

Brisingamen **D1**

Calendar **E2**

Catapult **B4-C4**

Eye of Odin **A2**

Fafnir the Dragon **A1**

Fenrir the Wolf **D6**

Frost Giant **B5-B6**

Great Cow **C4**

Hair of Sif **C6**

Hand of Tyr **A4**

Heimdall **A6**

Hela **B6**

Hodur **C6**

Horned Helmets (11) **A1, A6, B1, B1, B2, B4, C2-D2, C3, D1, D4, E6**

Hugin and Munin **A1, D2**

Jormungand **C3-C4**

Loki **C1**

Love Potion **D4**

Miniature Viking Ship **B2**

Mjolnir **E1**

Mouse **B6-C6**

Newt **E2**

Odin **A3-B3**

Otter **A4**

Portrait of Richard Wagner **C6**

Runes **B1-B2-C2**

Salmon **C4**

Scissors **B3**

Scroll **D6**

Shields (5) **A2, A3, B1, E3, E5**

Sif **D5-E5**

Skulls (5) **A6, B2, C3, C4, E6**

Sleipnir **B2**

Small Snake **A4**

Spears (5) **A3, B4, C2, C4, C4-D4**

Spider **B5**

Stinging Fly **C3**

Svadilfare the Horse **C1**

Thor **B5-C5**

Tyr **C5**

Valkyrie **C4-D4**

Wide-Brimmed Hat **B1**

Word: "Ragnarok" **C2**

# GLOSSARY OF IMPORTANT NAMES

**ÆSIR** ("spirits") a collective term for the race of gods who inhabit Asgard

**ASGARD** the home of the gods

**BALDER** ("lord") the most beloved of the gods, killed by his brother Hodur through the trickery of Loki

**BIFROST** the Rainbow Bridge that connects Asgard to Midgard

**BRAGI** ("song") god of poetry, husband of Iduna

**BRISINGAMEN** necklace forged by the dwarves for the goddess, Freya

**BRYNHILD** fallen valkyrie, love of Sigurd

**FAFNIR** son of Hreidmar the magician, dragon slain by Sigurd

**FENRIR** ("from the swamp") giant wolf sired by Loki

**FREY** ("the foremost") Vanir god, brother of Freya

**FREYA** ("lady, mistress") Vanir goddess of beauty, sister of Frey

**FRIGGA** ("lady, mistress") wife of Odin, mother of Balder

**GRAM** Sword of the Volsungs, given to Sigmund by Odin himself

**GRANI** Sigurd's noble steed

**HEIMDALL** ("rainbow") Watchman of the Gods

**HELA** ("concealer") daughter of Loki, half-living, half-dead ruler of the dead in Niflheim

**HJORDIS** wife of Sigmund, mother of Sigurd

**HODUR** blind brother of Balder

**HUGIN** ("thought") raven of Odin

**IDUNA** ("rejuvenation") goddess, keeper of the golden apples that give immortality to the gods

**JORMUNGAND** the Midgard serpent, son of Loki, encircles Midgard

**JOTUNHEIM** land of the frost giants

**JOTUNS** ("devourers") term for the frost giants

**LOKI** half-giant, half-god trickster, called "the doer of good and the doer of evil"

**MIDGARD** ("middle-earth") the world of men

**MIMIR** ("pondering") immortal guardian of the Well of Wisdom

**MJOLNIR** ("the flashing crusher") Thor's hammer, forged by the dwarves

**MUNIN** ("memory") raven of Odin

**MUSPELHEIM** ("home of destruction") the home of the fire giant, Surt, and his followers that lies on the other side of the sky

**NIFLHEIM** ("land of fog") realm of the dead, filled with a freezing fog

**NORNS** ("pronouncers") three immortal beings representing past, present, and future, similar to the Fates of Greek mythology

**ODIN** ("spirit, ecstasy") the All-Father of the Gods, leader of the Æsir

**RAGNAROK** ("destiny of the gods") the Day of Doom

**REGIN** guardian of Sigurd, blacksmith

**RUNES** ancient symbols used for magic and for writing, probably an ancient Germanic alphabet

**SIF** ("kinship") goddess of home and family, wife of Thor whose hair was shorn by Loki

**SIGGEIR** evil king of the Goths, husband of Signy

**SIGMUND** son of Volsung, received the sword Gram from the Branstock tree, father of Sigurd

**SIGNY** twin sister of Sigmund, mother of Sinfjotli

**SIGUNA** wife of Loki

**SIGURD** warrior, slayer of Fafnir and lover of Brynhild

**SINFJOTLI** son of Signy and her brother, Sigmund

**SLEIPNIR** Odin's eight-legged steed

**SURT** fire-demon giant whose followers will help bring about Ragnarok

**SVADILFARE** stallion that assists in the building of Asgard's walls

**SVARTALFHEIM** land of the dwarves

**THOR** ("thunder") god of thunder

**TYR** ("shining") god of single combat, sacrificed a hand to Fenrir

**URDA** one of the three Norns, protectors of a sacred well called the Well of Urd

**VALHALLA** ("hall of the slain") Odin's hall where the valiant warriors of Midgard are taken here to await Ragnarok, when they will fight side-by-side with the gods

**VALI** son of Odin sired to take revenge on Hodur for the death of Balder

**VALKYRIES** ("choosers of the fallen heroes") Odin's shieldmaidens, who by his command determined the course of mortal battles and lifted the spirits of those who died valiantly to Valhalla

**VANIR** ("friendly") another tribe of gods who once warred with the Æsir

**VOLSUNG** mighty king of Hunaland, his descendants are the Volsungs

**YGGDRASIL** ("Odin's steed") the World Tree, the support for the Nine Worlds. Some theorize the Christmas evergreen is a carry-over of this ancient sacred tree.

## PRONUNCIATION GUIDE

| | |
|---|---|
| Æsir | (Ā-SER) |
| Andvari | (AND-VAR-EE) |
| Angerboda | (ĀNG-ER-BŌ-DUH) |
| Asgard | (AZ-GARD) |
| Ask | (ASK) |
| Balder | (BAL-DER) |
| Bifrost | (BĪ-FRAWST) |
| Bragi | (BRA-GEE) |
| Brisingamen | (BRI-SING-UH-MEN) |
| Brokk | (BRAWK) |
| Brynhild | (BRIN-HILD) |
| Draupnir | (DRAWP-NEER) |
| Durin | (DOOR-EN) |
| Dvalin | (DVAL-EN) |
| Elli | (EL-EE) |
| Embla | (EM-BLUH) |
| Fafnir | (FAF-NEER) |
| Fenrir | (FEN-REER) |
| Frey | (FRĀY) |
| Freya | (FRĀY-UH) |
| Frigga | (FRIG-UH) |
| Garm | (GARM) |
| Gleipnir | (GLEEP-NEER) |
| Gnita | (NEET-UH) |
| Gram | (GRAWM) |
| Grani | (GRAW-NEE) |
| Grimhild | (GRIM-HILD) |
| Groa | (GRŌ-UH) |
| Gudrun | (GUD-RUN) |
| Gungnir | (GUNG-NEER) |
| Gunnar | (GOO-NAR) |
| Heimdall | (HĪM-DAL) |
| Hela | (HEL-UH) |
| Hermod | (HEER-MAWD) |
| Hjordis | (HYŌR-DIS) |
| Hodur | (HŌ-DER) |
| Hreidmar | (HRĪD-MAR) |
| Hrimfaxe | (HRIM-FAX-EE) |
| Hugin | (HEW-GEN) |
| Hunaland | (HUN-UH-LAND) |
| Hyrrokin | (HEER-RAWK-EN) |
| Iduna | (Ī-DOO-NUH) |
| Ifling | (IF-LEENG) |
| Jarnvid | (JARN-VID) |
| Jormungand | (YŌR-MUN-GAND) |
| Jotunheim | (YŌ-TUN-HĪM) |
| Lifthrasir | (LIF-THRUH-SEER) |
| Logi | (LŌ-GEE) |
| Loki | (LŌ-KEE) |
| Mani | (MA-NEE) |
| Midgard | (MID-GARD) |
| Mimir | (MI-MER) |
| Mjolnir | (MYŌL-NEER) |

| | |
|---|---|
| Munin | (MEW-NEN) |
| Muspelheim | (MUS-PEL-HĪM) |
| Nanna | (NA-NUH) |
| Nidhogg | (NID-HAWG) |
| Niflheim | (NIF-EL-HĪM) |
| Odin | (Ō-DEN) |
| Otter | (Ō-TER) |
| Ragnarok | (RAG-NUH-RAWK) |
| Ratatoskr | (RA-TAT-AWSK-ER) |
| Regin | (REE-GEN) |
| Sif | (SIF) |
| Siggeir | (SIG-EER) |
| Sigmund | (SIG-MUND) |
| Signy | (SIG-NEE) |
| Siguna | (SI-GOON-UH) |
| Sigurd | (SIG-ERD) |
| Sindri | (SIN-DREE) |
| Sinfjotli | (SINF-YAWT-LEE) |
| Skidbladnir | (SKID-BLAD-NEER) |
| Skinfaxe | (SKIN-FAX-EE) |
| Skrymir | (SKRĪ-MEER) |
| Skuld | (SKULD) |
| Sleipnir | (SLEEP-NEER) |
| Sol | (SŌL) |
| Surt | (SERT) |
| Svadilfare | (SVA-DIL-FAR-EE) |
| Svartalfheim | (SVART-ALF-HĪM) |
| Thialfi | (THEE-ALF-EE) |
| Thiazi | (THEE-A-ZEE) |
| Thor | (THŌR) |
| Thrym | (THRIM) |
| Tyr | (TEER) |
| Urd | (ERD) |
| Urda | (ERD-UH) |
| Utgard | (UT-GARD) |
| Valhalla | (VAL-HAL-UH) |
| Vali | (VAL-EE) |
| Valkyrie | (VAL-KUH-REE) |
| Vanir | (VA-NEER) |
| Vegtam | (VEG-TIM) |
| Verdandi | (VER-DAN-DEE) |
| Vidar | (VEE-DAR) |
| Vigard | (VĪ-GARD) |
| Volsung | (VŌL-SUNG) |
| Volva | (VŌL-VA) |
| Wagner | (VAWG-NER) |
| Yggdrasil | (IG-DRUH-SIL) |
| Ymir | (Ī-MEER) |

**NOTE:** These are my best guesses, for I could find no authoritative pronunciation guide for many of the Norse names. All vowel sounds should be considered short unless indicated by Ā, EE, Ī, Ō, or OO.

## ABOUT THE AUTHOR

Zachary "Zak" Hamby is a teacher of English in rural Missouri, where he has taught mythology for many years. In mythology he has seen the ability of ancient stories to capture the imaginations of young people today. For this reason he has created a variety of teaching materials (including textbooks, posters, and websites) that focus specifically on the teaching of mythology to young people. He is the author of two book series, the *Reaching Olympus* series and the *Mythology for Teens* series. He is also a professional illustrator. He resides in the Ozarks with his wife and children.

For more information and mythology products including textbooks, posters, and digital downloads visit his website **www.mythologyteacher.com.**

Contact him by email at **mr.mythology@gmail.com**

CPSIA information can be obtained at www.ICGtesting.com
Printed in the USA
BVOW03s0527030916

460759BV00006B/60/P